Philosophical Posthumanism

Theory

Series editor: Rosi Braidotti

Theory is back! The vitality of critical thinking in the world today is palpable, as is a spirit of insurgency that sustains it. Theoretical practice has exploded with renewed energy in media, society, the arts and the corporate world. New generations of critical "studies" areas have grown alongside the classical radical epistemologies of the 1970s: gender, feminist, queer, race, postcolonial and subaltern studies, cultural studies, film, television and media studies.

This series aims to present cartographic accounts of emerging critical theories and to reflect the vitality and inspirational force of on-going theoretical debates.

Editorial board

Stacy Alaimo (University of Texas at Arlington, USA)
Simone Bignall (Flinders University, Australia)
Judith Butler (University of Berkeley, USA)
Christine Daigle (Brock University, Canada)
Rick Dolphijn (Utrecht University, The Netherlands)
Matthew Fuller (Goldsmiths, University of London, UK)
Engin Isin (Queen Mary University of London, UK, and University of London Institute in Paris, France)
Patricia MacCormack (Anglia Ruskin University, UK)
Achille Mbembe (University Witwatersrand, South Africa)
Henrietta Moore (University College London, UK)

Titles in the series so far

Posthuman Glossary, edited by Rosi Braidotti and Maria Hlavajova
Conflicting Humanities, edited by Rosi Braidotti and Paul Gilroy
General Ecology, edited by Erich Hörl with James Burton

Philosophical Posthumanism

Francesca Ferrando

BLOOMSBURY ACADEMIC
LONDON • NEW YORK • OXFORD • NEW DELHI • SYDNEY

BLOOMSBURY ACADEMIC
Bloomsbury Publishing Plc
50 Bedford Square, London, WC1B 3DP, UK
1385 Broadway, New York, NY 10018, USA
29 Earlsfort Terrace, Dublin 2, Ireland

BLOOMSBURY, BLOOMSBURY ACADEMIC and the Diana logo are trademarks of
Bloomsbury Publishing Plc

First published in Great Britain 2019
Paperback edition published 2020
Reprinted 2020 (twice), 2021 (twice)

Copyright © Francesca Ferrando, 2019, 2020

A catalogue record for this book is available from the British Library.

A catalog record for this book is available from the Library of Congress.

ISBN: HB: 978-1-3500-5950-4
PB: 978-1-3501-8601-9
ePDF: 978-1-3500-5948-1
eBook: 978-1-3500-5949-8

Series: Theory in the New Humanities

Typeset by Jones Ltd, London
Printed and bound in Great Britain

To find out more about our authors and books visit www.bloomsbury.com
and sign up for our newsletters.

To us, human and posthuman beings.
To existence.

Contents

Acknowledgments   ix

Preface: The Posthuman as Exuberant Excess *Rosi Braidotti*   xi

Bibliographic Note   xvii

Introduction: From Human to Posthuman   1

Navigational Tool: A Glossary of Questions   7

Part One What Is Philosophical Posthumanism?

1   Premises   21

2   From Postmodern to Posthuman   24

3   Posthumanism and Its Others   27

4   The Birth of Transhumanism   29

5   Contemporary Transhumanism(s)   31

6   The Roots of Transhumanism   33

7   Transhumanism and Techno-Enchantment   35

8   Posthumanist Technologies as Ways of Revealing   39

9   Antihumanism and the *Übermensch*   45

10   Philosophical Posthumanism   54

Interlude 1   60

Part Two Of Which "Human" Is the Posthuman a "Post"?

11   The Power of the Hyphen   65

12   Humanizing   68

13   The Anthropological Machine   73

14   Almost, Human   77

15   Technologies of the Self as Posthumanist (Re)Sources   82

16   The Epiphany of Becoming Human   85

17   Where Does the Word "Human" Come From?   89

18   Mammals or *Homo sapiens*?   93

Interlude 2   98

Part Three Have Humans Always Been Posthuman?

19   Post-Anthropocentrism in the Anthropocene   103
20   Posthuman Life   109
     a. *Bios* and *Zoē*   109
     b. Animate/Inanimate   110
21   Artificial Life   115
22   Evolving Species   120
23   Posthumanities   124
24   Posthuman Bioethics   128
25   Human Enhancement   133
26   Cognitive Autopoiesis   140
27   Posthumanist Perspectivism   148
28   From New Materialisms to Object-Oriented Ontology   158
29   Philosophical Posthumanist Ontology   166
30   The Multiverse   171
     a. The Multiverse in Science   171
     b. The Multiverse in Philosophy   175
     c. A Thought Experiment: The Posthuman Multiverse   177
Interlude 3   183

Concluding Celebration   185
Notes   191
Bibliography   231
Index   259

Acknowledgments

My sincerest thanks to Prof. Rosi Braidotti, Prof. Francesca Brezzi, and Prof. Stefan Lorenz Sorgner, the trinity of wisdom.

Academic Tribe

Many thanks to Prof. Kevin Warwick, Prof. Achille Varzi, Prof. Luisa Passerini, Prof. Gianni Vattimo, Prof. Giacomo Marramao, Prof. Simona Marino, Prof. Angelo Morino, Prof. Evi Sampanikou, Dr. Natasha Vita-More, Prof. David Roden, and Jaime del Val, for their inestimable intellectual, human, and posthuman support. Many thanks to the Sainati Prize, the ETS publishing house, Bloomsbury, Frankie Mace, and the anonymous reviewers, for supporting this project with passion, vision, and patience. Many thanks to NYU-Liberal Studies, for believing in my work and offering me the ideal place to share, teach, and learn. Many thanks to all my amazing students, who inspire my life every day and who taught me how to teach the posthuman in clear and engaging ways: your feedback has been most precious in the articulation of this book.

Special thanks to the Beyond Humanism Network, the NY Posthuman Research Group, the co-organizers—(in alphabetic order): Kevin Lagrandeur, Farzad Mahootian, Jim McBride, and Yunus Tuncel—the World Posthuman Society, and Thomas Steinbuch, for nourishing the posthuman paradigm shift and constantly inspiring intellectual vision. I would also recognize my translators in other languages, for enabling the posthuman discussion to flourish outside of the English-speaking world—in particular Dr. Angela Balzano and Prof. Roman Stansiesko. My heartfelt thanks to the Department of Philosophy at the University of Roma Tre, Italy; the Department of Philosophy and the "IRWGS" Research Center of Columbia University, United States; the Department of Cybernetics at the University of Reading, England; "CIRSDe," the Center for Gender Studies at the University of Turin; and the Doctorate of Gender at the University of Naples Federico II, Italy.

Family Tribe

Special thanks, full of love and gratitude, to Sofia Sahara Shanti, for coming into my life—you are pure enlightenment; to Thomas Roby, for his support, love, and presence in my life; to Renata Prato, not only for having conceived me and loved me since my birth, but also for sending the book to the Sainati Prize; to Ugo Ferrando, for nurturing my love for philosophy and for believing in my ideas. I thank Tiziana Lacchio, for her love, strength, and precision; Ellen Delahunty Roby, for her generosity, love, and contribution to the development of my thought in English; Barbara and Federica Ferrando, for inspiring my life; Tom Roby and his family, for believing in my vision; Ida Bacigalupo, Agostino Prato, Caterina Manassero, and Giovanni Ferrando—you are always in my heart; Ridgewood, and all the amazing people at the Golden Oasis. I am also grateful to Tristan, Alisa and Remi, Garon and Gisella, Maria, Marisa and Eileen, for their presence in our life.

World Tribe

Much gratitude to the posthuman community worldwide—thanks for supporting my work and vision with your e-mails, feedbacks, comments, and likes. Thanks to all the philosophers who shaped my thought—in particular Friedrich Nietzsche and Rosi Braidotti. Thanks to feminism, anarchism, yoga, mindfulness, Buddhism, and other movements that have greatly influenced my life. Thanks to everyone in Italy and, in general, Europe, in New York and across the United States, in Costa Rica, Morocco, India, and across planet Earth, for supporting my existential research with great kindness; to my body, for sustaining the incandescent rhythms of philosophical writing; to you, who will read this work and share the exciting posthuman wave. Also, a special thanks to this book, *Philosophical Posthumanism*, which has exponentially expanded my existential awareness. And deep ontological gratitude to existence. Thank You.

Preface: The Posthuman as Exuberant Excess

Rosi Braidotti

Ferrando's brand of posthuman thought is as far removed from a sense of terminal crisis of the human, as posthumanism gets. What Ferrando enacts instead is a generous overflowing of ideas, affects, desires, and aspirations, which she operationalizes across a broad span of discourses within the humanities. They include strict disciplines, such as philosophy, and more interdisciplinary areas, such as media, gender, and postcolonial studies, but they are never limited to any one of them. Ferrando is both a classicist and a futurist thinker: erudite and upbeat, committed but critical, conceptual and poetic, at once; she combines and holds in balance potentially contradictory ideas and affects. In so doing, she forges an original argumentative style and produces texts that inform, stimulate, and provoke. What allows Francesca Ferrando to reconcile these tensions and lift them to a higher qualitative level of discourse is her appreciation of the paradoxical structure of the posthuman condition itself. I have defined the posthuman as a convergence phenomenon between post-humanism and post-anthropocentrism, that is to say, the critique of the universal ideal of the Man of reason on the one hand and the reject of species supremacy on the other. Ferrando's work is situated within this turbulent field and the force that inspires her to deterritorialize both humanism and anthropocentrism is exuberant excess.

Ferrando understands excess as a form of over-compilation and saturation of concepts that results in pushing them to their outmost boundaries and ends up exploding them. It is almost a methodological application of the concept of desire as overflowing, as opposed to desire as lack; that is to say, it resonates with Deleuze's position, not Lacan, with Spinoza, rather than Hegel. This exuberant mode, however, is not an end in itself, nor is it primarily or exclusively critical: it both expresses and sustains productive doses of creativity. What Ferrando aspires to—that is to say, the conceptual desire that animates her work—is to open up new horizons of thinking to express speculative insights that are still in the realm of the "not yet," and yet are urgently needed. This strategic use of excess therefore allows Francesca Ferrando to overflow the established structures of philosophical thinking in order to design the contour of a new image of thought and of the thinking subject. Thinking for Ferrando is not the exclusive prerogative of Man/ Anthropos, but is rather distributed across a wide spectrum of human and nonhuman entities. This produces also a new understanding of the human, not as an autonomous agent endowed with transcendental consciousness, but rather an immanent—embodied and embedded relational—entity that thinks with and through multiple connections to others, both human and nonhuman, organic and inorganic others. This vision of the subject, and the generous embrace of otherness that defines it, makes for heady reading at times, but the theoretical complexity exposed is compensated by the visionary force of Ferrando's text.

In Excess of Humanism

Over the last decades, while the academic humanities circles lived through the fallout of philosophical post-structuralism and deconstruction, and their respective brands of critical anti-humanism, many new developments also took place. A radical wave of theory that included feminist, postcolonial and anti-racist critical theory, environmental activists, disability rights advocates, queer and LGBT theorists questioned the scope, the founding principles, and the achievements of European humanism and its role in the project of Western modernity. These movements questioned more specifically the idea of the human that is implicit in the humanist ideal of "Man," as the alleged "measure of all things." This ideal combines individual physical perfection with intellectual and moral perfectibility. Over the centuries, it also has turned into an exceptionalist civilizational standard that claims privileged access to self-reflexive reason for the human species as a whole and for European culture more specifically. Faith in reason ties in with the teleological prospect of the rational progress of a Eurocentric vision of humanity through the deployment of science and technology. According to Foucault's sharp analysis of the *Death of Man* written in 1966, even Marxism, through the method of historical materialism, continued to assign to the subject of European thought a royal place as the motor of human social and cultural evolution. Moreover, rational self-assurance has also played a major historical role in both justifying and paving the ground for a civilizational model which equated Europe with the universal powers of reason and progress, a claim that became central to the colonial ideology of European expansion.

Ferrando's work is nurtured and inspired by these fundamental philosophical critiques of humanism, but not confined by them. Whereas the poststructuralist and the postmodern generations embraced anti-humanism as both a theoretical and political project, de-linking subjectivity from universalistic postures in order to produce more precise analyses of the power relations that structure it, other movements handled humanism with greater care. Feminist politics of location, for instance, valued both the lived experience and the specificity of female embodiment and took the "standpoint theory" approach as foundational. Although it paid great attention to the diversity among women, the subject of feminism was not relinquished, but rather re-cast as a nomadic non-unitary singularity. This subject produces embodied and embedded, affective and relational situated knowledges as both the method and the political tactic for grounding micro-political analyses of power and for positing workable alternatives.

This immanent and materialist approach, favored by feminist, anti-racist, and other social movements, developed its own variations of radical neo-humanism in a manner that shows up distinctly in different moments of Ferrando's work. The radical criticism of classical humanism had targeted two interrelated ideas: the self-other dialectics, on the one hand, and the notion of difference as pejoration, on the other. Otherness defined as the negative opposite of the dominant subject position and inscribed in a hierarchical scale that spells inferiority is challenged by a situated or an immanent method, inspired by Spinozist neo-materialism. The dialectics of difference in fact has dire consequences for real-life people who happen to coincide with categories of negative difference: women, indigenous, and earth "others," whose social and symbolic existence is precarious and exposed to all kinds of risk. Their own bodies raise crucial issues of power, domination, and exclusion that look to humanism as a possible solution.

A variety of forms of revised humanism is present also in postcolonial theory, inspired by the anticolonial phenomenology of Frantz Fanon and of his teacher, Aimé Césaire. They took humanism as an unfulfilled project in Europe, betrayed by imperialist violence and structural racism, but argued that there exist many other brands of humanism in other cultures. This position is echoed by environmental and transnational environmental justice activists, who combine the critique of the epistemic and physical violence of modernity with that of European colonialism. Ferrando's take on humanism, grounded in the classics of the Italian Renaissance and fuelled by contemporary post- and trans-humanist literature, is structured by all these critical concerns and yet is in excess of them. She spins her own web across multiple discursive communities, honoring them all, but pledging allegiance to none.

In Excess of Anthropocentrism

The debate on displacing anthropocentrism is of a different order and pertains to a different genealogical line from the critique of humanism, though it often intersects with it. The critique of species supremacy—the violent rule of Anthropos over this planet—opens another line of criticism of the parameters that define the human itself. "Man" is called to task as the representative of a hierarchical and violent species whose greed and rapacity are enhanced by a combination of scientific advances and global economic domination. As Ferrando's work clearly explains, neither "Man" as the universal humanistic measure of all things nor Anthropos as dominant species can claim the central position in the task of thinking. In the posthuman convergence that frames the contemporary world, the power of thinking is distributed across many species and often executed by technologically mediated knowledge production systems, run by networks and computational processes. Biogenetic and computational advances have challenged the separation of *bios*, as exclusively human life, from *zoē*, the life of animals and nonhuman entities. What comes to the fore instead is a human/nonhuman continuum, which is consolidated by pervasive technological mediation.

The political implications of this shift are significant. If the revisions of Humanism advanced by feminist, queer, anti-racist, ecological, and postcolonial critiques empowered the sexualized and racialized—but still human—"others," the crisis of Anthropos enlists the naturalized others. Animals, insects, plants, cells, bacteria, and in fact the planet and the cosmos are turned into a political arena. These nonhuman entities and agents play a significant role in Ferrando's work, where they are reviewed and reconceptualized like "conceptual personae." Their primary function is to challenge the nature-culture distinction and, with it, to claim the anthropocentric exceptionalism. What is striking about Ferrando's work is also her capacity to rejoice especially in the radical otherness of nonhuman species—their diversity becoming a source of wonder and admiration, rather than fear and control.

Another remarkable aspect of Francesca Ferrando's work is the gift of multiple literacies. The readers will be struck by the ease with which she transits from the culture of the humanities to that of science and technology, avoiding any dichotomy between the two. It is as if Ferrando demanded that history, literature, philosophy, and the study of religion should develop planetary perspectives in a geo-centered, mediated, and non-anthropocentric frame of reference. This demands a lot of the traditional humanities disciplines, because they are so deeply structured by anthropocentric habits that cannot easily contemplate the de-centering of anthropocentrism, let alone the specter of human extinction.

But Ferrando's scholarship has another level of complexity, in so far as it relies on radical interdisciplinary fields of enquiry like gender, feminist, queer, race, and postcolonial studies, as well as cultural studies, film, television, and media studies. These "studies" areas have exposed Eurocentrism, sexism, racism, and methodological nationalism as the major flaws at the core of the humanities. They expand and to some degree explode the boundaries of the humanities disciplines. It bears repeating, however, that acknowledging the compatibility of scientific reason and violence does not inevitably result in a refusal of humanism. What emerges instead is a set of alternative visions of the human and of the relational webs it is caught in, including innovative reformulations of a humanism for the twenty-first century.

Being profoundly technophilic, and at home in the mediated word of contemporary science and technology, Ferrando has perfected both the critique of humanism and the rejection of anthropocentrism. In keeping with the feminist tradition of integrating feminist body politics into science and technology studies, however, Ferrando aims to change the rules of the scientific game altogether. Following Haraway and Braidotti, she wants to replace anthropocentrism with a set of relational links to human and nonhuman others, including indigenous peoples, LGBT people, other species, technological artifacts, and cosmic others. The collective feminist exit from Anthropos does not mark a crisis, but the explosion of multiple new beginnings.

Although Ferrando is very aware of the inhuman(e) aspects of our technologically advanced historical condition, namely mass migration, wars, terrorism, evictions, xenophobia, and expulsions, or rather because of it, she stresses the importance of solidarity, empathy, and ultimately love.

There is a deep affective vein running through this book: it includes disloyalty to one's species, but is enriched by compassion and by the awareness that critical distance does not come easy, but requires collaborative effort. Even the most technophilic among us must admit that the liberating and even transgressive potential of the new technologies, more often than not, clashes with the entrenched conservatism of the financial and other social institutions that support them. The posthuman turn is charged with affective forces, even with passion, which, as we all know, includes pathologies and even suffering.

Furthermore, Ferrando's multispecies discursive universe invites us to rethink sexuality without and beyond genders, starting from a vitalist return to the polymorphous and perverse structure of human and nonhuman sexuality. Ever mindful of the Italian school of sexual difference, she also reappraises the generative powers of female embodiment, including its reproductive capacities—maternal materialism at work. Ferrando's approach reminds us that sexuality may be caught in the socialized sex-gender binary, but is not reducible to it. The binary mechanism of capture of the gender system moreover does not alter the fact that sexuality carries transversal, structural, and vital connotations. As life-force, sexuality provides a non-essentialist and trans-species ontological structure for the organization of human and nonhuman affectivity and desire. In Ferrando's intellectual universe, it involves a phantasmagoria of possible sexes and relations that include hybrid cross-fertilizations and generative encounters with multiple human and nonhuman others.

The affect that most struck me upon reading this text is the profound trust Ferrando expresses in critical thinking as a creative practice. She practices a joyful de-familiarization that can help us take distance from old habits of thought, such as anthropocentrism, and rejoice in them. She seduces us into unfamiliar territories, going with the flow of non-unitary reason, and is elated rather than frightened by the new horizons of thought and practice that she discovers. Ferrando's culture of methodological excess supports the process of re-composing what I call, citing Deleuze, a "missing" people. She longs for an intercultural, intraspecies, and mediated community that could be brought into being by a generous gesture of collective self-styling, or mutual specification. For her, the posthuman is never post-political, but ever transversal and relational.

This book demonstrates convincingly that dis-identification from familiar values—or de-territorializations—can not only be emotionally demanding but also enables creative nomadic shifts. They act like conceptual and affective stepping stones toward the new, the "not yet." For Francesca, this move is not a tragic break, but rather a rapturous departure—the line of flight of a queen bee.

Bibliographic Note

This work is a revised and updated translation of Dr. Francesca Ferrando's book *Il Postumanesimo filosofico e le sue alterità* published by ETS in 2016 and based on her PhD dissertation, which was the recipient of the "Sainati" Philosophical Prize awarded by the president of Italy, Giorgio Napolitano, in 2014.

Introduction: From Human to Posthuman

Posthumanism is the philosophy of our time. This shows in the great interest that is developing around the theme, in the multiplication of conferences, studies, and reflections around the world. "Posthuman" has become a key concept in the contemporary academic debate, to cope with the urgency for an integral redefinition of the notion of the human, following the onto-epistemological, as well as scientific and bio-technological developments, of the twentieth and twenty-first centuries. The philosophical landscape which has since developed includes several movements and schools of thought. The label "posthuman" is often evoked in a generic and all-inclusive way to indicate any of these different perspectives, creating methodological and theoretical confusion between experts and non-experts alike.[1] Specifically, "posthuman" has become an umbrella term to include Posthumanism (Philosophical, Cultural, and Critical); Transhumanism (in its variants as Extropianism, Liberal Transhumanism, and Democratic Transhumanism, among other currents); New Materialisms (a specific feminist development within the posthumanist frame); the heterogeneous landscape of Anti-humanism; the field of Object-Oriented Ontology; Posthumanities and Metahumanities. This book attempts, on one side, to highlight the similarities and differences between the various terms and schools of thought, tracing their genealogies, analogies, and overlaps. On the other, it offers an original contribution to Philosophical Posthumanism, developing its theoretical endeavors on ontological, epistemological, and ethical grounds. The book is divided into three parts developed around three thematic nodes, identified in the following questions:

1. What Is Philosophical Posthumanism?
2. Of Which "Human" Is the Posthuman a "Post"?
3. Have Humans Always Been Posthuman?

The three questions do not constitute sharp thematic divisions, but they shall be regarded as suggestions which inform the development of the discourse. For this reason, the chapters, through which each part is articulated, are successively numbered across the three parts, to emphasize the fluidity of the narrative path.

As a navigational tool, specific questions have been implemented throughout the text, to assist the readers as they move through the revealing narrative (the full list of questions is available at the end of this introduction). Notes section offer a necessary contribution to the text and shall be considered an integral part of narration. Going back to the three thematic nodes, a historical recollection of Philosophical Posthumanism (Chapters 1 to 10) corresponds to the first question. Philosophical Posthumanism is presented as a recent development of Critical and Cultural Posthumanism, which arose within the field of literary criticism— from the first appearance of the term (Hassan 1977) until the 1990s and the publication of the key text *How We Became Posthuman* (1999) by Katherine Hayles. With respect to Critical and Cultural Posthumanism, Philosophical Posthumanism, which is still a philosophy in the making, has developed a more strictly philosophical approach, from the first decade of the twenty-first century until today. Its genealogy, traced from the "Letter on Humanism" (1947) by Martin Heidegger, passes through Postmodernism, the studies of the difference (including, among others, gender studies, critical race studies, queer theory, postcolonial studies, disability studies), and cyborg theory. Philosophical Posthumanism is genealogically related to the radical deconstruction of the "human," which began as a political cause in the 1960s, turned into an academic project in the 1970s, and evolved into an epistemological approach in the 1990s, resulting in a multiplication of situated perspectives.

While aware of its epistemic limitations (as theorized by and for humans), the non-hierarchical perspective of the posthuman does not grant any primacy to the human and articulates the conditions for an epistemology concerned with nonhuman experience as site of knowledge—from the nonhuman animal (Wolfe 2010) to artificial intelligence, robotics, and even unknown forms of life (Badmington 2004). Such a comprehensive approach is rooted in the recognition that the difference is already constitutive of the human species, with all of its gendered, ethnic, social, and individual varieties. In other words, the posthuman recognition of nonhuman alterities starts with the recognition of human alterities. Posthumanism can be considered as a second generation of Postmodernism, leading the deconstruction of the human to its extreme consequences by bringing to its theoretical revision speciesism, that is, the privilege of some species over others. The onto-epistemological openness of Posthumanism is placed in a hybrid vision of humanity itself: through the cyborg,[2] specifically located in the critical reflection of Donna Haraway (1985), Posthumanism has internalized the hybrid as its point of departure (that is, an origin which has no origin[3]). On the one hand, Posthumanism can be seen as a "post-humanism," that is, a radical critique of humanism and anthropocentrism; on the other hand, in its significations as a "posthuman-ism," it recognizes those aspects which are constitutively human, and nevertheless, beyond the constitutive limits of the human in the strict sense of the term. Posthumanism is a praxis, as well as a philosophy of mediation, which manifests post-dualistic, post-centralizing, comprehensive, and "acknowledging" types of approaches, in the sense that they acknowledge alterity and recognize themselves in alterity (this term is particularly suitable because of its double signification of acknowledging and expressing gratitude—modalities paired in the philosophy of "acknowledgment").

Posthumanism will then be compared with other currents of thought (Chapter 3), starting with the main distinction between Posthumanism and Transhumanism (Chapters 4 to 7). Both movements arose more clearly in the 1990s, orientating their interests around similar topics, but they share neither the same roots nor perspectives. While Posthumanism generated out of Postmodernism, Transhumanism seeks its origins in the Enlightenment, and therefore does not expropriate humanism; on the contrary, it can be defined as an "ultra-humanism" (Onishi 2011). In order to greatly enhance human abilities, Transhumanism opts for a radical transformation of the human condition by existing, emerging, and speculative technologies (as in the case of regenerative medicine, radical life extension, mind uploading, and cryonics). For some transhumanists, human beings may eventually transform themselves so radically as to become posthuman (the concept of posthuman itself is interpreted in a specific transhumanist way). Here, it is important to note that Transhumanism is not an homogeneous movement. In particular, we will present some of the main voices of Extropianism (More 1990, 1998) (Vita-More 2004), Democratic Transhumanism (Hughes 2004), and the Singularity (Kurzweil 2005). These various currents, while differing on certain aspects, share the main goal of Transhumanism, which is human enhancement. More in general, if the strength of the transhumanist vision consists in its openness to the possibilities offered by science and technology, therein lays its weakness, which can be detected in a techno-reductionist assimilation of existence, and in a progressivist approach that does not leave space to deconstructionist practices.

If rationality and progress are at the core of the transhumanist postulation, a radical critique of those same notions is the kernel of Antihumanism, a philosophical position which, although sharing its roots in Postmodernity with the posthuman, should not be assimilated to it (Chapter 9). The deconstruction of the human, which is almost absent in the transhumanist reflection, is crucial to Antihumanism. This is one of its main points in common with Posthumanism, while their main distinction is already embedded in their morphologies and, specifically, in their composition: the structural opposition implied by the prefix "anti-" has been challenged by the posthumanist post-dualistic process-ontological horizon. Posthumanism, after all, is aware of the fact that hierarchical humanistic presumptions cannot be easily dismissed or erased. In this respect, more than with Foucault's death of Man, the posthuman is in tune with Derrida's deconstructive approach (1967). In this chapter, the *Übermensch* of Friedrich Nietzsche (1882; 1883–5) will be related, from different perspectives, to both Post- and Trans- and Anti-Humanism. Another aspect which will be presented in a comparative way within the posthuman scenario (understood here in its broadest sense) is technology and its potentials offered to the revisitation of the notion of the human (Chapter 8). In the transhumanist reflection, such a focus is mostly centralized and instrumentalized: technology resolves as a means and an end for obtaining specific goals—from increasingly advanced technology to immortality, redefined as radical life extension. Philosophical Posthumanism, on one side, explores technology as a mode of revealing, passing through "The Question Concerning Technology" (1953) by Martin Heidegger, and thus re-accessing its ontological and existential potentials; on the other, the notion of technologies of the self (Foucault 1988) becomes significant in a posthumanist scenario which has deconstructed the dualism Self/Others (Chapter 10).

We can now address the second question: *Of which "human" is the posthuman a "post"?* Historically, the recognition of the human status has been regularly switched on and off. In Western history, for instance, the concept of the "human" has been reinscribed within categories marked by exclusionary practices. Sexism, racism, classism, ageism, homophobia, and ableism, alongside other forms of discrimination, have informed the written and unwritten laws of recognition as to who was to be considered human. For instance, slaves and women, among many other categories, have represented the margins of the human, the chaos, the non-disciplinable (Chapter 14). In Western history, "human" referred, more specifically, to white, male, heterosexual and propertied citizens, who would comply with institutionalized norms, as well as with ethnic, cultural, and physical characteristics. In order to comply with a comprehensive and "acknowledging" approach to the notion of the human, one consequent question needs to be asked: How have the (categories of) humans who have been repeatedly dehumanized dealt with their humanness? How have they reconfigured such a denied status? In order to conceive a posthumanist approach, it is first necessary to reflect on the meaning of the notion of the "human," both by investigating on the technologies of the self historically developed by the human "others" (Chapter 15) and by disclosing the ways by which its hegemonic groups have formed and established. We will inquire into the process of humanizing—here conceived as a verb, "to humanize" (Chapter 12) rather than as an "anthropological machine" (Agamben 2002) (Chapter 13)—and then delve into the semantics and pragmatics supporting the term "human" (Chapter 16). Specifically, the human will be investigated both in its Latin etymology (*Humanitas*) (Chapter 17) and in its taxonomic classification as *Homo sapiens* (Chapter 18). Such inquiries are necessary in order to reflect upon the relevance of postulating a "post" to the notion of the human. On the one hand, the posthuman must be aware of its genealogical relationship to the human, and thus delve into the historical as well as philosophical meanings of what this may entail. On the other hand, Posthumanism successfully manifests its critical commitment and establishes its approach through the conditions of the "post" (Chapter 11).

The posthuman destabilizes the limits and symbolic borders posed by the notion of the human. Dualisms such as human/animal, human/machine, and, more in general, human/nonhuman are re-investigated through a perception which does not work on oppositional schemata. In the same way, the posthuman deconstructs the clear division between life/death, organic/synthetic, and natural/artificial. We are now entering the domain of the third question: *Have humans always been posthuman?* Here, we will investigate the "bio" realm: life and biology (Chapters 19 to 22) as well as bioethics and the biotechnological evolutions of posthumanities (Chapters 23 to 25). The anthropocentric choice of privileging *bios*, instead of *zoē*, exposes the exclusivist domain of "life" itself, which is more clearly presented as a human notion based on the human cognitive apparatus. In this part, the posthuman perspectivist approach will be acknowledged in its embodied character, delineated historically through the proposal of Friedrich Nietzsche (1887; 1901/6) (Chapter 27) and biologically through a critical appraisal of the concept of "autopoiesis" (Maturana/Varela 1972) (Chapter 26). Ultimately, Posthumanism challenges biocentrism, sentiocentrism, vitalism, and the concept of life itself, blurring the boundaries between the animate and the inanimate, in a quantum approach to the physics of existence. It is now time to access the third level of reconfiguration of the posthuman, which is more specifically ontological. We will start by investigating the dynamic and pluralistic natureculture[4] of matter (Chapter 29) through quantum physics and the string theory, philosophically explored within the frame of New Materialisms (Chapter 28), and in particular, through the reflection of Karen Barad (2007) and her relational ontology. Within this frame, the human is perceived not as a single agent, but as part of a semiotic, material, as well as multidimensional network (Latour 1987, 2005); in this sense, the human is already posthuman. Evolution, in its materialist configurations, can be approached as a technology of existence; every material manifestation may be perceived as nodes of becoming, in a pluralistic monist, as well as a monistic pluralist approach to the multiverse.

The notion of the multiverse (Chapter 30) refers to the scientific investigations on matter from the micro to the macro level of materialization, which recently brought different fields (from quantum physics to cosmology and astrophysics) to the same hypothetical conclusion: this universe might be one of many. The hypothesis of the multiverse is inherently posthuman; it not only stretches any universe-centric perspective (problematizing the inclusive, but still centralized, notion of a universe), but materializes the dissolution of strict binaries, dualistic modes, and exclusivist approaches. And still, despite the undoubtedly nonhuman-centric character of this notion, the hypothesis of the multiverse has been mostly developed in human-centric and solipsistic terms, both scientifically (Everett 1956) and philosophically (Lewis 1986). Instead, we will revisit such a notion through the rhizome (Deleuze and Guattari 1987), and develop it speculatively, not by counting on any essentialism, polarity, or strict dualism but by relying on a hybrid, mediated, and process-ontological perspective. We will present such an interpretation of the multiverse, which we will refer to as the "posthuman multiverse," as both a thought experiment, which might expand a speculative perception of the self, and a material hypothesis, which may conceal a possible physics outfit of the actual multiverse. Such a hypothesis, based on the deconstruction of the Self/Others paradigm, entails that matter, while constituting this universe, it would also be actualizing an indefinite number of other universes, in a process of both relationality and autonomy. This original acquisition of meaning of the multiverse reveals itself inductive for a posthuman ontology which materializes the posthumanist overcoming of any strict dichotomy.

Navigational Tool: A Glossary of Questions

This is a glossary of the main questions that the book covers in each section.

Part 1 What Is Philosophical Posthumanism?

1. Premises

a.   Are these scenarios inducing a paradigm shift in the ontological and epistemological perception of the human? Is this shift "post-human"?
b.   Where does this easiness on the use of the "post" come from?
c.   How to define Philosophical Posthumanism?

2. From Postmodern to Posthuman

a.   What does Posthumanism mean?
b.   Where does Posthumanism come from?
c.   When was the term "posthuman" coined?
d.   What is Critical Posthumanism?
e.   What is Cultural Posthumanism?
f.   Which movements go under the umbrella term "posthuman"?

3. Posthumanism and Its Others

a.   Within the umbrella term "posthuman," which movements are more often confused?
b.   What are the main differences between Transhumanism and Posthumanism?
c.   Are "we" already posthuman?

4. The Birth of Transhumanism

a.   What are the genealogical roots of Transhumanism?
b.   Why was Julian Huxley's vision anthropocentric?

5. Contemporary Transhumanism(s)

a. What is Transhumanism?
b. What do all these movements share?
c. How can human enhancement be achieved?
d. What is Extropianism?

6. The Roots of Transhumanism

a. Where does Transhumanism come from?
b. Why is the transhumanist embracing of the humanist tradition of the
    Enlightenment problematic, from a posthumanist standpoint?

7. Transhumanism and Techno-Enchantment

a. Why is technology central to the discussion on Transhumanism?
b. How can the human be redesigned, according to Transhumanism?
c. How are the histories and herstories of the historical human body going to
    affect our posthuman future?

8. Posthumanist Technologies as Ways of Revealing

a. Why is technology relevant to the discussion on Posthumanism?
b. Why Heidegger?
c. What is technology?
d. Do we really know what we are talking about when we reflect on technology?
e. What does "poiesis" mean?
f. Why is modern technology an *Enframing*?
g. What is this danger that Heidegger is referring to?
h. When did this switch in worldviews take place?

9. Antihumanism and the *Übermensch*

a. What is the main characteristic of Antihumanism?
b. In what do Antihumanism and Posthumanism harmonize, and in what do
    they differ?
c. What does *episteme* mean, according to Foucault?
d. If, according to Foucault, the current notion of "man" is near its end, when
    did such a notion come along?

e.   What does *Übermensch* mean?

f.   Why is Nietzsche's *Übermensch* relevant to the posthuman discussion?

g.   What are the metamorphoses of the spirit, according to Nietzsche?

h.   Would Nietzsche have supported human enhancement?

i.   What about the overhuman in relation to Philosophical Posthumanism?

j.   Why is Zarathustra the one to proclaim the death of God?

k.   Why did Nietzsche proclaim the death of God?

l.   How can Nietzsche be relevant in our daily life?

m.   What if your life was going to come back exactly the same forever?

n.   Does Posthumanism support the death of God?

o.   If God and Man are dead, who killed them?

p.   What are some of the other movements related to the posthuman turn?

10. Philosophical Posthumanism

a.   What is Philosophical Posthumanism?

b.   Where does Philosophical Posthumanism come from?

c.   What are the sources of this specific take of Philosophical Posthumanism?

Interlude 1

a.   What about post-dualism?

b.   What kind of dualism is deconstructed by Philosophical Posthumanism?

c.   Why is post-dualism important?

d.   What are the genealogical sources of post-dualism in relation to Philosophical Posthumanism?

e.   Why is the prefix "post" relevant? Where does the notion of the "human" come from? More specifically: of which "human" is the posthuman a "post"?

Part 2 Of Which "Human" Is the Posthuman a "Post"?

11. The Power of the Hyphen

a.   Where does the term "human" come from?

b.   Why are the "post" and the hyphen "-" relevant to the discussion on the posthuman?

c.   Why is "post-" needed in the emergence of Post(-)humanism?

d.   When and how have we become "human"?

12. Humanizing

a. Is the "human" a notion (i.e., a noun) or a process (i.e., a verb)?
b. Why does de Beauvoir refer to the Woman as the "Other"?
c. Why was the reaction of the intellectual establishment so extreme to Irigaray's ideas?
d. Is there a subject enacting the process of humanizing? Is humanizing a process or a project (or both)?

13. The Anthropological Machine

a. Who were these humans, and who set the standards of the "human"?
b. "Who" is humanizing "whom"?
c. Is language "that" important in the formulation of philosophical accounts?

14. Almost, Human

a. How to achieve a comprehensive analysis of the process of humanizing?
b. How did the excluded subjectivities perceive themselves in relation to the notion of the human?
c. Which humans have been excluded from the notion of the human?
d. Why are we going back to the time of the *Conquista*?
e. How may genocide result out of processes of dehumanization?
f. Have all the human "outsiders" been considered less-than human?

15. Technologies of the Self as Posthumanist (Re)Sources

a. How have the (categories of) humans who have been repeatedly dehumanized dealt with their humanness? How have they reconfigured such a denied status?
b. How to account for the outsiders of the discourse?
c. What are the technologies of the self?
d. How to access non-hegemonic perspectives on the notion of the human?
e. What about spirituality?

16. The Epiphany of Becoming Human

a. What are some of the possible outcomes of the process of humanizing?

b. How can we detect a purpose for the human(s) as a species if the human is not one but many?
c. Why is the overview effect significant to the posthuman approach?
d. When and how did humans become "human"?
e. Is the notion of the human inherently biased?
f. What is the human?

17. Where Does the Word "Human" Come From?

a. When and how did the Latin notion of "*humanus*" emerge?
b. If "*humanus*" was coined in the age of the Roman Republican, which writers started to employ this term?

18. Mammals or *Homo sapiens*?

a. How are humans classified in biology?
b. When and how were humans first classified as *Homo sapiens*?
c. Are there any biased assumptions in Linnaeus's system? If so, do they allow for an impartial comprehension of all human beings under the notion of *Homo sapiens*?

Interlude 2

a. Of which human is the posthuman a "post"?

Part 3 Have Humans Always Been Posthuman?

19. Post-Anthropocentrism in the Anthropocene

a. Why is anthropocentrism a problem?
b. When can we trace the beginning of the informal geological era of the Anthropocene?
c. Has the notion of the Anthropocene been contested?
d. How can we achieve a post-anthropocentric paradigm shift?
e. What is the Earth? Can a planet be considered an organism?
f. What is the Gaia hypothesis?
g. What kind of issues does the Gaia theory raise?
h. How can life and death coexist?

20. Posthuman Life

a.   Does the notion of "life" offer the ultimate border between animate and inanimate?

20a. Bios and Zoē

a.   What is the scientific definition of life?

20b. Animate/Inanimate

c.   What is life?
d.   What does it mean that life is a "relative" category of classification?
e.   Why is animism relevant?
f.   Are machines animate?
g.   What is the relationship between humans and robots?
h.   Are robots alive?

21. Artificial Life

a.   Can life be artificial?
b.   Does life need to be embodied?
c.   Why is Biological AI a turning point?
d.   Is the interest on Artificial Life taking away from nonhuman animals? In other words, is Philosophical Posthumanism technocentric?
e.   Does artificial life presume a new ontological primacy?
f.   What does "eco-technology" mean?
g.   Is their material cycle separated from the notion of technology?

22. Evolving Species

a.   What is "life" from an evolutionary standpoint?
b.   Why is the discussion on the origin of life significant from a posthumanist perspective?
c.   What does the notion of "species" mean from a genetic perspective?
d.   What does the notion of "species" infer? In other words, is the notion of "species" implicitly speciesist?
e.   Why is Vandana Shiva critical of the notion of the cyborg?
f.   Why is advanced capitalism perversely post-anthropocentric?

23. Posthumanities

a. Will humans evolve into different species?
b. How does evolution work?
c. What does "posthumanities" mean?
d. Who was Lamarck and how is Lamarckism re-entering the conversation on evolution?
e. What is epigenetics?
f. How does epigenetics occur?
g. Why is epigenetics relevant to Philosophical Posthumanism?

24. Posthuman Bioethics

a. To be or not to be genetically modified?
b. What is CRISPR?
c. What does eugenics mean?
d. Should we, as a society, proceed in this path toward a future of designer babies?
e. What is the difference between bio-conservatives and bio-liberals?
f. Why is the separation between "therapy" and "enhancement" slippery?

25. Human Enhancement

a. How to regulate human enhancement?
b. What is human enhancement?
c. Are the outcomes of genetic engineering fully predictable?
d. What is genetic discrimination?
e. What is the precautionary principle?
f. Precautionary or proactionary?
g. What is the proactionary principle?
h. What is the bioethical standpoint of Posthumanism in relation to human enhancement?
i. Is Posthumanism against human enhancement?
j. Is this take on human enhancement valid for all the thinkers who define themselves as posthumanists?
k. What is Speculative Posthumanism?
l. Is "life" an adequate term to refer to these hypothetical evolutionary scenarios?

26. Cognitive Autopoiesis

a. Are there alternatives to the notion of "life"?
b. Is the internet alive?
c. Are robots nonhuman persons?
d. What does "autopoiesis" mean?
e. Where did the concept of autopoiesis first appear?
f. Is the notion of autopoiesis exhaustive from a posthuman perspective?
g. What is Maturana and Varela's cognitive approach?
h. What is the difference between cognitive science and epistemology?
i. Where does the notion of autopoiesis come from?
j. What about animal testing?
k. Is a post-anthropocentric reading of the frog experiment ahistorical?
l. What are the explicit and implicit assumptions of the frog experiment?
m. Which kind of criticisms did Maturana and Varela's theories receive?
n. What is solipsism?
o. What is the polite convention, according to Alan Turing?
p. What is cognitive anthropocentrism?
q. What is the difference between relativism and perspectivism?
r. What is that "something else" which is presupposed by the notion of "relative"?

27. Posthumanist Perspectivism

a. Where does perspectivism come from?
b. What are the roots of perspectivism in Western philosophy?
c. Is Nietzsche's perspectivism human-centric?
d. Does Posthumanism sustain the notion of "fact"?
e. What does pluralism imply from a philosophical posthumanist perspective?
f. What is feminist epistemology?
g. What is the standpoint theory?
h. What about nonhuman perspectives?
i. Affinity or Identity?
j. What is "strategic essentialism"?
k. What is the relation between perspectivism and embodiment?
l. Do embodiments have to be physical and/or biological?
m. What is the will to power?

n. What about alternative types of embodiments?
o. What about dream embodiments?

28. From New Materialisms to Object-Oriented Ontology

a. What is New Materialism?
b. Does New Materialism come from historical materialism?
c. Who coined the term "New Materialism"?
d. Where does New Materialism come from?
e. What is agential realism?
f. What are some of the risks run by new materialist thinkers?
g. What is vitalism?
h. What is Spinoza's conatus?
i. What is "vital materiality"?
j. Why is Bennett's notion of nonhuman agency relevant to Philosophical Posthumanism?
k. What are some of the differences of Bennett's proposal from Philosophical Posthumanism?
l. How does vitalism differ from Barad's agential realism?
m. What is Object-Oriented Ontology (OOO)?
n. What are the main similarities between OOO and Philosophical Posthumanism?
o. What are the main differences between OOO and Philosophical Posthumanism?
p. What are flat ontologies?
q. How can we have flat ontologies if there are always perspectives?

29. Philosophical Posthumanist Ontology

a. What is matter?
b. What is string theory, and why is it relevant to Philosophical Posthumanism?
c. Monism or pluralism?
d. What is the wave-particle duality?
e. What kind of ontology does quantum physics suggest?
f. What is reductionism?
g. What is the problem with reductionism?

h.   What kind of posthumanist philosophical insights emerge out of string theory?
i.   What does Susskind mean by the "landscape"?
j.   How is string theory related to the hypothesis of the multiverse?

30. The Multiverse

a.   What is the multiverse?

30a. The Multiverse in Science

a.   What are the four main views of the multiverse?
b.   Is the notion of the multiverse posthuman?
c.   Why focus on the narcissistic projection that the human realm is flourishing somewhere?
d.   Why "the wastefulness worry," in the hypothesis of the multiverse, cannot be easily dismissed?

30b. The Multiverse in Philosophy

a.   What about the notion of the multiverse in the field of philosophy?
b.   What about contemporary philosophy?
c.   If other words exist, do these worlds share something in common?
d.   What is the posthuman multiverse?

30c. A Thought Experiment: The Posthuman Multiverse

a.   Why a thought experiment?
b.   What does this thought experiment entail?
c.   What does this thought experiment mean in relation to "you"?
d.   What if our way of existing had multidimensional ripple effects?
e.   What is a rhizome?
f.   Why is notion of the rhizome relevant to Philosophical Posthumanism?
g.   What is the difference between the metaphor of the rhizome and metaphor of the multiverse?
h.   What are humans, within a posthumanist multiverse?
i.   What is posthuman agency?

Interlude 3

a. What is post-anthropocentrism? And, what is post-dualism?
b. How does matter materialize?
c. What does "ethics" mean?
d. How can we exist, as posthumanists?

Concluding Celebration

a. How can we exist, as posthumanists?
b. Can we be posthuman now?
c. How can we become posthuman?
d. Can humans be posthuman?
e. What does it mean to be posthuman in relation to other species?
f. Why is technology relevant to the discussion on Philosophical Posthumanism?
g. Is this the era of Philosophical Posthumanism?
h. What are the fields of investigation of Philosophical Posthumanism?
i. Is Philosophical Posthumanism a praxis?
j. Why Philosophical Posthumanism?
k. Is it time to say goodbye to the human?
l. How can alterity be within the self?

Part One

What Is Philosophical Posthumanism?

1

Premises

The twenty-first century has ushered in a redefinition of the body by cybernetic and biotechnological developments; the concept of "human" has been broadly challenged, while "posthuman" and "transhuman" have become terms of philosophical and scientific enquiry. Physicality no longer represents the primary space for social interaction, as the growing issue of internet addiction seems to suggest. Human cloning has approached bioethical disputes, and surrogate motherhood is deconstructing natural conception. The semantic demarcation between humans and cyborgs[1] has blurred. On the one side, electronic pacemakers, high-tech prostheses, and plastic surgery have become accepted practices of body reconfiguration. On the other, in a pioneer experimentation[2] toward technological enhancement, a growing number of people have implanted RFIDs under their skin. *Are these scenarios inducing a paradigm shift in the ontological and epistemological perception of the human? Is this shift "posthuman"?* Philosophical Posthumanism is flourishing in an era which has been, and still is, generating a proliferation of "post-s": from post-modern to post-postmodern, from postcolonial to post-capitalist, from post-feminist to post-racial, from post-democracy to the hyperbolic post-truth, and so on. We shall locate the posthuman within this need for "post-s"—an urgency to express something which seems to escape each and every singular "post," and which should be investigated, more generally, through the significance of the "post" itself. *Where does this easiness on the use of the "post" come from?* There are many traditions of thought which could be held responsible for this tendency: the integral deconstruction of fixed categories invested by postmodernity; the epistemological impact of quantum physics; and the increased role of technology in the formation of human identity,[3] with a lead to hybridization as a constitutive technology of the self.[4] Philosophical Posthumanism reflects upon the broader signification of technological developments, but it does not exhaust its analysis there. Actually, considering that a large number of the population worldwide is still engaged in the attempt of surviving, if Philosophical Posthumanism was reduced to a reflection on the technological kinship of the human revisited in its specific technical endeavors, such a preference would confine it to a classist and techno-centric academic movement.[5] In fact, the posthuman turn cannot be accounted only in relation to the human or to technology, but it should be engaged per se.

How to define Philosophical Posthumanism? Philosophical Posthumanism is an onto-epistemological approach, as well as an ethical one, manifesting as a philosophy of mediation,[6] which discharges any confrontational dualisms and hierarchical legacies; this is why it can be approached as a post-humanism, a post-anthropocentrism, and a post-dualism. Historically, it can be seen as the philosophical approach which suits the informal geological time of the Anthropocene (Crutzen and Stoermer 2000). While Philosophical Posthumanism focuses on decentering the human from the center of the discourse, the Anthropocene marks the extent of the impact of human activities on a planetary level, and thus stresses the urgency for humans to become aware of pertaining to an ecosystem which, when damaged, negatively affects the human condition as well. Posthumanism exceeds the particular tradition of Western academic thought, and it can be traced and enacted in different cultures as well as in different modes.[7] In a similar way, it should be noted that Posthumanism is not only an academic perspective but a transhistorical attitude which has been a part of human cultures, trans-spaces, and eras. Hybrid representations can be traced as early as the upper paleolithic age—for instance, the lion-headed figurine of the Hohlenstein-Stadel (Germany), which is determined to be about 32,000 years old, is the oldest known zoomorphic sculpture that has been found in the world till present (Hahn 1993). Hybrid imageries have been part of the human symbolic heritage since the very beginning of recorded civilization; highlighted as cultural and ontological metaphors by Postmodernism,[8] they developed a further significance within Posthumanism and the rise of biotechnological cultures (think, for instance, of genetic chimeras). On one side, due to genetic engineering and nanotechnology, life itself has become more and more of a "biotechnological assemblage" (Waldby 2000); on the other, the environmental concerns of posthuman ethics, which invest in recycling policies and sustainability, spontaneously delve into such tradition. This book will deal mostly with a contemporary Western philosophical genealogy of the posthuman; this location, far from essential, shall be seen as a part of an ongoing choral process unraveling the global genealogies of the posthuman. It is important to emphasize this non-reducibility of sources so as not to fall into any parochial or culturally biased foundational myth. Before delving into the meanings and possibilities of the posthuman approach, we should also mention its species-specific epistemological premises. In the economy of knowledge, humans are both subjects and objects[9]: even when trying to avoid anthropocentric positions, humans are still communicating specific and situated human understandings in a human language to other human beings. Posthumanism shares with humanism the fact that it is still enacted by human beings, but accesses such an epistemological standpoint through the feminist policies of situating the self,[10] and also by acknowledging the self as plural and relational. Posthumanism postulates a specific self-awareness,[11] which recognizes its own embodied location without placing it at the top of any epistemological hierarchy.[12] Andy Miah, in "A Critical History of Posthumanism" (2008), underlines this aspect, as he states: "A crucial premise of posthumanism is its critical stance towards the idea that humans are a superior species in the natural order" (77). In the following, he clarifies, "In this sense, the 'post' of posthumanism need not imply moving beyond humanness in some biological or evolutionary manner. Rather, the starting point should be an attempt to understand what has been omitted from an anthropocentric worldview" (*ibidem*). From a philosophical posthumanist perspective based on mediation, we can interpret Posthumanism as both a reflection on what has been omitted from the notion of the human and a speculation about the possible developments of the human species. The two perspectives are connected: the speculative aspect relies upon a critical understanding of what the notion of the human implies. A critical revision of the human is necessary to the development of a posthumanist agenda.[13]

2

From Postmodern to Posthuman

What does Posthumanism mean? The term "Posthumanism" may refer, more specifically, to Critical Posthumanism, Cultural Posthumanism, and Philosophical Posthumanism. In this chapter, we will present and explain each movement; within the book, the term "Posthumanism" will be implemented to include them all. *Where does Posthumanism come from?* Posthumanism came along within and after Postmodernism, generated out of the radical deconstruction[1] of the "human," which began as a philosophical as well as a political project in the late 1960s and turned into an epistemological one in the 1990s. Posthumanism is a "post" to the notion of the "human," located within the historical occurrence of "humanism" (which was founded on hierarchical schemata),[2] and in an uncritical acceptance of "anthropocentrism," founded upon another hierarchical construct based on speciesist assumptions.[3] Both the notion of the "human" and the historical occurrence of "humanism," have been sustained by reiterative formulations of symbolic "others," which have functioned as markers of the shifting borders of who and what would be considered "human": non-Europeans, non-whites, women, queers, freaks, animals, and automata, among others, have historically represented such oppositional terms. As Rosi Braidotti puts it, in *Metamorphoses: Towards a Materialist Theory of Becoming* (2002): "Postmodernity is notoriously the age of proliferating differences. The devalued 'others' which constituted the specular complement of the modern subject—woman, the ethnic or racialized other and nature or 'earth-others'— return with a vengeance" (174). Posthumanism may arise once the need for such a "vengeance" has been fulfilled, and the voices of the subjectivities which have been historically reduced to the realm of the "Other," have been acknowledged. Posthumanism is inextricably related to the studies of the differences, referring to the fields of research which developed out of the deconstruction of the "neutral subject" of Western onto-epistemologies.[4] The deconstruction enacted, within the historical and philosophical frame of Postmodernism, by feminist, black, gay and lesbian, postcolonial, and chicana theorists, together with differently abled activists and other outsiders, pointed out the partiality of the construction of the Discourse.[5] In order to postulate a post- to the human, the differences which are constitutive to the human, and which have been historically erased by the self-claimed objectivity of hegemonic accounts, have to be acknowledged. Posthumanism is indebted to the reflections developed out of the "margins" of such a centralized human subject, because of their emphasis on the human as a process, more than a given, inherently characterized by differences and shifting identities.

When was the term "posthuman" coined? The genealogical trace between the posthuman and the postmodern is not only an epistemological and historical affiliation. The terms "posthuman" and "Posthumanism" first appeared within postmodern literature. In particular, literary theorist Ihab Hassan, was among the first to use it in the article "Prometheus as Performer: Toward a Posthumanist Culture?" (1977), to then develop it in *The Postmodern Turn* (1987), where he pointed out some crucial aspects within this specific linguistic asset: "I see a pattern that many others have also seen: a vast, revisionary will in the Western world, unsettling/resettling codes, canons, procedures, beliefs—intimating a post-humanism?" (XVI). The pattern Hassan defines as a "post-humanism" resonates with the contemporary urgency to express something which seems to escape each and every singular "post," debated previously. Hassan thus foresaw how the postmodern investigation could turn into a Posthumanism. Referring to Postmodernism, he stated: "On some deeper level of its transformations, it still reaches for something larger, something other, which some call posthumanism" (XVII). Throughout the text, Hassan highlighted some key aspects of Posthumanism, such as investing in a post-dualistic approach,[6] and calling for an inclusive notion of the human, which would result in a "posthuman vision": "The cardinal question of course remains: how in practice to found a human or posthuman vision—call it inclusively human—or an anxious order of knowledge?" (82) Although the term "inclusive"—which, in order to *in*-clude, consequently *ex*-cludes others—can still be criticized,[7] Hassan outlined some of the focal points of Posthumanism, such as: the further deconstruction of the human, an openness through the possibilities of the "post," and a post-dualistic approach which proceed through recognitions, instead of assimilations.

What is Critical Posthumanism? The specific take on the posthuman developed within the field of literary criticism is sometimes referred to as Critical Posthumanism. A text which was crucial to the development of this approach was *How We Became Posthuman: Virtual Bodies in Cybernetics, Literature and Informatics* (1999) by Katherine Hayles. Her criticism of disembodied narratives within cybernetic and informatic literature paved the way for a posthumanist approach rooted within feminist and postmodern practices.[8]

What is Cultural Posthumanism? The posthumanist turn, as enacted within the field of literary theory in the 1990s, was also embraced by cultural studies, producing a specific take on the posthuman, which has been defined as Cultural Posthumanism.[9] A crucial contribution to it was given by cyborg theory, inaugurated by the success of "A Manifesto for Cyborgs: Science, Technology, and Socialist Feminism in the 1980s" (1985), where Donna Haraway problematized notions of human fixity and introduced the inquiry into the hybrid in positive and generative terms: "By the late twentieth century, our time, a mythic time, we are all chimeras, theorized and fabricated hybrids of machine and organism; in short, we are cyborgs. The cyborg is our ontology; it gives us our politics" (50). Haraway was also a main influence in the development of an academic field which became focal within Cultural Posthumanism, which is animal studies (for instance, Haraway 1989, 1991, 1996a, 2003, 2007). It has to be noted, though, that animal studies per se do not necessarily imply a posthumanist approach, as Cary Wolfe notices in *What is Posthumanism?* (2010), in which he exposes the risks of an uncritical type of pluralism, which thus becomes "incorporation."[10] *Which movements go under the umbrella term "posthuman"?* Although these different takes on Posthumanism—such as Critical, Cultural, and Philosophical Posthumanism—cannot be seen as separated but inherently related, the notion of the posthuman per se has developed in profoundly different ways, within the frame of not only Posthumanism (to be considered in its broadest sense), but also Transhumanism and Antihumanism (in all of their variants); Metahumanism, Posthumanities, and Metahumanities; Object-Oriented Ontology and the nonhuman turn; among other currents. The rich variety of movements going under the umbrella term "posthuman" demonstrates the growing interest on this topic, as well as generates confusion between experts and non-experts alike.

Posthumanism and Its Others

Within the umbrella term "posthuman," which movements are more often confused?
The most confused areas of signification are the ones shared by Transhumanism
and Posthumanism; the most common misunderstandings are generated by
the ways the term "posthuman" has been employed within posthumanist and
transhumanist discourses[1]. In fact, while within trashumanist literature, the
term "posthuman" may refer to the next phase of (human) evolution, within
posthumanist literature, it may refer to the symbolic move of going beyond
the human, embracing a post-anthropocentric approach which acknowledges
technology and the environment, among others, as defining aspects of the human.
What are the main differences between Transhumanism and Posthumanism?
Both Transhumanism and Posthumanism arose in the late 1980s/early 1990s,
orientating their interests around similar topics, but they generally do not
share either the same roots or perspectives, even if they do share a common
perception of the human as a non-fixed and mutable condition. Transhumanism
problematizes the current understanding of the human not necessarily through
its past and present legacies, but through the possibilities inscribed within its
biological evolution, and in particular, its physical and cognitive enhancement.
The concept of Posthumanism itself is interpreted in a specific transhumanist way.
In order to greatly enhance human abilities, Transhumanism opts for a radical
transformation of the human condition by existing, emerging, and speculative
technologies (as in the case of regenerative medicine, radical life extension, mind
uploading,[2] and cryonics); it thus suggests that diversity and multiplicity will
replace the notion of existing within a single system, such as a biological body.[3]
For some transhumanists, human beings may eventually transform themselves
so radically as to become "posthuman" (a condition which will follow the current
transhuman era). For instance, transhumanist philosopher Max More declares:
"By thoughtfully, carefully, and yet boldly applying technology to ourselves,
we can become something no longer accurately described as human—we can
become posthuman" (More 2013: 4).

Let's then ask the important question: *Are "we" already posthuman?* According to Transhumanism, the answer is: no, we are not posthuman yet. We were humans; some of us can be currently defined as transhuman—for instance, by merging more and more with technology, and by approaching the human as an open project that can be redesigned (Vita-More 2004). Eventually, according to Transhumanism, some may become posthuman;[4] for instance, in the close future, the speculative technology of mind uploading may manifest in hybrid co-emergences of human consciousness and machinic assemblages which could not be considered "human" anymore—humans, for instance, have (and are) biological bodies; still, they would be intrinsically related to the human species, since the phenomenological genealogy of their own consciousness would have had originated out of embodied human experiences. Going back to our question if we are already posthuman, the answer may vary, depending on the philosophical movement we are contemplating. According to Transhumanism, the answer is: not yet, some may become posthuman in the close future. On the contrary, according to Posthumanism, the answer is: yes, we can already be posthuman now, by fully embracing the consequences of the historical and material deconstruction of the notion of the human. Posthumanism does not contemplate a linear notion of time; today, yesterday, and tomorrow are not separated. We, posthumans, cannot think of the future without thinking of the present and of the past—this is why a genealogical approach to the human is relevant. Equally, we cannot think of the past without the future and the present. For instance, only now we can fully see the environmental damage brought by the Industrial Revolution, along with other aspects, such as better living conditions for some of the humans who are currently living in industrialized nations, and so on. Posthumanism addresses the posthuman not only as an onto-epistemology, but also as a perspectivism and a praxis. According to Posthumanism, we can be posthuman now in the ways we are existing, in our modes of enactment, in our relating to others and to ourselves as "others," through the deconstruction of the human approached in light of post-humanism, post-anthropocentrism, and post-dualism. It is time to delve into this fascinating movement, focusing first on its differences and similarities with Transhumanism and Antihumanism.[5]

The Birth of Transhumanism

What are the genealogical roots of Transhumanism? Let's start our inquiry into Transhumanism[1] by examining the roots of the term itself. The verb "trasumanar," that is, going beyond the human, can be already traced in the *Comedìa* (1304–21)—later known as *La Divina Commedia*, written by Dante Alighieri (1265–1321). The way Dante employed the verb, though, is very different from its current use: the specific state of "trasumanar," that is, transcending the human, is experienced by Dante (as the subject of the *Comedìa*) in the presence of God.[2] In a similar way, T. S. Eliot (1888–1965) uses the term in his play *The Cocktail Party* (1950) to refer to the risks of the human journey in becoming illuminated.[3] The term "trans-humanizing" can also be found in the paper "The Essence of the Democratic Idea: A Biological Approach" (1949) included in the posthumous collection *The Future of Mankind* (1959), by the philosopher Pierre Teilhard de Chardin (1881–1955), in an extensive signification related to the ethical, political, and spiritual realms.[4] The impact of Teilhard de Chardin on Transhumanism has been underestimated (Steinhart 2008). The transhumanist movement notably recognizes the closest reference to Transhumanism as the current philosophical attitude in the writings of Julian Huxley (1887–1975), the evolutionary biologist and the brother of Aldous Huxley (1894–1963). The intellectual exchange between Teilhard de Chardin and Huxley is often ignored, but it is important to note that Huxley endorsed Teilhard de Chardin's approach to evolution as a process leading to an expansion of consciousness and wrote the introduction to Teilhard de Chardin's seminal work *The Phenomenon of Man* (1955). Inspired by this exchange, Huxley coined the term "Transhumanism," giving it as the title of one of the chapters of his book *New Bottles for New Wine* (1957). This is how the chapter begins: "As a result of a thousand million years of evolution, the universe is becoming conscious of itself, able to understand something of its past history and its possible future. *This cosmic self-awareness is being realized in one tiny fragment of the universe—in a few of us human beings* [Emphasis mine]" (13). It is important to note that this expansion of consciousness is not decentralized: Huxley's Transhumanism is anthropocentric, based on human exceptionalism. In his vision, human specificity is unique; such an ontological primacy will be mostly left intact in the current developments of Transhumanism, as we will soon see.

Why was Julian Huxley's vision anthropocentric? Human exceptionalism is remarked throughout the chapter to the point where "man's responsibility and destiny" is "to be an agent for the rest of the world" (*ibidem*). Huxley affirms: "It is as if man had been suddenly appointed managing director of the biggest business of all, the business of evolution. . . . What is more, he can't refuse the job" (13–14). Humans (more specifically, "men" in a language that preceded gender-neutral grammatical preferences) are in charge. This is an aspect that will be greatly challenged by Posthumanism, which critically reflects on the notion of the Anthropocene and the anthropocentric habits and discourses sustaining the privilege of the human, and can be thus defined as a post-anthropocentrism. On the other side, if anthropocentrism per se has not been substantially challenged by contemporary Transhumanism, there is a specific aspect of Huxley's proposal which may distantiate it from the current transhumanist reflection, as he stated: "We need a name for this new belief. Perhaps transhumanism will serve; *man remaining man* [Emphasis mine], but transcending himself, by realizing new possibilities of and for his human nature" (17). One of the main points of contemporary Transhumanism is that humanity is undergoing a historical transcendence, which will lead them to the next step in evolutionary terms. Huxley shared this vision ("the human species will be on the threshold of a new kind of existence" (*ibidem*), but for him "man will remain man," while, for contemporary transhumanists, some human beings will turn into different species through the advance of different types of technologies.[5] Let's understand this point more clearly by reflecting on the contemporary transhumanist scenario.

Contemporary Transhumanism(s)

It is time to address the question: *What is Transhumanism?* To begin with, it is important to clarify that Transhumanism should not be seen as one homogeneous movement, but formed by many different schools of thought, and this is why we can actually talk of Transhumanism(s). Distinctive currents coexist, such as Libertarian Transhumanism, Democratic Transhumanism, Extropianism, and Singularitarianism. *What do all these movements share?* They share the goal of human enhancement, which is why the main online platform to discuss transhumanist ideas is called H+, where "H" stands for "Humanity" and "Plus" refers to enhancement. *How can human enhancement be achieved?* According to Transhumanism(s), the main assets of reformulation of the human that can bring along human enhancement are science and technology (in their current and speculative frames). Science and technology are the main focus of interest for all these positions, with different takes. Libertarian Transhumanism, for instance, advocates free market as the best guarantor of the right to human enhancement (see, among others, Bailey 2005); one of his affiliates, Zoltan Istvan, ran for president of the United States in the 2016 elections to raise awareness for transhumanist political issues.[1] Democratic Transhumanism calls for an equal access to technological enhancements, which could otherwise be limited to certain sociopolitical classes and related to economic power, consequently encoding racial and sexual politics (Hughes 2004). As James Hughes, one of the leading voices, argues: "We are critical of the way that unequal power in society, based on gender, race, class, religion and so on, distorts the democratic process. . . . But, as transhumanists, we also believe that democratic societies need to adapt to emerging technologies" (2009: n. pg.).[2] Democratic transhumanists equally emphasize the urgency of finding feasible solutions to social issues and fully supporting technological advancements, for instance, by embracing universal basic income as a needed response to technological unemployment (Lagrandeur and Hughes 2017).

What is Extropianism? If Libertarian and Democratic Transhumanism can be most clearly defined through their social, political, and economic agendas, Extropianism, another current within the transhumanist scenario, can be approached more distinctively as a philosophy related to the individual and self-transformation. According to Max More, one of the main theorists of Transhumanism and the founder of Extropianism, it can be considered the "first fully developed transhumanist philosophy" (2013: 5); this is why, although the Extropy Institute closed in 2006, such an approach is still relevant. Its main principles can be summarized as perpetual progress, self-transformation, practical optimism, intelligent technology, open society (information and democracy), self-direction, rational thinking (More 2003). The uncritical emphasis on notions such as rationality, progress, and optimism should not be unexpected, given the fact that Transhumanism does not fully acknowledge the philosophical contribution of postmodernity, but it seeks its origins in science and technology, philosophically rooting itself in the Enlightenment, and so it does not expropriate rational humanism. This is an important aspect that we must not overlook.

6

The Roots of Transhumanism

Let's then take a step back and ask the genealogical question: *Where does Transhumanism come from?* The roots of Transhumanism can be traced back to the philosophical tradition of the age of the Enlightenment, which spread in Europe in the eighteenth century.[1] James Hughes, for instance, sees in the "Transhumanist Declaration" (2002) the moment when the legacy with the Enlightenment was explicitly affirmed: "With the Declaration transhumanists were embracing their continuity with the Enlightenment, with democracy and humanism" (2004: 178). The aspiration to progress and rationality at the core of the Enlightenment ideals is still embraced by Transhumanism, which locates itself in the humanist tradition.[2] Humanism is not only reaffirmed but radicalized. In "Extropian Principles: A Transhumanist Declaration" (1998), More states: "Like humanists, transhumanists favor reason, progress, and values centered on our well being rather than on an external religious authority. Transhumanists take humanism further by challenging human limits by means of science and technology combined with critical and creative thinking" (1). The starting point of Transhumanism is humanism, and still, these two approaches cannot be assimilated. The main distance from humanism can be found in the transhumanist ontological endorsement of science and technology, as More further explains: "Transhumanism differs from humanism in recognizing and anticipating the radical alterations in the nature and possibilities of our lives resulting from various sciences and technologies" (*ibidem*). By "taking humanism further," Transhumanism cannot be simply defined as a humanism, but can be addressed as an "ultra-humanism" (Onishi 2011):[3] this is one of the main differences between Posthumanism and Transhumanism. If Posthumanism is a post-humanism (and also, a post-anthropocentrism and a post-dualism), Transhumanism is not; on the contrary, the humanist understanding of the human is not undermined by Transhumanism, but augmented; thus Transhumanism can also be addressed as an "ultra-humanism."

Why is the transhumanist embracing of the humanist tradition of the Enlightenment problematic, from a posthumanist standpoint? Transhumanism does not seem to critically engage either with this genealogical affiliation to the Enlightenment or with the values associated with it.[4] Philosophical narratives, social discourses, and knowledge, as Michel Foucault underlined (1975), are not neutral, but are tied to politics, historical occurrences, macro- and micro-physics of power.[5] Moreover, notions are not univocal, but relational. For instance, the notion of "progress" has been widely criticized after the Second World War, when the impact of the atomic bomb on humans and on planet Earth made many realize that the manifestation of progress and regress is not necessarily separated; some technologies may cause both progress and regress at the same time. In this sense, if the discovery of nuclear energy brought (some) progress to (some) human societies, the consequences of the atomic bomb on the human species and, more currently, of nuclear waste on the environment have caused regress in the praxis of coexistence between humans (for instance, think of the cancer increase and birth defects of the residents of Hiroshima and Nagasaki after the atomic bombing, 1945) and in the praxis of sharing the planet between human and nonhuman species (think of the devastating effects of radioactivity on the wildlife at Chernobyl, 1986, and Fukushima, 2011). Another notion that has been taken for granted within the transhumanist tradition is "reason." And still, critical race studies, feminism, and animal studies, among other fields, have clearly demonstrated how the emphasis on the human as a rational animal has been a powerful discursive tool to historically enslave, mistreat, and dominate some humans and most nonhuman animals. For instance, women and slaves have been historically defined as "irrational," "emotional," and "natural" (in contraposition to "cultural"); the notion of rational animal would not apply to them, but would refer to privileged categories of men (such as adult males in patriarchal societies and masters/owners in slave economies).[6] Such a discourse, far from being neutral, would generate, sustain, and justify social inequalities, political discriminations, and legal violence. From a posthumanist perspective, Transhumanism would benefit from implementing a substantial critical approach not only to the humanist paradigm but also to the notion of technology, which is at the core of the age of Transhumanism.

Transhumanism and Techno-Enchantment

Why is technology central to the discussion on Transhumanism? Although there are many schools of thought within the transhumanist scenario, they all share the deepest interest and emphasis on technology, which is recognized as key in the evolutionary drive toward the "next" stage of the human. Technology may allow humans to transcend the finitude of life by reaccessing their biological bodies, which are perceived as ongoing projects for potential progression. Technology is pivotal in the strive toward radical life extension and digital immortality; it is also indispensable in re-envisioning life as it is. Utilitarian transhumanist philosopher David Pearce is a proponent of the "hedonistic imperative," which "outlines how genetic engineering and nanotechnology will abolish suffering in all sentient life"[1] (1995: n. pg.). Pearce defines as "Paradise engineering" "the complete abolition of suffering in *Homo sapiens*" (*ibidem*). Pearce, in fact, goes further, arguing that "the circle of compassion" should eventually include "other animals via ecosystem redesign and genetic engineering." In sum: "The option of . . . redesigning the global ecosystem, extends the prospect of paradise-engineering to the rest of the living world" (*ibidem*). Although we can sympathize with Pearce's attempt to alleviate suffering, the prospect of (some) humans redesigning the global ecosystem, according to their perception of relative and culture-specific notions, such as "happiness" and "paradise," is rooted in a hyperbolic form of humanistic exceptionalism, moral anthropocentrism, and absolutism, which, from a posthumanist critical perspective, is far from desirable. Within the transhumanist discourse, which is supposedly anchored on atheist assumptions,[2] technology becomes the drive to fulfill desires,[3] a generic answer for hopes in the constitution of "better"[4] individuals and ecosystems, as well as the golden key to access the forbidden fruit: immortality, later renamed, within transhumanist literature, as radical life extension.[5] There are many interesting parallels which can be drawn between the transhumanist take on technology and religions (Tirosh-Samuelson and Mossman 2012). Critical historian David

Noble, in his book *The Religion of Technology: The Divinity of Man and the Spirit of Invention* (1997), states:

> The present enchantment with things technological—the very measure of modern enlightenment—is rooted in religious myths and ancient imaginings. Although today's technologists, in their sober pursuit of utility, power, and profit, seem to set society's standard for rationality, they are driven also by distant dreams, spiritual yearnings for supernatural redemption. However dazzling and daunting their display of worldly wisdom, their true inspiration lies elsewhere, in an enduring, other-worldly quest for transcendence and salvation. (4)

Noble's description of the current techno-enchantment can be comfortably applied to the transhumanist discourse on technology. The specific tradition in which Transhumanism locates itself is the Enlightenment; as we have noticed in our previous chapter, the notions of progress and rationality are left untouched within the transhumanist technological paradigm. Technology becomes a hierarchical project, based on rational thought, and is driven toward progression; the human notion of time, in this epistemological set, turns into the ontological nourishment of technology, which needs the chronological future in order to successfully develop its transcendental projects, one of which is of crucial relevance to Transhumanism: human enhancement.

How can the human be redesigned, according to Transhumanism? Many transhumanist thinkers have contributed to this topic. Max More, for instance, defines morphological freedom as "the ability to alter bodily form at will through technologies such as surgery, genetic engineering, nanotechnology, uploading" (1993: n. pg.). The concept of morphological freedom has been widely endorsed by the biohacking community to address the right to self-modification; to this conversation, transhumanist ethicist Anders Sandberg adds a distinction between morphological freedom and self-harm, adding that "there are legitimate limits of morphological freedom when it causes harm to others or harm to oneself" (Sandberg 2011: n. pg.). Natasha Vita-More, a leading voice within the transhumanist movement, has been working on the design of a posthuman body for more than ten years; her artistic and philosophical project, called "Primo Posthuman" (1997 to present), is one of a visionary mind. And still, the way she presents "nature," "biology," and "technology" resonates with a dualistic mindset which transhumanist thinkers tend to leave intact. As Vita-More states: "Affected by this state of progress, human nature is at a crossroads. The bonds that tie us to nature's biological ancient, accidental design are rapidly dissolving. We are questioning our human biology and challenging what it means to be biological"

(2004: n. pg.). Note that nature is presented as an "accidental design," while "we" (as separated from nature) are challenging our own biology. In the table which represents some of the differences between the human body and the twenty-first-century Primo Prototype, Primo figures as "ageless," with "replaceable genes" and "upgrades" (2013: n. pg.). The human body, instead, is defined by "limited lifespan," "legacy genes," and by the fact that it "wears out," among other terms. Gender is marked as "restricted" (compared with Primo Posthuman's "changeability"); race is not mentioned; age must be overcome. But this human body does not seem to be situated or belong to a genealogy. A pertinent question from a posthumanist critical standpoint to this seemingly "neutral" body being redesigned is: *How are the histories and herstories of the historical human body going to affect our posthuman future?*[6] The "human" is not one but many,[7] and the human "body," as a biological and figurative locus of sociopolitical interactions, is hardly neutral; reaffirming its discontinuities, emphasizing differences rather than erasing them, will set a more strategic terminus a quo to envision forthcoming posthumanities. More in general, talking of human embodiment as an outfit which can be conveniently reshaped reveals a reductionist approach, based on the Cartesian body/mind dualism, according to which "I" *am* my mind, while "I" *have* a body that can be replaced without much loss. The famous *cogito* set the privilege of the mind over the body: "I think, therefore I am." Although dualism does not have to be hierarchical,[8] in the history of Western thought the two sides have been placed in a value system according to which one side would be the positive, the other the negative.

The transhumanist overemphasis on technology often results in a technocentric transcendence of biology. For instance, in *The Singularity Is Near: When Humans Transcend Biology* (2005), Ray Kurzweil, the father of the Singularity movement, predicts on human evolution: "We will continue to have human bodies, but they will become morphable projections of our intelligence. . . . Ultimately software-based humans will be vastly extended beyond the severe limitations of humans as we know them today" (324–5). There is certainly a high degree of futuristic sensitivity and acumen in these predictions, although, from a posthumanist perspective, they are sustained on an ontological flaw which weakens their impact. Kurzweil's language denotes a dualistic perception of being: "we" (the minds) versus "they" (the bodies). By de-fleshing human existence and becoming "morphable projections of our intelligence," "we" will have thus overcome "the severe limitations of humans as we know them today": such limitations are, more strictly talking, our fleshy bodies.[9] Most of the transhumanist debate is directed in rethinking the human through technology, which is thus invested of an ontological primary role toward the next step in human evolution. In *The Age of Spiritual Machines* (1999), Kurzweil states: "The introduction of technology is not merely the private affair of one of the Earth's innumerable species. It is a pivotal event in the history of the planet. Evolution's grandest creation—human intelligence—is providing the means for the next stage of evolution, which is technology" (35). In his evolutionary interpretation, human intelligence becomes "evolution's grandest creation" (to which, we could humbly ask: according to whom?), and technology is determined to be its worthy successor.[10] In the era of the Anthropocene, when between hundreds to thousands of nonhuman species go extinct every year due to human activities (cf. Chivian and Bernstein 2008), Kurzweil's triumphalist approach to evolution, based on anthropocentric and technocentric premises, may not satisfy all audiences. If Posthumanism and Transhumanism share a common interest in technology, the ways in which they reflect upon this notion is divergent. Transhumanism offers a deep and visionary reflection on technology, which should be cherished by anyone interested in exploring the current, and hypothetical, potentialities of technology; some of its limits, though, are found in the uncritical perpetuation of anthropocentric and dualistic tendencies, which might lead to technocentric biases and delusions. The posthumanist critical reflection on technology may add some layers of understanding, through notions such as embodiment and "poiesis." Let's see how.

Posthumanist Technologies as Ways of Revealing

Why is technology relevant to the discussion on Posthumanism? The historical and ontological dimension of technology is a crucial issue when it comes to a proper understanding of the posthumanist agenda. Yet, Posthumanism is a post-*centralizing*, in the sense that it does not recognize one specific center of interest. Posthumanism sees technology as a trait of the human outfit, but not its main focus, which would reduce its own theoretical attempt to a form of techno-reductionism. Technology is neither the "other" to be feared and to rebel against, in a sort of neo-luddite attitude; nor does it sustain the God-like characteristics which some schools of thought in Transhumanism attributes to it, addressing technology as an external source which might guarantee humanity a place in post-biological futures. What Transhumanism and Posthumanism share is the notion of technogenesis, as Katherine Hayles, in "Wrestling with Transhumanism" (2008), points out: "Technology is involved in a spiraling dynamic of coevolution with human development. This assumption, known as technogenesis, seems to me compelling and indeed virtually irrefutable" (2011: 216).[1] The non-separateness between the human and the techno realm is of key importance to the understanding of the posthuman, and shall be investigated not only as an anthropological (cf. Gehlen 1957) and paleontological issue (cf. Leroi-Gourhan 1943, 1964), but also as an ontological one. The "techno" of tehnogenesis, within this frame, will be interpreted through the work of Martin Heidegger (1889–1976).

Why Heidegger? Before we start our reflection, we should mention the fact that Heidegger has been highly disputed for his unethical behaviors and political choices: an unrepentant Nazi, a narcissist who had sexual relations with many of his female students (Chessick 1995) (Badiou and Cassin 2016). It is true that Posthumanism is a praxis, that is, theory and practice cannot be approached in separation (Ferrando 2012), but it is also true that Heidegger never claimed to be a posthumanist (the term had not even been coined at the time). Heidegger's reflection does shed some important light by bringing the conversation on technology to the realm of ontology, that is, by approaching it from the question on Being: *What is technology?* He is the first philosopher to radically and convincingly move in this direction; this is why it is important to reflect on his work, as much as it is important to acknowledge his controversial biography. In his essay "The Question Concerning Technology" (1953; Engl. Transl. 1977), Heidegger engages in an ontological reflection which is of great relevance to the posthumanist understanding of technology. Here, we should note that this essay was written after the end of the Second World War, in which technology played a key role, to the point of impacting its final outcome.

Understanding the relevance of technology in contemporary society, as a committed philosopher, Heidegger asks a crucial question, which can be summarized as: *Do we really know what we are talking about, when we reflect on technology?* More specifically, instead of trying to support or condemn technology, Heidegger wishes to answer to the question which is often given for granted: *What is technology?* To this question, he finds two common answers: technology is usually defined as "a means to an end" and "a human activity" (4). According to Heidegger, these answers are not wrong, but they are not enough to understand the essence of technology. Being trained in ancient Western philosophy, he goes back to the Greeks, addressing technology through not only its etymology (*technē* and *logos*, that is, the "discourse" on "techne") but also its semantic legacies; by doing this, Heidegger brings to our attention something very interesting—the fact that in ancient Greek literature and philosophy, the term "techne" was necessarily associated with two other notions: *poiēsis*[2] and *epistēmē*.[3] In ancient Greek, "techne" referred to both handcrafts and arts. The semantic relation to "episteme"—that is, the domain of "knowledge," more specifically associated with the domain of "scientific knowledge"[4]—does not come as a surprise to our modern understanding of technology; the two terms, that is, "technological" and "scientific" knowledge, are often found in relations (think, for instance, of the field of science and technology studies). The relation that may come to our modern understanding of technology as a surprise is the one with *poiēsis*. The term itself may even sound obsolete to readers who are not familiar with ancient Greek, so let's first ask the question: *What does "poiesis" mean?*

To understand the notion of "poiesis" we can refer to different examples such as poetry, a jam session, or a blooming flower. When we start writing a poem, or when we are going to jam with some other musicians, we do not know what the outcomes are going to be. We may have a framework of reference (for instance, soloing scales for chords in jazz improvisation), or some topic we would like to address (for instance, writing a poem about life), but we do not know what the exact outcome is going to be. Often, when we listen back to the recorded jam session, or when we read the final poem, we feel a sense of surprise which exceeds our initial expectation: this is the creative process being revealed. It is important to underline the fact that, according to Heidegger, "not only handcraft manufacture, not only artistic and poetical bringing into appearance" (10) is a "poiesis"; also "*Physis*," that is, nature, "is a bringing-forth, *poiesis*" (*ibidem*). Think, for instance, of the "bursting of a blossom into bloom" (*ibidem*): this is "poiesis" "in the highest sense" (*ibidem*). According to the ancient Greeks, the creative process was something sacred, related to the Gods and Goddesses; it was a moment of truth, of revealing: *aletheia*, in Greek, that is, "bringing something concealed . . . into unconcealment" (12).

Let's now go back to technology and its relation with "poiesis," and ask with Heidegger: "What has the essence of technology to do with revealing? The answer: everything" (*ibidem*). According to Heidegger: "Technology is therefore no mere means. Technology is a way of revealing" (12). He reiterates this crucial statement throughout the essay.[5] And still, modern societies have lost this understanding of "techne" as "poiesis"; this is why, although modern technology is also a way of revealing, Heidegger describes modern technology as an "Enframing."[6] Heidegger sees modern technology as a limitation of the potentials of its revealing, as he states,

> What is modern technology? Is too is a revealing. . . . And yet the revealing that holds sway throughout modern technology does not unfold into a bringing-forth in the sense of *poiēsis*. The revealing that rules in modern technology is a challenging, which puts to nature the unreasonable demand that it supply [*sic*] energy that can be extracted and stored as such. . . . The earth now reveals itself as a coal mining district, the soil as a mineral deposit. (14)

Why is modern technology an Enframing? Our modern understanding of technology is "based on modern physics as an exact science" (14) and addressed primarily from a utilitarian point of view. The sense of mystery, which allows for the creative process to take place, is gone, and the poietic aspect has been lost. Everything becomes measurable and available. Nature becomes a "standing reserve" (p. 17) for human use: "The earth now reveals itself as a coal mining district, the soil as a mineral deposit" (14); "the sun's warmth is challenged forth for heat" (15); "what the river is now, namely, a water power supplier" (16). To go back to the example of the blossoming flower, instead of a poietic act, modern society would invest it as site of honey production. Modern technology is different from ancient technology because of the way society is now approaching science and technology. Modern technology has been systematized and "humanized" as an ordering regulated on human factual needs, in a reductionist approach which limits its possibilities as a mode of revealing. In the book *Technica and Time, 1: The Fault of Epimetheus* (1994), French philosopher Bernard Stiegler sharply comments on Heidegger's standpoint: "Technics becomes modern when metaphysics expresses and completes itself as the project of calculative reason with a view to the mastery and possession of nature" (1998: 10). *When did this switch in worldviews take place?* Heidegger traces back such a shift to the seventeenth century and the second half of the eighteen century,[7] in the time frame of the Enlightenment and the Industrial Revolution, which is precisely where Transhumanism sets it roots. We can now start seeing more clearly why the ways Posthumanism and Transhumanism address technology are divergent. If Transhumanism, with its emphasis on reason, progress, and mastery, might be a suited example for Heidegger's criticism and Stiegler's reflection, the way Posthumanism engages in technology might leave space for other possibilities.

Posthumanism follows on Heidegger's reflection that technology cannot be reduced to mere means, nor to a reification, and thus cannot be "mastered." This reflection shall be addressed within the contemporary fear of AI takeover, that is, the hypothetical scenario where technological beings (for instance, robots and artificial intelligence) will be dominant on Earth, replacing human mastery (see, for instance, Bostrom 2014). To this discussion, Heidegger's reflection may add some different level of understanding, as he states: "We will, as we say 'get' technology 'spiritually in hand.' We will master it. The will to mastery becomes all the more urgent the more technology threatens to slip from human control. / But suppose now that technology were no mere means, how would it stand with the will to master it?" (1977: 5). Heidegger is sometimes portrayed as a luddite who chose the rural life of the Black Forest in Germany, and viewed technology as "dangerous," but this may be a misleading interpretation of his words. Heidegger's vision of technology is beyond good or evil. Technology per se is not the problem; the problem lays in how human societies approach it, that is, the sociocultural oblivion of the poietic power of technology is the problem. In Heidegger's words, "What is dangerous is not technology. There is no demonry in technology, but rather there is the mystery of its essence. The essence of technology, as a destining of revealing, is the danger" (28). Heidegger underlines the fact that "the threat to man does not come in the first instance from the potentially lethal machines and apparatus of technology. The actual threat has already affected man in his essence" (*ibidem*). *What is this danger that Heidegger is referring to?* The danger is that, out of all the potential of existence, "the rule of Enframing threatens man with the possibility that it could be denied to him to enter into a more original revealing and hence to experience the call of a more primal truth" (*ibidem*). This passage is dense with meaning, not surprisingly as Heidegger is considered one of the most complex thinkers in the history of Western philosophy. Let's then bring some examples to make this point more clear and vivid.

Let's imagine that we are sculptors and we have a large block of raw marble to work with. Out of this piece of marble, we can sculpt many different things, such as the statue of philosopher Hannah Arendt, the statue of Sophia the robot,[8] or the statue of a unicorn. This piece of marble, in other worlds, is full potential. Of all these possibilities, we decide to make a statue of Sophia the robot. We work very hard on it and complete the task. Once the statue of Sophia is ready, there is no way back: of all the possible statues we could have made, only one was actualized. Let's now think of the movie *Wall-E* (2008),[9] where future humans are portrayed as extremely obese, with short legs and arms, not able to walk and fully dependent on technology. Although it is hard to predict how humans will look like in the future, the way technology has been developed may have a role in it. For instance, currently the use of computers is mostly exercised by sitting on a desk, using our hands. Although technology per se is full potentiality,[10] and computers could be developed very differently, the way computers are being designed is already having a direct effect on our bodies, postures, and health (for instance, sitting too long in front of a computer can lead to back pain, poor circulation, and headaches, among other issues).

Let's go back to the piece of marble and think of technology in a similar tone, meditating on all the possible ways that computers could be developed. For instance, instead of static laptops, we could imagine machines that do not need electric power but are charged through kinetic movement and solar energy. These hypothetical machines would operate by moving in outdoor spaces, where they would be able to collect much solar energy. They would have neither screens nor keyboards; they would receive human inputs verbally in similar ways to smart speaker Alexa (Amazon 2016). To interact with their virtual assistants, humans would have to constantly walk and, possibly, spend most time outdoors. In this hypothetical scenario, the humans using this type of technology would eventually develop very muscular legs and may not suffer in vitamin D deficiency, although their skin would eventually need some protection from solar exposure. This simple example demonstrates that the ways we are developing technology are not neutral, but have deeper consequences, if thought relationally. We can state that a computer is not just a computer: out of the unlimited potential of revealing, what we are bringing forth is relevant to the whole spectrum of ontological intra-acting within the frame of existence.

To summarize, more than a functional tool for "obtaining" (energy; more sophisticated technology; or even immortality), technology arrives to the posthumanist debate through the mediation of some key thinkers, such as Martin Heidegger, Michel Foucault, and Donna Haraway. After presenting Heidegger, we should mention that feminism, in particular, can be seen as pivotal in the posthuman approach to technology, not only through its emphasis on embodiment,[11] but also through Donna Haraway's cyborg (1985) and her dismantling of dualisms and boundaries, in particular: the boundary between animal-human (organism) and machine; the boundary between the physical and nonphysical; and ultimately, the boundary between technology and the self. Posthumanism investigates technology as a mode of revealing, thus re-accessing its ontological significations in a scenario where technology had been repeatedly reduced to its technical endeavors.[12] Another key notion of the posthuman approach to technology, and actually one of the ways in which, to go back to Heidegger, revealing has not been necessarily confined to an Enframing, can be found in the technologies of the self, as reflected upon by Michel Foucault (1926–84) in its later production.[13] The notion of the technologies of the self is crucial to the posthuman: since the dualism self/other has been re-accessed through a relational ontology, as we will see later, the technologies of the self play a substantial role in the process of existential revealing. The technologies of the self allow for a reflection on a posthuman praxis which may transcend the written/spoken paradigm, impregnating modes of existing and relating, and opening the debate to posthuman ethics and applied philosophy. We will delve into these points in Chapter 15. Let's now go back to our unraveling of the differences between the movements and standpoints which currently characterize the posthuman scenario in order to further define and situate the perspective of Philosophical Posthumanism.

Antihumanism and the *Übermensch*

If modern rationality and progress are at the core of the transhumanist postulation, a radical critique of those same notions is at the core of Antihumanism,[1] a philosophical position which, although sharing its roots in postmodernity with Posthumanism, should not be assimilated to it. Before proceeding, we should also mention that Antihumanism is not an homogeneous movement (Han-Pile 2010: 119); here, we will mostly focus on the philosophical current developed out of the Nietzschean-Foucauldian legacies, but we shall mention that there are different antihumanist perspectives, such as the one rooted in Marxism and developed by philosophers such as Louis Althusser (1918–90) and György Lukàcs (1885–1971).[2] *What is the main characteristic of Antihumanism?* The critical undermining of the human, which is almost absent in the transhumanist reflection, is crucial to Antihumanism. Both Antihumanism and Posthumanism abandon the universalist rhetoric of humanism; "we" are not the same, we are actually all very different, but being different does not mean being better or worse; difference is not hierarchical. In this sense, pluralism does not equal relativism[3]: we can be united in our differences and by our differences.[4] To this point, we can see an essential similitude between Antihumanism and Posthumanism, but do they share the same orientation? More specifically, *In what do Antihumanism and Posthumanism harmonize, and in what do they differ?*

Both Posthumanism and Antihumanism distantiate themselves from a singular and generalized approach to the human. This means that there is no one specific type of human who can impose their own experiences, views, and perspectives as absolute characteristics of the human species as a whole.[5] In this sense, what has been postulated as the "neutral" subject in the history of Western philosophy reveals the inherent assumption that participating in the white, male, Western-centric historical experience is the central position to describe the (universal) human experience. According to this onto-epistemological perspective, the historically privileged humans could describe the "others"—

such as women and non-Europeans—based on an un-embodied and indirect experience of what it meant to exist as a "woman" or as a "non-European," thus projecting their own expectations and biases. In this narrational structure, the positive connotations would typically apply to the first element of the hierarchical dualism—which also represented the subject formulating the discourse, that is, the describer—while the second element (the described) would be negatively recreated around the positive constitution of the first. We can think, for instance, how the notion of the "Orient" was constructed to feed Western prejudices and stereotypes, as Edward Said underlined in his influential book *Orientalism* (1978);[6] or how the notion of "Woman" was created to sustain a canon based on sexist biases and presumption, as Simone de Beauvoir (1949) and Luce Irigaray (1974) cleary revealed.[7] In the 1960s and 1970s the political and theoretical deconstruction (as Derrida will call it) of the human starts taking place. The year 1968 marks a symbolic date: an onto-epistemological evolution is manifesting, in the vibrant momentum gained by the political and social revolution initiated by the civil rights movement, the hippie counterculture, feminism, and many other waves of social, political, and ecological activism. "The private is political," as feminism will state, life is the political arena: the way we live is a political act. Posthumanism and Antihumanism share a radical and undermining critique to the absolutist and universalist hegemonic accreditation and recognition of the human, which actually proved to be reflective of the subjectivities involved in the intellectual postulation of such "neutral" human. This type of revealing and this form of historical "poiesis" enacted not only an epistemological shift in the system of philosophical thought,[8] but a political one in the history of social consciousness: the realization that *this* had to change and was already changing.

If these are some of the main points in common between Posthumanism and Antihumanism, their main distinction is already embedded in their morphologies, and specifically, in their composition as a "post-" and as an "anti-." In this sense, their genealogy speaks for itself. Antihumanism fully acknowledges the consequences of the "death of man," as delineated by some post-structuralist theorists, in particular Michel Foucault who, in *The Order of Things: An Archeology of the Human Sciences* (1966), stated: "Man is neither the oldest nor the most constant problem that has been posed for human knowledge. . . . As the archeology of our thought easily shows, man is an invention of recent date. And one perhaps nearing its end" (1970: 386–87). Note that "man" here refers to humankind, although the French term Foucault employs is in the masculine form (in French, *homme* means both "man" and "human being").

By stating that man is near its end, Foucault does not mean that humans are at risk of extinction. In fact, Foucault is not referring to the human as a bio-evolutionary animal, but as a historical notion, more specifically, a sociocultural construction accepted within a specific "episteme." *What does* episteme *mean, according to Foucault?* We have previously addressed this notion in relation to Heidegger;[9] this is why we shall note that Michel Foucault employs it, more specifically, to refer to the scientific knowledge that is recognized as such in each era.[10] In fact, what is considered science in a specific era may not be considered science in another time. Let's clarify this important point with a current example. If you told your friends that you were going to study the Science of Angels at NYU, many would not believe you: angels, in our society, are not considered objects of scientific disquisition. Differently, in the Middle Ages, Angelology was the branch of Christian theology that tried to explain the origin and qualities of these spiritual beings; it played a major role in bringing about the transformation from the monastic to the scholastic method,[11] which gave birth to the rise of academia as we currently know it, and eventually became a required course of study (Keck 1998). With this example, we want to clarify the fact that what is considered science may change according to the specific beliefs of each era, that is, the social and cultural discourse which Foucault would define as "episteme."

If, according to Foucault, the current notion of "man" is near its end, when did such a notion come along? It is important to note that Foucault traces the historical birth of this specific "man" in the Enlightenment—and not, as Béatrice Han-Pile points out, in "the revival and reinterpretation of the Ciceronian notion of *humanitates* during the Renaissance" (2010: 122).[12] If the transhumanist cultural notion of the human is traced back to the Enlightenment, according to Foucault, that same notion is near its end. Moreover, if the symbolic birth of this dying man can be traced to the Enlightenment, Foucault identifies his symbolic death with the philosophical occurrence of Friedrich Nietzsche's *Übermensch*,[13] the overhuman. *What does* Übermensch *mean?* First found in *The Gay Science* (1882), the notion of the *Übermensch* was fully developed by Nietzsche in his philosophical, and epic, novel *Thus Spoke Zarathustra: A Book for All and None* (1883–85). It can be epitomized in the notable words by the main character Zarathustra, an alter-ego of the author:[14] "*I teach you the overman.*[15] Human being is something that shall be overcome. What have you done to overcome him?" (2006: 5). Before delving into the notion of the overhuman, we shall note that the masculine form "overman," as a translation of *Übermensch,* is not correct.[16] *Mensch* in German is gender-neutral and means "humanity," while *Mann* means "man, male," and *Frau* means "woman, female"; this is why *Übermensch* should be translated as "overhuman."

Why is Nietzsche's Übermensch *relevant to the posthuman discussion?* The notion of the overhuman has been recognized as a source of inspiration by Transhumanism, Posthumanism, and Antihumanism, for different reasons and with divergent interpretations. As far as Antihumanism is concerned, in its specific Foucauldian terms, the death of God proclaimed by Nietzsche is necessarily followed by the death of Man. More specifically, this dying "Man" Foucault is thinking of can be found in the notion of man as historically shaped within the Enlightenment—a tradition which, antithetically, is precisely the one that the transhumanist philosophical movement sees as its antecedent.[17] As far as Transhumanism is concerned,[18] between 2009 and 2010 an interesting debate followed the publication of the article "Nietzsche, the Overhuman, and Transhumanism" (2009) by Stefan Lorenz Sorgner, in which Sorgner contested Nick Bostrom, who had dismissed Nietzsche as a significant source of inspiration for Transhumanism.[19] Max More replied to Sorgner's article with the paper "The Overhuman in the Transhuman" (2010), where he shared Sorgner's position, and stated that "transhumanist ideas were directly influenced by Nietzsche" (1).[20] Recently, the publication of *Nietzsche and Transhumanism: Precursor or Enemy?* (Tuncel 2017) kept the conversation rolling, with different Nietzschean scholars supporting, or undermining, the view of Nietzsche as a precursor of transhumanist ideals, asking the question: *Would Nietzsche have supported human enhancement?* There are many possible answers to this question. We can state, more in general, that, even though Nietzsche may not have been against possible developments in biotechnologies and genetic engineering, he did not approach science as the path leading to the *Übermensch*. In fact, you are not born, you rather become an *Übermensch*: the *Übermensch* is the result of an individual process, which is defined by Nietzsche through the metamorphoses of the spirit. Let's delve into this aspect more thoroughly.

What are the metamorphoses of the spirit, according to Nietzsche? As accounted in the First Part of *Thus Spoke Zarathustra*, the metamorphoses of the spirit develop in three stages. The first stage is the camel, which represents that stage in our life in which we are depending on external authorities. The camel is an animal which is often seen carrying humans, or human belongings, on their backs; most likely, the camel would rather be free from this task, but they cannot liberate themselves yet. This is why the camel says "yes," but would rather say "no." An example of this stage can be the student, who is like a camel, walking with their heavy books on their back: even though the student would probably much rather say "no, I do not want to take the exam," they have to say "yes, I will take the exam" or they will not get their degrees. The camel is an important stage; like the student, when we are camels, we are learning about society by accepting external authorities, but this stage cannot be permanent, can only be temporary on the path of becoming the *Übermensch*: the camel eventually turns into the lion. As Zarathustra affirms: "Like the camel that, burdened, speeds into the desert, thus the spirit speeds into its desert. / In the loneliest desert, however, the second metamorphosis occurs: here the spirit becomes a lion who would conquer his freedom and be master in his own desert" (138). The lion represents rebellion and freedom. The lion says "no" and wants to say "no." An example of the lion is the teenager who tries to find their voice in separation from the one of their parents. You can also relate the lion to the idea of fighting for your rights. Let's think, for instance, of people who have been discriminated against and who, at one point, realize that enough is enough: they will respond with a "no" the next time someone tries to discriminate against them. A consequence of this delicate situation is that these people need to be constantly protecting their space of freedom, or their rights may be suddenly taken away again. This is an important stage on the path of becoming the *Übermensch*, but the lion is too busy trying to protect their freedom, so that, according to Nietzsche, the lion cannot create yet.

The third and last metamorphosis of the spirit is the child, who only says "yes" when they want to say "yes." Let's think, for instance, of a very young child (six or seven months). If this child is hungry, they will eat, and they will cry if there is no food; if they are not hungry, they will not eat, even if their parents try to feed them. Moreover, the creativity of this young child is not restricted by rules or expectations. For instance, if you give a book to such a young child, they will not think of the book as a book; instead, they will explore it in its full potential by touching it, opening it, moving it in all directions, smelling it, they may even try to taste it; and then, suddenly, they may move on, throwing the book on the ground and focusing their attention on something else. They are fully in the moment, open to any possibility; this is why they can create new values. "The child—according to Nietzsche—is innocence and forgetting, a new beginning, a game, a self-propelled wheel, a first movement, a sacred 'Yes' " (139). The child represents the *Übermensch*—here we should clarify that Nietzsche is not claiming that all children are *Übermensch*; this is just a metaphor. In fact, the *Übermensch* is a process (the child was a camel, and then a lion) and a choice. For these reasons, it may not be possible to genetically engineer an *Übermensch*. Moreover, although Nietzsche may not have opposed our latest developments in science and technology, the project of genetically engineering a child to be an *Übermensch* may sound like an imposition upon the individual from an external authority (such as the parents or the scientists involved). It is true that Nietzsche repeatedly talks of *amor fati* (love of one's fate),[21] but the destiny Nietzsche is referring to is the one that you have created for yourself, not the one imposed upon you by God, your parents, or a geneticist. This is a very important point in Nietzsche's philosophy. We will explore this point more clearly in the next paragraphs, by addressing the notion of the death of God.

First, though, let's ask a crucial question for our philosophical investigation: *What about the overhuman in relation to Philosophical Posthumanism?* From a posthumanist perspective, even though Nietzsche is a major influence in the development of Philosophical Posthumanism,[22] the acceptance of the *Übermensch* cannot be taken for granted. On one side, the way Nietzsche portrays the human being as a "a bridge and not a purpose"[23] is crucial to Posthumanism; such an interpretation of the human echoes particularly well with notions such as *la frontera* (Anzaldúa 1987), *nomadic subjects* (Braidotti 1994), and the *cyborg* (Haraway 1985), developed within feminist postmodern theory, which represents one of the direct genealogical sources of Posthumanism. On the other side, the *Übermensch* can be criticized for being posed through a hierarchical symbolism, displayed in the ape-human-overhuman compound,[24] as Zarathustra proclaims: "What is the ape to a human? A laughing stock or a painful embarrassment. And this is exactly what the human should be to the overhuman: a laughing stock or a painful embarrassment" (2006: 6). From a critical posthumanist perspective, the inherent anthropocentrism of Nietzsche's notion of the overhuman is problematic. Another point of difference is its reliance on the killing of God: this symbolic death, in Nietzsche's view, is necessary to the birth of the *Übermensch*. Before addressing the death of God, let's take a step back and ask: *Why is Zarathustra the one to proclaim the death of God?* Founder of the Zoroastrian[25] religion, Zarathustra (or Zoraster in Greek) was a prophet who lived around the sixth century BCE[26] in ancient Persia; he was the first one to proclaim the unity of God, or God as one, universal, and transcendent (defined as "Ahura Mazda," meaning in Avestan language: "Lord" and "Wisdom"), marking the passage from a politheistic society to a monotheistic one. Nietzsche, in tune with the ancient Greek[27] notion of time, regarded time as cyclical, instead of linear; in a circular notion of time, we can suggest that only the prophet who proclaimed the birth of God can eventually proclaim the death of God.[28]

Why did Nietzsche proclaim the death of God? Nietzsche was born and raised in a rigid society, where being religious was not by choice but by necessity. In the nineteenth century, in Europe being Christian was considered an implicit, and explicit, requirement to be a part of civil society; the role of religion was so relevant that anyone who would undermine its premises would have been considered dangerous, mad, or even heretic. This is one of the reasons why, for instance, Darwin waited twenty-three years to present his work *On the Origin of Species* (1859) to the public, because its main argument, that species had evolved from one another, seemed to be in contrast with the creation account, as listed in the Bible, Gen 1:1–2:3. Here, we should underline that, when Nietzsche proclaims the death of God, he is referring not only to religion, but also to science, if it becomes the final authority to be revered and blindly accepted.[29] Nietzsche's God should be intended broadly, as any external authority imposing their Truth to the individual. More in general, the death of God should be approached as a metaphor to reject any external imposition about our own life, trying to find instead our individual voice: different perspectives should be respected and cultivated.[30] The death of any external Truth allows for the birth of the *Übermensch*—or, of the fully empowered individual. This is an extraordinary gift that Nietzsche has given us all.

How can Nietzsche be relevant in our daily life? In order to understand if we are living the life we want to be living, he proposes the powerful thought experiment of "the eternal recurrence of the same."[31] Let's try to do it now. Please take a seat and close your eyes. Now think of your life exactly the way it is. *What if your life was going to come back exactly the same, and we mean* exactly *the same, forever?* Every thought you have ever had; every person you have ever met; every action you have ever taken; every dream you have ever had: everything, exactly, the same. Nothing different. Would you be thrilled at this idea? Would you be terrified? Would you be happy? Would you be in despair? Now take a minute and think of your emotional reaction to this thought experiment: How did you react? According to Nietzsche, the person that can joyfully accept this thought experiment is the *Übermensch.* This is something that we can also apply to our daily life; for instance, when we are not sure about some important decisions, we can ask ourselves: *What if... I had to experience this forever?* It may help us choose what it really matters to us.

Does Posthumanism support the death of God? Posthumanism supports the end of any external Truths imposed upon the individual, although the specificities of the death of God, as described by Nietzsche, may not be in line with the mediated approach of Posthumanism. Different from Antihumanism, Posthumanism does not necessary rely on the death of God nor, passing through Foucault's approach, on the death of Man. On the one side, the assumptions of a "death" are already based on the recognition of the symbolic dualism dead/alive, which has been challenged by the posthumanist reflection.[32] More importantly, according to Nietzsche, God didn't just die: "We have killed him."[33] *If God and Man are dead, who killed them? Who is this "we"? Did you kill God?* This is a relevant question, given the simple fact that if someone is talking about their deaths, it means that someone has survived: *Who is the survivor?* The death of God, as well as the death of Man, can be seen as a symbolic sacrifice of redemption, which is perceived as unnecessary within a posthumanist frame. In this sense, we can talk more properly of the end of any external Truth through an individual evolution that does not rely on a violent killing (which, as such, would necessarily bring back a vengeance). While Antihumanism is characterized by an oppositional attitude, pertaining to the social and cultural agenda in which it developed (the 1960s as a symbolic decade), Posthumanism, which developed more clearly in the 1990s, is a philosophy of mediation that relocates hegemonic modes of thinking close to resistant ones (Ferrando 2012);[34] none of them are fully dismissed, but they are recognized as functional acts of the philosophical drama, and, more in general, as contributors to the historical formation of the notion of the human.

Posthumanism, after all, is aware of the fact that its own standpoints are formulated by human beings formed within a specific "episteme,"[35] expressed in a historically situated human language to other human readers, and that humanistic views and assumptions are structurally embedded within such a human-related scenario; consequently, they cannot be easily dismissed or erased. In this respect, more than with Foucault's death of Man, the posthuman is in tune with Derrida's deconstructive approach (1967). As Neil Badmington points out in his anthology *Posthumanism* (2000): "While the anti-humanists were declaring a departure from the legacy of humanism, Derrida was patiently pointing out the difficulties of making such a break. Precisely because Western philosophy is steeped in humanist assumptions, he observed, the end of Man is bound to be written in the language of Man" (9). Badmington further explains: "There is no pure outside to which 'we' can leap. To oppose humanism by claiming to have left it behind is to overlook the very way that opposition is articulated. / It does not follow, however, that poststructuralism is content to confirm the status quo, for Derrida's work repeatedly shows how systems are always self-contradictory, forever deconstructing themselves *from within*" (ibidem). Different from Antihumanism, Posthumanism, although not recognizing any onto-epistemological primacy to the human, actually resumes the possibility for human agency in a deconstructive and relational form.

What are some of the other movements related to the posthuman turn? Before focalizing our attention on Philosophical Posthumanism, let's mention some other movements. Connected to New Realism, Speculative Realism, and the nonhuman turn, Object-Oriented Ontology (OOO) is an area of study which shares with Posthumanism a post-anthropocentric turn, although the ways post-anthropocentrism is accessed are different.[36] In the third part of this book, which focuses more directly on ontology, we will not only analyze the differences between Posthumanism and OOO, but also delve into the posthumanist area of New Materialism. Metahumanism is a recent approach attempting to mediate between the Post- and Trans-tendencies (Del Val and Sorgner 2010); it should not be confused with Metahumanity, a term which started to appear in the 1980s within comics narratives[37] and role-playing games, to refer to superheros and mutants, and has been since employed specifically in the context of cultural studies. One final remark is that the notion of Posthumanities has been welcomed in academia to emphasize an internal shift (from the "Humanities" to the "Posthumanities"[38]), extending the study of the human condition to the posthuman, but it also refers to future generations of beings related to the human species and to the connected field of Speculative Posthumanism.[39] In the last decade, a number of other interesting terms have flourished, such as ahuman theory (MacCormack 2012), inhuman epistemology (Hird 2012), environmental humanities (Neimanis et al. 2015), among other proposals, showing the richness of the ongoing discussion.[40] Overall, it can be stated that Posthumanism, by itself, has become an umbrella term to include different, even antithetical, perspectives, in an era where the symbolic boundaries of the "human" have been ultimately challenged.

Philosophical Posthumanism

It is now time to ask the question at the core of this investigation: *What is Philosophical Posthumanism?* Philosophical Posthumanism can be defined as a post-humanism, as a post-anthropocentrism, and as a post-dualism: these three aspects should be addressed in conjunction, which means an account based on a philosophical posthumanist approach shall have a posthumanist sensitivity as well as a post-anthropocentric and a post-dualistic one. Let's clarify each term. Post-humanism implies the understanding of the plurality of the human experience; the human is not recognized as one but as many, that is, human(s)—thus undermining the humanist tradition based on a generalized and universalized approach to the human.[1] Post-anthropocentrism refers to decentering the human in relation to the nonhuman; it is based on the realization that the human species has been placed in a hierarchical scale and has been granted an ontological privilege in the large majority of the historical accounts on the human. Post-dualism relies on the awareness that dualism has been employed as a rigid way to define identity, based on a closed notion of the self and actualized in symbolic dichotomies, such as "us"/"them," "friend"/"foe," "civilized"/"barbarian" and so on.[2] *From where did this substantial revisitation of the human originate?* More generally, *where does Philosophical Posthumanism come from?*

There are many ways to trace genealogical relationalities. One is by following the chronology in relation to the birth of the term. As we underlined in Chapter 2, Posthumanism can be traced back to its postmodern embryonic stage, that is, to the coining of the term by Ihab Hassan (1977). Nurtured by gender studies, cultural studies, and literary criticism, by the end of the 1990s, a specific take on the posthuman shift historically developed out of the feminist reflection. The key text which brought what would be later defined as Critical Posthumanism to the attention of mainstream academia was *How We Became Posthuman* (1999), written in a critical feminist tone by Katherine K. Hayles. The momentum gained by Critical Posthumanism was accompanied by the wave of Cultural Posthumanism, with publications such as *Posthuman Bodies* (Halberstam and Livingston 1995) and the reader in Cultural Criticism *Posthumanism* (Badmington 2000). Posthumanism evolved into a specific philosophical inquiry in the decade following the year 2000, merging different fields of reflection, such as the humanities, science, and environmentalism. Philosophical Posthumanism is an ongoing reflection which is developing rapidly, gaining much attention in and outside of academia; it shall be seen not as a homogeneous movement, but as a pluralistic approach developed by related currents. On one side, following the posthuman dismantling of traditional dualities such as alive and not alive, human and nonhuman, male and female, physical and virtual, black and white, nature and culture, among others, a specifically feminist approach, which has been defined as New Materialisms,[3] has been engaging into a sophisticated inquiry into matter, directly investigating scientific fields such as theoretical physics, quantum physics, and cosmology; we will fully embrace New Materialism in the third part of this book, dedicated to matter. Here, we will address more clearly the current of Philosophical Posthumanism which is redefining the Western hegemonic discourse, in a comprehensive attempt to re-access each field of philosophical investigation through this acquired awareness of the limits of previous humanistic, anthropocentric, and dualistic assumptions: from epistemology to ontology, from bioethics to an existential inquiry.

Posthumanism has been primarily defined as a *post-humanism* and a *post-anthropocentrism*. Rosi Braidotti, for instance, in one of the key texts of Philosophical Posthumanism, that is, *The Posthuman* (2013), divides the narrational flow into four chapters entitled "Posthumanism: Life beyond the Self"; "Post-Anthropocentrism: Life beyond the Species"; "The Inhuman: Life beyond Death"; "Posthuman Humanities: Life beyond Theory." This map is significant in emphasizing the main aspects of Philosophical Posthumanism, which decentralizes the human, with respect to both the "nonhuman" and the human "others" (that is, all the human categories that historically have not been recognized as such). On the other hand, it employs a critical post-dualism that leaves no room for the strict separation between life and death; finally, it opens its reflection to the future evolutions of posthumanities, both in its political ramifications and in its genetic ones.[4] Consequently, the academic studies previously defined as "human sciences, or humanities" may reflect this turning point as "post-human sciences or posthumanities." Robert Pepperell, one of the early thinkers of the posthuman philosophical approach, well summarized these

aspects in his "The Posthuman Manifesto," published as an appendix to his book
The Posthuman Condition: Consciousness Beyond the Brain (1995):

1. It is now clear that Humans are no longer the most important things in
    the Universe. This is something the Humanists have yet to accept.
2. All technological progress of Human society is geared towards the
    redundancy of the Human species as we currently know it.
3. In the Posthuman era many beliefs become redundant—not least the belief
    in Human Being.
4. Human beings, like Gods, only exist in as much as we believe them to
    exist. (2003: 177)

In Pepperell's perspective, post-anthropocentrism, the developments of
technology and the dissolution of God(s), as well as of the dissolution of
human beings, go hand in hand. Here, we shall open a parenthesis and notice
that the posthuman overcoming of human primacy is not to be replaced with
other types of primacies (such as the one of the machines). More in general,
Philosophical Posthumanism can be seen as both a *post-centrism*[5] and a *post-
exclusivism*. It does not rely on oppositions, but can be appointed as an empirical
philosophy of mediation, which offers a reconciliation of existence in its broadest
significations. It does not employ any frontal dualism or antithesis, demystifying
ontological polarizations through the postmodern practice of deconstruction.
Posthumanism is not obsessed with proving the originality of its own proposal,
and thus can be seen as a *post-exceptionalism* as well. It implies an assimilation
of the "dissolution of the new," which philosopher Gianni Vattimo in *The End
of Modernity: Nihilism and Hermeneutics in Postmodern Culture* (1985; Trans.
Engl. 1991) identified as a specific trait of the postmodern.[6] In order to postulate
the "new," the center of the discourse has to be located, so that the question *"New
to what?"* shall be answered. But the novelty of human thought is relative and
situated: what is considered "new" in one society might be common knowledge
in another.[7] Moreover, hegemonic perspectives do not explicitly acknowledge all
the resistant standpoints which coexist within each specific cultural-historical
paradigm, thus failing in recognizing the discontinuities embedded within any
discursive formation. What Posthumanism puts at stake is not only the identity
of the "center" of the Western discourse, which has already been radically
deconstructed by its own "peripheries" (feminists, black, queer, postcolonial
theorists, to name a few). Posthumanism, as a post-humanism, dismisses the
centrality of the center in its singular form, both in its hegemonic and in its
resistant modes (Ferrando 2012). Posthumanism might recognize centers of

interests; its centers, though, are mutable, nomadic, ephemeral. Its perspectives have to be pluralistic, multilayered, and as comprehensive as possible in order to remain open – including exclusivism which, for instance, would preclude such a strategy.

What are the sources of this specific take of Philosophical Posthumanism? Within the contemporary history of Western philosophy, a relevant source can be found in the "Letter on Humanism" (1947; Engl. Transl. 2001) by Martin Heidegger. In this text, the German philosopher traces the etymological roots of the human in the Roman concept of *humanitas* (242), and reflects upon the historical significance of humanism, which is not reduced to Renaissance humanism, but it is located further back in Roman humanism.[8] In so doing, Heidegger brings our attention to the significance of the essence of man:

> The first humanism, Roman Humanism, and every kind that has emerged from that time to the present, has presupposed the most universal "essence" of man to be obvious. Man is considered to be an *animal rationale*. This definition is not simply the Latin translation of the Greek *zōon logon echon* but rather a metaphysical interpretation of it. . . . Above and beyond everything else, however, it finally remains to ask whether the essence of man primordially and most decisively lies in the dimension of *animalitas* at all. Are we really on the right track toward the essence of man as long as we set him off as one living creature among others in contrast to plants, beasts, and God? (243)

In this passage, Heidegger has pointed out a key aspect of Philosophical Posthumanism, which consists precisely in accessing the human through alternative strategies, rather than establishing *his*[9] essence through the traditional contrast or opposition with the "others" (not only plants, beasts, and Gods, but also women, slaves, and machines, among many others).[10]

It is important to note that a form of anthropocentrism remains in Heidegger, according to whom: "Man is not the Lord of beings. Man is the shepherd of Being. Man loses nothing in this 'less'; rather, he gains in that he attains the truth of Being" (*ivi*: 254). Although Man is not the "Lord of beings anymore," he is still granted the privileged position of "shepherd of Being." This "guardianship, that is, the care of Being" (255) comes to man through language: "Thinking accomplishes the relation of Being to the essence of man . . . in thinking Being comes to language. Language is the house of Being. In its home man dwells. Those who think and those who create with words are the guardians of this home" (*ivi*: 238). This relocation of man, this newly recognized position, still relies on an ontological privilege, although such a privilege is not absolute, but based on a relation.[11] Within the history of the Western hegemonic[12] philosophical tradition, which has posed and sustained the absolute onto-epistemological privilege of the human,[13] this is a significant switch. And still, Posthumanism, as a post-humanism, does not stand on a hierarchical standpoint; there are no higher and lower degrees of alterity, when formulating a posthuman standpoint, so that the nonhuman differences are no more compelling than the human ones. For instance, Italian posthumanist philosopher Roberto Marchesini[14] in his book *Il Tramonto dell'Uomo. La Prospettiva Post-Umanista* (2009) states: "The human is no longer the emanation or the expression of man, but the result of man's hybridization with non-human otherness" (2009).[15] We can rephrase this point by saying: the human is no longer the expression of man, because "man," as a universal concept, has been deconstructed. It is only through such a deconstruction that the human can be accessed as a process of hybridization with the nonhuman.

From a metanarrative[16] perspective, such a critique manifests itself as a "post," instead of coining a new term. Posthumanism does not sustain an opposition to the previous episteme, an act which would be based on the logics of the symbolic concave mirror:[17] "we are right, because they were wrong" or "our philosophy is new, because their philosophy had become obsolete." This attitude results in the fact that what is supposed to be counteracted turns into a necessary vehicle to the hermeneutics of the new paradigm: the notion of "post-modern" is posed through a rejection of some determining elements of Modernism,[18] while Modernism can trace its own narratives by opposing elements related both to the Enlightenment and to Romanticism (Lewis 2007), and so on. On one side, presenting a history of ideas through rejections may sound like a simplification; a different history could be successfully assembled as an evolution or a metamorphosis from one movement to the other.[19] And still, it is significant to observe that, within Western schemata, a recognition of a movement is often established through its oppositions to previous ones. For instance, Thomas Kuhn (1922–96) in his influential book *The Structure of Scientific Revolutions* (1962) has thus characterized the epistemological shift from a scientific paradigm to another: "A crisis may end with the emergence of a new paradigm and with the ensuing battle over its acceptance" (2012: 84). Note that although Kuhn saw the characteristic of one reigning paradigm as specific of the sciences, the mechanism of the shift may apply to the social sciences as well.

In the specific case of Posthumanism, there is no need for a symbolic sacrifice. Posthumanism does not reject the previous episteme, but it actually follows on the track set upon by postmodern and post-structuralist practices,[20] in a development which is in a constant dialogue with past, present, and future acknowledgments and possibilities. Posthumanism has embedded feminist horizontal practices and approaches, thus it is able to manifest as a generation rather than as a symbolic killing followed by a redemption. A reflection on its metanarratives is particularly significant since Posthumanism does not mark a separation between "theory," "poiesis," and "praxis";[21] the processes embedded in revealing knowledge, production, and action are intrinsically and extrinsically cohabiting each other. In this sense, the metanarratives of Posthumanism are a recognition and a location: the ways the posthuman accesses the recorded histories and herstories of ideas are as significant as its theoretical formulations, thus moving beyond dualism from a meta-perspective as well.

Interlude 1

Posthumanism can be defined as a post-anthropocentrism, as a post-humanism, and as a post-dualism. The first two terms, that is, post-humanism and post-anthropocentrism, have been emphasized clearly in the formation of Philosophical Posthumanism; we have analyzed some of their genealogical references and discussed their contributions and limits. *What about post-dualism?* The third term of reference, post-dualism, has not been engaged fully and needs a deeper reflection. Before entering into this discussion, we shall ask the question: *What kind of dualism is deconstructed by Philosophical Posthumanism?* Although dualism does not have to be hierarchical, in the history of Western thought, the two sides have been placed in a value system according to which one would be the positive and the other the negative. More clearly, the type of dualism deconstructed by Philosophical Posthumanism is a strict, rigid, and absolute form of dualism, and not the liquid, shifting, and intra-changing form of duality as practiced, for instance, in the Tao. In Taoism, according to philosopher Alan Watts: "The yin-yang principle is not . . . what we would ordinarily call a dualism, but rather an explicit duality expressing an implicit unity" (1976: 26). Lao-Tzu, the reputed author of the classic text *Tao Te Ching* (sixth century BCE ca.), for example, notably reveres water as the most suited metaphor for the all-encompassing dynamic balance of the Tao.[1] [2]

Why is post-dualism important? Post-dualism is a necessary step in the final deconstruction of the human. We, as a society, may eventually overcome racism, sexism, and even anthropocentrism, but if we do not address the rigid form of dualistic mindset that allows for hierarchical sociopolitical constructions, then new forms of discrimination will emerge, such as portraying robots as the new "others."[3] *What are the genealogical sources of post-dualism, in relation to Philosophical Posthumanism?* In order to access post-dualism, considering that such an onto-epistemological approach finds revealing parallels in ancient Asian traditions, such as Buddhism, Jainism, and Advaita Vedanta,[4] we shall look for sources outside of the Western tradition.[5] Posthumanism, in fact, extends over the boundaries of the academic, technological, and scientific domains, and can be genealogically traced in different types of knowledges and understandings. Currently, nondualism is attracting an increasing interest from scholars working on bridging modern knowledge and ancient wisdom. In Western science, for instance, the term is used to refer to an interconnectedness which, in tune with the posthuman approach, rejects Cartesian dualism. Such an approach stands on the path opened by Fritjof Capra with his groundbreaking work *The Tao of Physics* (1975), which highlighted "the parallels between the worldview of physicists and mystics" (7) and demonstrated "the profound harmony" (10) between ideas and concepts as expressed in quantum physics and Eastern practices. This shift has been paired by the rapidly growing interest in mindfulness and meditation in many industrialized countries, for instance, in the United States (Burke and Gonzalez 2011). The contemporary attempt to rethink science, technology, and spirituality in a natural-cultural continuum honors the ontology of the cyborg, to use Donna Haraway's terminology, and highlights Posthumanism as a suited philosophical platform of discussion in the contemporary academic debate; *but should Posthumanism and nondualism be assimilated?* No, they cannot be seen as synonyms. Posthumanism recognizes its own standpoints as post-dualistic, rather than non-dualistic, in the sense that, within hegemonic systems of thought, the episteme has been repeatedly dualistic—think of the classic sets: body/mind, female/male, black/white, east/west, master/slave, colonizer/colonized, human/machine, human/animals, just to mention a few. In tune with a deconstructive approach, Posthumanism is aware of the fact that such dualistic presumptions cannot be easily dismissed; the impact of the historical redundancy on reductionist and dualistic approaches in human thoughts and actions are still pervasive. To understand such an impact more clearly, in Part 2, we are going to embark on a linguistic and semantic journey, where we will approach the following related questions: *Why is the prefix "post" relevant? Where does the notion of the "human" come from? More specifically: of which "human" is the posthuman a "post"?*

Part Two

Of Which "Human" Is the Posthuman a "Post"?

The Power of the Hyphen

In the first part of this book we have embarked on a deep and fascinating journey into some of the main schools of thought which go under the umbrella term "posthuman," such as: Transhumanism, Antihumanism and (Critical, Cultural and Philosophical) Posthumanism. We have addressed them through their significance in the contemporary debate and through their genealogical references. In this second part, we would like to explain why the concept "posthuman" is fitting in addressing the contemporary revisitation of the notion of the human. In order to do this, we will analyze the term itself, in its three main components: "post," "-" (hyphen), and "human." Of the three, a major emphasis has been placed on the "human," and so, as we have previously mentioned, the posthuman has been often defined as a post-humanism and a post-anthropocentrism; to these points, we have added the crucial aspect of post-dualism, which will be more clearly analyzed in Part 3. Here, in Part 2, we will engage more thoroughly with the notion of the human: *Where does the term "human" come from? Is it a notion (i.e., a noun: "human") or a process (i.e., a verb: "humanizing")? Is it symbolically exclusive, or is it comprehensive?* Before focusing on the "human" (as related to both the human species and the humanistic tradition), we have to address the two elements which precede it, in the constitution of the post/-/human/. More specifically, let's ask the question: *Why are the "post" and the hyphen "-" relevant to the discussion on the posthuman?* In the first part of this book, we have stressed the relevance of the "post" in the configuration of the posthuman, as a marker of differentiation from other perspectives previously analyzed, such as Trans(-)humanism and Anti(-)humanism, each of them relying on their prefixes to define their own specificities.

Let's then ask the question: *Why is "post-" needed in the emergence of Post(-)humanism?* Different from the prefix "anti," "post" does not comply with oppositional ontologies, thus overcoming dualisms such as self/other, subject/object, animate/inanimate, human/animal, human/robot, male/female, physical/virtual, flesh/machine, citizen/alien, and normal/pathological. *"Post"* in Latin means both "behind" (if related to space) and "after" (if related to time). As an "after," "post" does not mark a sharp break from which a blank page to be filled can be established, such as the elaboration of a new term might suggest. "Post" implies a continuity, a discontinuity, and a transcendence (in its literal meaning of exceeding) of the term to which it is a "post," and so it necessarily reconciles its own identity to it in a symbiotic relation. The emphasis can be differently posed on the "post" as a reaction (such as "post-modern"), as a continuity (such as "post-feminist," as employed by some contemporary feminist theorists), or as a transcendence (such as "post-apocalyptic" could suggest).

Locating the posthuman as one more "post" in this crowded scenario is crucial in order to contextualize it. And still, the risk of focusing excessively on the politics of the "post" consists in losing its referential terms. The "post" by itself eventually dismembers in the openness which it postulates; it becomes a passage from somewhere to everywhere, in other words, a nowhere (such as in the case of "post-truth").[1] More appropriately, the "post" of the post-human has to be approached as a "post-." The hyphen is the term of mediation; it communicates the fact that there is another term, or other terms, which shall be acknowledged, and so it situates the "post" within a multiplicity of possibilities. The hyphen can be grammatically used in different ways: it can divide a single word in separate parts for the purpose of line-wrapping; it can serve as a "hanging" hyphen, with the second term omitted, and thus manifesting as a suspension. It can be employed to join different notions into a single one, when its manifestation occurs between terms; it is preceded and proceeded, emphasizing a relationality which, as we will see, is specific to the posthuman approach. The hyphen is a relation which can introduce any other term, including a repetition of the self, the mirror, that is, another "post," as in the term "post-postmodernism" (Jameson 1991; Nealon 2012), in a game of reflections which has virtually no end. The hyphen can manifest through its presence as well as through its absence: sometimes it disappears. Specifically, when the use of a term becomes more common, it tends to be omitted: post-modern becomes postmodern, post-feminist turns into postfeminist, post-human into posthuman. Its relevance, though, should not be dismissed. The fact that its presence can be substituted with its absence without a significant loss makes of it a suited mark for the post-dualistic approach of the posthuman; the hyphen does not have to be one or the other: it can be both or neither. Once we have explained why "post" has been selected in the formulation of the posthuman, and why the presence, and disappearance, of the hyphen is emblematic to this approach, we can now start our journey into the human. *When and how have we become "human"?* Through the following reflection, we will underline the fact that "we" have not always been "human." The "human" is a historical notion referring to a culturally specific take on the processes which have brought the emergence of what will be later defined as the human species, that is, the process(es) of humanizing.

12

Humanizing

After analyzing the "post" and the hyphen, let's now engage in a critical analysis of the third constituent of the posthuman: the human. *Is the "human" a notion (i.e., a noun) or a process (i.e., a verb)?* First of all, it is important to emphasize that, more than a noun, the human should be expressed as a verb: to humanize. In order to explain this, we will rely on the genealogy of gender, following feminist theorist Donna Haraway, who stated: "Gender is a verb, not a noun" (2004: 328–29).[1] There are a lot of parallels to be drawn between the ways gender and the human have been historically constituted; this is due to the fact that the same hegemonic subjectivities that had symbolic access to the normativization of epistemic roles and social functions assigned to different genders were also the (only) ones that were granted access to the definition of the human per se. In order to explain this point further, we will offer a brief summary of some key points within feminist theory, which may prove helpful to critically engage with the notion of the human as well. Let's start with existentialist philosopher[2] Simone de Beauvoir (1908–86) who, in her influential book *The Second Sex* (1949; Eng. Transl. 1974), which became a milestone in feminist philosophy, famously affirmed: "One is not born, but rather becomes a woman" (1974: 301). As she further explains: "No biological, psychological, or economic fate determines the figure that the human female presents in society; it is civilization as a whole that produces this creature, intermediate between male and eunuch, which is described as feminine. Only the intervention of someone else can establish an individual as an *Other*" (*ibidem*). De Beauvoir is describing the notion of the woman as a process, rather than an essence, in what would later become the difference between sex and gender. According to de Beauvoir, being born as a female and becoming a woman are two different things: the first term is related to biology, the second to culture. Each cultural paradigm relies on a set of assumptions and biases posed by those humans who are setting the cultural norms, and who, until recently, had been men.

Why does de Beauvoir refer to the Woman as the "Other"? De Beauvoir highlights how the construction of the notion of the "woman" has been shaped to fit as the structural Other of the subject of Western, and non-Western, accounts. In other words, the "woman" is the Other through which the "man" is able to achieve his identity: man is man because the woman is not. According to such cultural premises, the identity of the woman is contingent to the one of the man. De Beauvoir emphasizes the symbolic role of the woman as the Other in numerous passages[3] such as "to be a 'true woman' she must accept herself as the Other" (295). This notion of the Other is related to the traditional separations: nature/culture; body/mind; woman/man, according to which the "woman" is relegated to the aspects that have been considered inferior, such as "nature"—in an anthropocentric episteme which has historically emphasized "culture" as what makes us human—and "body"—in the Cartesian split, according to which the primacy has been given to the mind: "I think, therefore I am." De Beauvoir underlines that, more specifically, the woman has been defined to its (potential) sexual relation to man: "She appears essentially to the male as a sexual being. For him she is sex—absolute sex, no less. She is defined and differentiated with reference to man and not he with reference to her; she is the incidental, the inessential as opposed to the essential" (XIX). Although this text was written many years ago (in 1949), this statement still holds true of our society.

For instance, Hollywood movies can be presented as a fitted example of this redundancy of the female character and her reduction to a sexual prize for the male hero. A large majority of female characters serve the role of the sexual object to be conquered, aesthetically designed for the heterosexual male eye.[4] In the 1990s, after the popularization of politically correct policies, females were granted another possible role to the one of object of sexual desire; now, they could be the talented sexy assistant who may rescue the hero, along with the patriarchal schemata: accepting the secondary role with honor and devotion, she will not run for the crown. In the sexist movie industry, women do not get founded. Movies are mostly directed by males, and the few exceptions do not always challenge the white/male/heterosexual paradigm. For instance, Kathryn Bigelow's *Strange Days* (1995) is a remarkable movie, revealing and original on many different levels; and still, its approach to gender roles is not challenging. The movie portrays "Nero," the main character (acted by Ralph Fiennes), as a dystopian white male hero in love with "Faith," a charming over-sexualized punk girl, performed with excellence by Juliette Lewis. His assistant, "Mace," acted by Angela Bassett, is a highly talented African-American woman who, devoted to her love for Nero, saves him on many occasions. Faith is a good example of the female role of sexual object; Mace is a fine example of the talented assistant who will not threaten the patriarchal asset. Cultural industries such as Hollywood are reinforcing sexist biases in both their storytelling and their practices: female actresses, for instance, receive lower salaries than males (Lauzen 2017). Moreover, the culture of complicity which surrounded the sexual assaults of hundreds of women by Hollywood producers and actors (see, for instance, the scandal and arrest of the co-founder of Miramax production company, Harvey Weinstein, 2017–18) reveals that sexist representations and sexist practices are not separated. Reversing such discriminatory practices will release different cultural products: Hollywood is ready for a change, and so it's the audience. For instance, films which have passed the Bechdel test—that is, a test for which a work of fiction has to feature at least two women who talk to each other about something else other than a man (Bechdel 1985)—are usually produced on a lower budget than others, and still have comparable or better financial performance.[5]

As we can see, de Beauvoir's analysis is still very relevant to our society; and yet, there is an aspect of her criticism that we might have to confront, from a posthumanist perspective. According to the existentialist thinker, "the category of the *Other* is as primordial as consciousness itself" (*ibidem*) and "Otherness is the fundamental category of human thought" (*ivi*: XIX).[6] De Beauvoir underlines how this "Otherness" is not posed as an absolute, but as a relation: "As a matter of fact, wars, festivals, trading, treaties and contests among tribes, nations and classes tend to deprive the concept of the Other of its absolute sense and to make manifest its relativity; willy-nilly, individuals and groups are forced to realize the reciprocity of their relations" (*ivi*: XX).[7] From a posthumanist perspective, claiming that "alterity is the fundamental category of human thought" (2009: 26) is problematic, because it reflects a cultural preference which cannot be essentialized for the human species as a whole. Once we underline the human not as one but as many, some may emphasize that other notions and practices— such as interdependence, symbiosis, affinity, and so on—are as fundamental as the category of alterity, and that these categories are co-constructing each other.[8]

Another thinker who saw these settings as problematic was feminist psychoanalyst Luce Irigaray (born 1930), who gave a specific twist to the concept of the woman as the Other. The publication of her groundbreaking work *Speculum of the Other Woman* (1974) caused her expulsion from the University of Vincennes, and the break with psychoanalyst Jacques Lacan (1901–81) and the

Ecole Freudienne de Paris. *Why was the reaction of the intellectual establishment so extreme to Irigaray's ideas?* Let's try to access the theoretical consequences of her perspective. According to Irigaray, the woman is not the difference, is not the "Other," as in de Beauvoir's account, but is an absence, or better, the absence to be filled with male projections; "she" has not been granted an identity of her own, not even as the Object in the submissive relation to the Subject—that is, the Man. As Irigaray famously posed it, she is not just a mirror, but a "concave mirror"[9] out of which generative potentials can also be explored: "But perhaps through this specular surface which sustains discourse is found not the void of nothingness but the dazzle of multifaceted speleology. A scintillating and incandescent concavity, of language also, that threatens to set fire to fetish-objects and eyes plugged with gold" (*ivi*: 143). In Irigaray's perspective, the woman is not essentialized in her differences from the man, but it is posed as an absence to validate the existence of man through male terms and projections;[10] this concavity, though, is also "scintillating and incandescent" and cannot be reduced to a mere vacuum. Both de Beauvoir and Irigaray are explicit references[11] in the work of postmodern feminist philosopher Judith Butler, whose groundbreaking study *Gender Trouble* (1990) has had a tremendous impact on feminist theory for its exhaustive representation of gender as performative and reiterative. As Butler explains it:

> The action of gender requires a performance that is *repeated*. This repetition is at once a reenactment and reexperiencing of a set of meanings already socially established; and it is the mundane and ritualized form of their legitimation. Although there are individual bodies that enact these significations by becoming stylized into gendered modes, this "action" is a public action. (1990: 178–79)

With this gained perspective on the public ritualized constitution of gender, let's now go back to the human, and revisit it through the different insights we have just presented. The human, in tune with de Beauvoir, is not an essence, but a process: one is not born, but rather becomes human through experience, socialization, reception, and retention (or refusal) of human normative assets. Simultaneously, revisiting Irigaray, the human has been established in the ontological denial of the nonhuman; the recognition of the human has been sustained by a negative reduction of the others—or better, by the absence of a real acknowledgment of embodied alterity and onto-epistemological plurality—through related concomitant exclusions, marked as the inhuman, the subhuman, the less-than-human, and so on.[12] Lastly, the performative and historical manifestation of the notion of the human can be interpreted, in accordance with Butler, as a repeated performance which establishes and consolidates the subject, that is, the human: as gender is gendering, human is humanizing. Addressing the human as a verb has some important consequences. First of all, we should ask the questions: *Is there a subject enacting the process of humanizing? Is humanizing a process or a project (or both)?* To access these points, the concept of the anthropological machine may be of help.

13

The Anthropological Machine

In *The Open: Man and Animal* (2002), philosopher Giorgio Agamben underlines something crucial to the posthuman approach, that is, the historical construction of the human. In his words: "Homo sapiens, then, is neither a clearly defined species nor a substance; it is, rather, a machine or devise for producing the recognition of the human" (2004: 26). Agamben is engaging upon a topic of prime relevance to the posthuman, and still, from a posthumanist critical approach, there are some limits to his proposal. According to Agamben, the human has been strategically produced through a separation from the animal, which is what he calls the "anthropological machine":

> The anthropogenic (or—taking up Furio Jesi's expression—we might say anthropological) machine . . . is an optical machine constructed in a series of mirrors in which man, looking at himself, sees his own image always already deformed in the features of an ape. *Homo* is a constitutively "anthropomorphous" animal . . . who must recognize himself in a non-man in order to be human. (*ivi*: 26–27)

First of all, it is important to note that the animal that is constructed in this negative dialectic is based on the absence of the actual animal, resulting in a speciesist monologue in which the (human) subject has co-created their own image through the absence of what has been posed as the radical difference (of the nonhuman animal). The production of this "ape" which deforms the image of the human is based on some, partial, human experience of the ape,[1] which does not inform us about the ape itself, but about the formulation of human systems of knowledge. Furthermore, the animal should not be accessed in isolation, but as a gradient of a more complex pyramidal structure, according to which some humans have been considered more similar to nonhuman animals than to other humans. *Who were these humans, and who set the standards of the "human"?* By answering to these questions, we will problematize some aspects of Agamben's proposal, specifically, the risk of disembodiment in the notion of "machine," and the assimilation of "man" and "human" (both linguistically and ontologically) throughout the text.

Despite the importance of Agamben's reflection, which has destabilized the ahistorical notion of the human by underlining its processual constitution, the use of the term "machine" may suggest a dissociation between the enactment of humanizing and the subjectivities who have had access to the defining terms of such a process.[2] An "anthropological machine" may recall a neutralized apparatus, which has lost its human embodiment. As Judith Butler underlines in *Undoing Gender* (2004): "If gender is a kind of a doing, an incessant activity performed, in part, without one's knowing and without one's willing, it is not for that reason automatic or mechanical" (1). We can borrow from Butler's understanding of the social performativity of gender in order to access the process of humanizing and critically address the notion of the anthropological machine, which may evoke a mechanical and/or automatic activity. Following, the risk of disembodiment brought about by this notion, and the consequent loss of its biological legacies, are not redeemable. For this reason, we shall rather use the term "humanizing," which leaves its human agents intact, with its embedded question: *"Who" is humanizing "whom"?* Humanizing is an embodied process; moreover, the embodiment of such doing is strictly human (nonhuman animals or machines have had no direct agential access to such redefinition, yet). Before proceeding further, we should clarify that, here, we are not trying to postulate a frontal antithesis between the subjects and objects of such a process, between the oppressors and the oppressed, since both pertain to the same cultural apparatus: power, as Michel Foucault pointed out in *Discipline and Punish: the Birth of the Prison* (1975), is not acquired, but is tactical and strategic.[3] Instead, we wish to emphasize that the notion of a "machine" itself can be misleading, on one side, by annihilating its embodied specificities; on the other, by de-humanizing the overall process and tapping into the old legacy based on the dualism human/machine, which evokes other ones, such as man/woman, white/black, Western/Eastern, among others.

In the historical process of humanizing the human, the animal has been placed, more than as the antithesis of "man," as another gradient in a hierarchy which would pose a whole spectrum of human others between the animal and the human, so that women, nonwhites, queers, "freaks," among others, would be placed accordingly. Agamben refers to this aspect when he states, "[The anthropological machine] functions by excluding as not (yet) human an already human being from itself, that is, by animalizing the human, by isolating the nonhuman within the human" (37). Soon after, he presents the Jew as "the non-human produced within the man" (37) and then refer to concentration camps as "an extreme and monstrous attempt to decide between the human and the inhuman" (22). This is a very effective example of the inhuman in the human, but is not exhaustive for his critical account on the nonhuman "within the man," as we will see in the next chapter. Throughout the text, the exclusion of women by the anthropological machine is not mentioned once; there is no reference to any feminist critique on alterity: considering the crucial contribution given by feminist theorists to the political and ontological reflection on the "Other," as previously pointed out, this omission is particularly significant. This lack of a feminist awareness is reflected in the uncritical use of a language which is not gender-neutral, in the indiscriminate use of "he" as a neutral subject, and "Man"[4] to refer to humankind.[5] And still, Agamben is offering us many precious insights, so shall we close an eye and view this linguistic fallacy as irrelevant? In other words: *Is language "that" important in the formulation of philosophical accounts?* To answer to this question, we shall open a parenthesis which is relevant to not only Agamben but other philosophers quoted in this book.

Let's take a step back and mention that the unconditional use of the masculine form has been widely criticized by feminist linguistics since the 1970s. In 1980, Casey Miller and Kate Swift published their successful *Handbook of Nonsexist Writing*; by the 1990s, the policies of equal opportunities had internationally evolved into institutionalized attempts to create a non-discriminatory language, based on gender-neutrality, race-neutrality, ethnic-neutrality, and so on, in a comprehensive attempt which resonates with a posthumanist sensitivity. The use of a language which is aware of its own implications is even more crucial for philosophers. *Why is that?* As Virginia L. Warren in her "Guidelines for Non-Sexist Use of Language" (1986)[6] brightly suggests:

> For several reasons we, as philosophers, should be particularly sensitive to the issue of nonsexist language. . . . First, our profession has long focused on language. Accordingly, we are attuned to the emotive force of words and to the ways in which language influences thought and behavior. Second, we pride ourselves on our willingness to question assumptions. Yet the uncritical use of sexist language may blind us to our having adopted a particular value-laden perspective. Such blindness may systematically distort our theories. . . . Third, as scholars and teachers we pursue truth wherever it leads: to the reform of our ordinary concepts and beliefs and, if necessary, of our everyday language. Our readers and listeners may have been receiving a message that we never intended to send. Rather than encouraging a superficial recasting of words, these guidelines are designed to foster a deeper appreciation of how easily bias slips into our thoughts and theories. (471)

The use of non-discriminatory language is extremely important in the constitution of posthuman narratives, where the "what" and the "how" are not disjunct: in the posthuman post-dualistic practice, the message is the means, to quote McLuhan (1964). Let's take, for instance, the example of Hollywood, as we have underlined in our previous chapter: the messages embedded in its cultural products are not separated from their production practices. The what is the how. Given that Agamben aims to reveal the privilege of the human, his lack of critique of the notion of "man" inherently weakens his attempt. We shall strive for the use of a language that is fully mindful of its own implications; this is why using the verb "humanizing" may be a better fit for our attempt to emphasize the human as a process that is constantly enacted and re-enacted, according to specific cultural modes and social norms that are co-constituted in the process. In summary, even though the notion of an anthropological machine may be a good starting point to address the human in dynamic terms, it intrinsically reaffirms humanistic assumptions, while erasing the particular embodied aspects of the process. By critically engaging with this notion, we also wished to demonstrate that the methods of a research are not separated from its theoretical endeavors. Posthumanism is a praxis; its perspectives should be embedded in its methodologies.

14

Almost, Human

How to achieve a comprehensive analysis of the process of humanizing? A very important point to be stressed here is that a posthumanist approach shall not focus its analysis merely on hegemonic traditions: such a choice would activate a different light on the same centers of power which have been already at the core of the humanistic tradition, living the rest in the shade again. For instance, in the case of the historical humanization of specific categories of humans, a posthumanist approach should add to its inquiry questions such as: *How did the excluded subjectivities perceive themselves in relation to the notion of the human?* Before delving into these aspects, we should offer a brief overview on whom we may be referring to by that generic "they," focusing on some of the categories of humans which have been repeatedly denied full recognition as human beings. In our previous chapter, we have reflected on the forming of the humanizing process through the nonhuman; as we have repeatedly underlined, not every human being has been considered human. We shall thus ask: *Which humans have been excluded from the notion of the human?* Historically, the recognition of the human status has been regularly switched on and off. In order to clarify this point, we will present four significant trans-historical occurrences, among many others, which shall function as examples of denials in the process of humanizing. Far from a complete map of all the subjectivities which have been denied (or excluded from) the human status, these examples shall serve as trajectories in order to better understand the implication of the project of the human. Considering the vastness of the subject, it is not our intent to present a complete recollection; instead, we will reflect on a few specific cases such as: chattel slavery, genocides, freak shows, and witch trials. For each, we will only offer one specific historical background, even though all four cases have repeatedly and consistently re-emerged within the history of humanity.

Let's start with slavery, specifically, chattel slavery—a system where humans are reduced to property, chattels, and commodities. In the American system of slavery, for instance, captives were considered property to the extent that, in some cases, owners had legal rights to kill them. In 1740, South Carolina passed the "Negro Act," which made it legal for slave owners to kill rebellious slaves.[1] As historian Mark Smith affirms, "This 1740 'Negro Act' redefined slaves as personal chattels (they had been considered freehold property until then)" (2005: 20). In his book *How America's First Settlers Invented Chattel Slavery: Dehumanizing Native Americans and Africans with Language, Laws, Guns, and Religion* (2005), David O'Rourke offers interesting insights on the ways settlers responded to the natives' different cultures in the New World, through the human/less-than human paradigm and the semiotics of the "Other":

> It is common to see these cultural clashes as encounters with "the other." The question of otherness is not simply a distinction between being human and being other. It is more complex. It begins with wondering whether these people are like us or not like us. And if they are not like us, if they are something else, or other, then what are they? Are they human—still a question whether, in some way at least, they are like us—or are they less than human? . . . in nearly all cases "not like us" meant "less than us." (15)

This reflection directly relates to the Valladolid debate, which took place in Valladolid, Spain, between 1550 and 1551, concerning the treatment of the Native Americans in the New World. *Why are we going back to the time of the Conquista?* Because we can trace there a crucial moment in the development of the moral debate on what we can now call the process of humanizing. The main protagonists of the controversy were the Dominican friar Bartolomé de las Casas (1484–1566) and the Renaissance humanist Juan Ginés de Sepúlveda (1494–1573). The central issue at stake was whether the Indians were, by Aristotle's definition, "natural slaves" in need of a master, thus justifying a "just" war for civilization (Diamond 2016). According to Sepúlveda, Native Americans were naturally inferior beings, barbarians to be Christianized, as political theorist Andrew Vincent affirms: "Indians were thus regarded as subhuman. Sepúlveda sees them as different to humans as monkeys. The Spaniards, on the other hand, were viewed as pure and full of humanity" (2010: 62). On the contrary, according to de las Casas, Native Americans were fully human and thus, they had the right to be treated with dignity. The goal of his *Apologetic History of the Indies* (written most likely in the 1550[2]) was to demonstrate that Native Americans were not barbarians but rational beings, and that their laws and costumes equaled or even surpassed those of the ancient Western civilizations, such as the Greeks and the Romans. In sum, as he argued in the *History of the Indies* (1527–61), his

"Spanish nation . . . [was] denying to Indians the condition of human beings" (1971: 10). It is important to note that, while de las Casas had direct contact with Native Americans and experienced the New World first hand, Sepúlveda never traveled to America and his accounts were based on secondary sources. Sepúlveda's fundamental division between "us" (the plus) and "them" (the minus) is at the base of any historical process of dehumanization.

How may genocide result out of processes of dehumanization? In the article "The Eight Stages of Genocide" (1998), anthropologist Gregory Stanton identified eight stages through which a genocide may develop. The first one, which is "classification," is precisely based on this foundational division: "All cultures have categories to distinguish people into 'us and them' by ethnicity, race, religion or nationality: German and Jew, Hutu and Tutsi. Bipolar societies that lack mixed categories, such as Rwanda and Burundi are the most likely to have genocide" (n. pg.). The other seven stages which may lead toward a genocide, as accounted by Stanton, offer precious insights for our inquiry into the human. After the second stage, which is "symbolization," the third is "dehumanization," that is, "one group denies the humanity of the other group. Members of it are equated with animals, vermin, insects, or diseases. Dehumanization overcomes the normal human revulsion against murder" (*ibidem*). After "organization," "polarization," and "preparation," we encounter the seventh stage, which is "extermination";[3] the eighth and final stage is "denial." To summarize, the process starts with the dualism "us/them" (stage 1); through stages 2, 3, and 5, the humanness of "them" is denied to the point that their extermination can be enacted in virtue of their not humanness (stage 7), to which follows the denial of what happened. The technics of a genocide are based upon a dehumanization of the victims. We can clearly trace such a pattern in Nazi Germany (1933–45). As historian Kathleen Kete in *Animals and Ideology: The Politics of Animal Protection in Europe* (2002) has stated,

> The Nazis worked within a new paradigm. Accepting the logics of modernism, they abolished the line separating human and animal and articulated a new hierarchy based on race, which placed certain species—races—of animals above "races" of humans—eagles and wolves and pigs in the new human hierarchy were placed above Poles and rats and Jews. (20)

The process of dehumanization of certain categories of humans, enacted through the dissolution of the animal/human divide (Sax 2002), among other types of ideological propaganda, was sealed in blood. The Nazis exterminated approximately six million[4] European Jews and millions of others, including

Germans with mental and physical disabilities,[5] homosexuals, Roma ("Gypsies"), Poles, Jehovah's witnesses, and Soviet prisoners of war.

More in general, it can be claimed that, in the case of both slavery and genocide, some categories of humans are subjected to a symbolic dehumanization through the division us/them. But in the historical process of humanizing, not every human category excluded from the hegemonic notion of the human can be accounted under this type of dualistic procedure. Leslie Fiedler, in his classic study *Freaks: Myths and Images of the Secret Self* (1978), notes how the freak has historically challenged the us/them paradigm: "He is one of us, the human child of human parents, however altered by forces we do not quite understand into something mythic and mysterious" (24). For instance, dwarfs "were considered beast/human hybrids" (*ibidem*: 72), and thus frequently "portrayed side by side with monkeys and dogs" (*ibidem*). Fiedler importantly underlines the symbolic significance of the "freak" in Western culture, as that human which cannot be reduced to a fixed entity, but represents the bridge, the dissolution of strict binaries: "Only the true Freak challenges the conventional boundaries between male and female, sexed and sexless, animal and human, large and small, self and other, and consequently between reality and illusion, experience and fantasy, fact and myth" (24). Fiedler also notes how freaks have been functional in defining the "normal" human:[6] "Their long exclusion and exploitation by other humans, who defining them thus [as freaks] have by the same token defined themselves as 'normal'" (*ivi*: 13). A "normal" human, in other words, meant a body that had been posed as the human norm in separation from other less-than, or more-than, human bodies. In "Signs of Wonder and Traces of Doubt: On Teratology and Embodied Differences" (1996a), Rosi Braidotti redefines the figure of the human "monster" as "a process without a stable object" (150), pointing out the superstitious roots of teratology, which often attributed the manifestation of these not normalized embodiments to supernatural causes, such as women's power to create—and consequently deform—life (136).

Have all the human "outsiders" been considered less-than human? No, this is not always the case. The feminization of magic is one of the key elements in the European witch trials of the late Middle Ages/early Modern period, which ended in an estimation of sixty thousand[7] executions, a large majority of women.[8] The witch hunt proved superstition[9] as one of the hidden forces behind law-making apparatuses, next to biological determinism, scientific racism, and ethnocentrism, proving another discontinuity within the human frame: not only the lives of those humans considered inferior should be taken, but also the ones of those who were believed to have supernatural powers shall be sacrificed, in order to keep the human realm safe. In this sense, not only the critical deconstructive approach of Posthumanism but also the trajectory toward human enhancement of the transhuman may escape the normalizing dynamics of the historical process, and project, of humanizing. Geo-historically situated, the human body can be perceived as a symbolic text of cognitive and social processes. The establishment of a discourse of perversion (Foucault 1976) and the consequent practices of normalization of the perverse, such as the Nazi genocide, the freak shows, and the witch hunt, are embedded to its genealogy, in a recurring paradigm of human abjection.[10] While the monster and the supernatural stand as social and mythical archetypes delimiting the domain of the comprehensible body, it can be argued that the "human"[11] project has formed, historically and theoretically, through the construction of the "Other": animals, automata, children, women, freaks, people of color other than white,[12] queers,[13] and so on marking the shifting borders of what would become "the human" through processes of performative rejections.[14]

Technologies of the Self as Posthumanist (Re)Sources

The posthumanist perspective aims to attain a comprehensive understanding of the process of humanizing. As we have seen, not every embodied human being has been historically granted such a recognition. One necessary question which needs to be posed in order to achieve a more comprehensive approach is: *How have the (categories of) humans who have been repeatedly dehumanized dealt with their humanness? How have they reconfigured such a denied status?* Accounting for the techniques of the self developed by the outsiders of different historical configurations of the human in order to deal with their own dehumanization is necessary to the posthuman approach, which otherwise would be still entrapped in redemption practices. Let's explain this point further. Even though postulated as a radical critique, the act of revisiting hegemonic traditions to demonstrate the way the human has been performed through exclusions is necessary, but not finalizing. Actually, such an approach, on the long run, proves instrumental to the survival of those same traditions, which achieve their own redemptions through the radical critiques enacted from within: usually, by their rebel "biological" sons.[1] Limiting the analysis to the critique of hegemonic traditions is a centralized type of approach, in the sense that it has successfully recognized a specific center of the discourse to be criticized, and so it does not fit the nomadicity and decentralization of the posthuman. The next step toward a posthumanist analysis would be experiencing different *foci* of interest through the subjectivities which have been excluded from such a centralized perspective. Here we should clarify that the point is not inclusion per se. Inclusion should be viewed as a strategy in order to attain a comprehensive relational epistemology: accounting for a plurality of standpoints draws a multilayered picture, offering a deeper understanding on the manifestation of being, as we will see in Part 3.

How to account for the outsiders of the discourse? The technologies of the self employed by the outsiders of the hegemonic notion of the human might be a good starting point. *What are the technologies of the self?* The technologies of the self are a concept conceived by Michel Foucault, who resumed technology by configuring it in four categories, which should not been perceived as independent from each other, but rather co-constituting each other.[2] The first ones are the "technologies of production, which permit us to produce, transform, or manipulate things" (1988: 17); the second ones are the "technologies of sign systems, which permit us to use signs, meanings, symbols, or signification" (*ibidem*). The third ones are the "technologies of power, which determine the conduct of individuals and submit them to certain ends or domination, an objectivizing of the subject" (*ibidem*). The forth ones are the "technologies of the self, which permit individuals to effect by their own means or with the help of others a certain number of operations on their own bodies and souls, thoughts, conduct, and way of being, so as to transform themselves in order to attain a certain state of happiness, purity, wisdom, perfection, or immortality" (18). In short, the technologies of the self are employed by individuals "to transform themselves." Some may argue that, from a posthumanist methodological standpoint, such technologies may be hard to access, since the resistance/acceptance/reconfiguration of the exclusivist delimitations of the human status by its outsiders might have left no official records behind.

How to access non-hegemonic perspectives on the notion of the human? There are ways to deal with such a challenge in retrieving sources. The posthuman, in its attempt to recollect a comprehensive notion of the human, can rely on the pioneer work developed within different fields, such as African-American studies, gender studies, and postcolonial studies, among others. Aware of the difficulties related to historically documenting non-hegemonic perspectives, these fields have posed increasing interest in alternative sources, such as oral history, performative practice, and folk art. As historian Joan Sangster in her article "Telling our Stories: Feminist Debates and the Use of Oral History" (1994), affirms: "The feminist embrace of oral history emerged from a recognition that traditional sources have often neglected the lives of women" (5). If oral history has been recognized by women's studies and African-American studies as a valid source to retrieve information on non-hegemonic standpoints, the significance of practices such as satire and parody in identity formation has been investigated within queer theory. In particular, the performative aspects of the masquerade,[3] cross-dressing, and transvestitism have been acknowledged as "subversive bodily acts" to heteronormative scenarios.[4]

Moreover, a posthumanist approach should revisit the subversive value of social modes such as the carnivalesque (Bakhtin 1941) and the sacrilegious laughter, as employed within anarchist traditions and their "ironic praxis."[5] Such attitudes, which can be explored in both sociopolitical and existential terms, can be perceived as ways to demystify hegemonic dynamics of social discourses, including normative connotations of the human. Music and dance traditions should also count as alternative sources to be investigated. In the case of American slavery, for instance, slaves, in order to deal with the dehumanization they were experiencing, developed techniques of the self in modes of day-to-day resistance (Bauer and Bauer 1942); they also expressed their feelings through songs characterized by the recurring theme of a trusting faith in the life after, as attested in the specific tradition of slave spirituals. In "Veiled Testimony: Negro Spirituals and the Slave Experience," John White offers a reflection on the significance of the development of Negro spirituals by slaves, as a "distinctive culture which, to a large (but indeterminate) extent protected them from the dehumanizing effects of servitude" (1983: 251).

What about spirituality? Ultimately, the resisting side of spirituality, which can be silently expressed during the most challenging circumstances, should not be underestimated. A history of beliefs, visions, prayers, and rituals has accompanied the historical outcomes of the most oppressed categories of human beings and can be recollected throughout extremely challenging times (during slavery, for instance, as well as by women in highly misogynist eras[6]). Spiritual practices can be viewed, from a posthumanist perspective, as techniques which offer hybridization in contexts where essentialism has been employed to configure fixed categories and hierarchies, and may silently destabilize such a state of things through an existential attitude which moves beyond historical conventions. Here, we shall clarify that the history of spiritual practices shall not be assimilated to the history of the religions enacting them. Religions are most commonly characterized by a set of principles (dogmas), which define its specificities in respect to other religions, and are empirically sustained by hierarchical structures based on acquired knowledges, which are needed in order to preserve those same teachings through historical changes.[7] Spirituality, on the other side, refers to a human tendency to conceive existence more extensively than the ordinarily perception of individual beings. Spirituality contemplates a non-separation between the inner and the outer worlds, and may culminate in mystical experiences, which offer non-mediated perceptions of transcending. The realm of spirituality[8] can be investigated as one of the genealogies of the posthuman.[9]

The Epiphany of Becoming Human

What are some of the possible outcomes of the process of humanizing? By presenting the human as a verb, humanizing, we aim to emphasize its performative dynamics and its potentials, which may spark different outcomes. Until now, we have underlined how humanizing can be experienced as an act of self-identity by the subjectivities enacting it (in other terms: "I am human, because the others are not"), and developed through the us/them paradigm. Such an attitude carries the related risk of developing into a fetishism of existential primacy, which may consequently justify social discrepancies sustained by exclusivist paradigms; in its extreme forms, it may eventually lead to practices of dehumanization and denial, such as slavery and genocide. But there are other possible outcomes, one of which is what we will refer to as the epiphany of becoming human. In this other possible outcome, the act of humanizing per se manifests as a location, as a connector, and as a revelation. In other words: "I *am*, in my embodied human experience, and, in relation to others." In this sense, the recognition of alterity as necessary to the manifestation of the self brings along ethical responsibilities and deontic significations. In *Totality and Infinity: An Essay on Exteriority* (1961), French philosopher Emmanuel Lévinas (1906–95) elaborated on the human to human encounter as a face-to-face epiphany, which can be epitomized in this sentence, to be found in his essay "Diachrony and Representation" (1985; Engl. Trans. 1969): "Responsibility for the Other—the face signifying to me 'thou shalt not kill,' and consequently also 'you are responsible for the life of this absolutely other Other'—is responsibility for the unique one" (1994: 107–08). It has to be noticed that, to Lévinas, this "Other" is an absolute Other to which "I" can unilaterally open; Lévinas takes this stand in response to the subjectivistic tradition of Western philosophy which, according to him, has predominantly enacted "a reduction of the Other to the Same" (1969: 43). Although Philosophical Posthumanism also problematizes such unredeemable reduction, it does not respond to it with the configuration of an absolute Otherness outside of mediation,[1] but with a pluralistic-monistic deconstruction,[2] according to which the Other(s) maintain their specific alterity, as well as their shared relationality to the Self. A relation does not have to comply with a reduction (for instance, during pregnancy the two bodies of the mother and of the fetus are in a necessary relation that does not resolve in an assimilation). We shall also mention that, according to Lévinas, the face of the Other is strictly human, while from a posthumanist approach, this humanist assumption can only be challenged.[3]

In fact, there are different types of epiphanies. Roberto Marchesini, for instance, presents the notion of "animal epiphany" (2014) to refer to the sense of revelation, fascination, and/or terror (but not indifference), that humans have always experienced toward nonhuman animals, and that has been silenced in the historical categorization of the nonhuman animal as inferior, and/or as an absence. Another posthumanist epiphany to be addressed, among others,[4] can be epitomized in the encounter of the human with the "face" of the planet. For instance, in his book *The Overview Effect: Space Exploration and Human Evolution* (1998), Frank White defines as "the overview effect" the series of epiphanies experienced by astronauts looking at the Earth from outer space. To White, the overview effect is so significant that he affirms: "The Overview Effect may point to humankind's purpose as a species" (5). Although evocative, this teleological outcome may be challenged by addressing the human as a plural notion, that is: *How can we detect a purpose for the human(s) as a species, if the human is not one but many?* This question can be answered in different ways. Nietzsche, for instance, saw the human as a bridge, as constant potential,[5] focusing mainly on individual drives. Julian Huxley underlined, more specifically, the great potentials in "the advancement of our species as a whole" (1957: n. pg.), affirming: "The human species can, if it wishes, transcend itself—not just sporadically, an individual here in one way, an individual there in another way, but in its entirety, as humanity" (*ibidem*). In mediated terms, Teilhard de Chardin in his paper "From the Pre-Human to the Ultra-Human: The Phases of a Living Planet" (later published in the book *The Future of Man*, 1959, Engl. Trans. 1964) sustained that "the human multitude is moving as time passes not toward any slackening but rather toward a superstate of psychic tension" (296–97). More in general, we can claim that humans are related through their biological intra-actions, and still, they are all very different; from a naturalcultural standpoint, generalizations on the species may not fully account for personal and historical specificities.

Why is the overview effect significant to the posthuman approach? The realization of the non-separateness of the human and the planet is particularly relevant in the era of the Anthropocene, when human activities are heavily impacting the Earth. Furthermore, White relates this epiphanic shift in consciousness to the specific geographical perspective,[6] stating: "Mental processes and views of life cannot be separated from physical location" (3). The significance of the specific location of the embodied human perspective will be understood in depth in Part 3, when perspectivism will be presented as an important component of a philosophical posthumanist epistemology. Before proceeding further in our reflection on the possible evolutionary, as well as epistemological, consequences of space migration, we first need to proceed in our investigation on the third constituent of the "post-human," which is the human, and ask the question: *When and how did humans become "human"?* As we have underlined, the historical outcomes of the notion of the human have not comprehended all the beings who, for instance, would genetically count as humans. We shall thus wonder if the historical exclusivism which has characterized the humanizing process is interconnected to the linguistic, semantic, and etymological mechanisms which have sustained the notion of the "human." In other words: *Is the notion of the human inherently biased?* This reflection is crucial to Philosophical Posthumanism, in order to understand if its configuration as a "post" is only a strategic one—a "post" which, once reaffirmed a comprehensive and non-hierarchical approach of the "human," could be erased again (that is, getting rid of the "post" and going back to the "human"). Or, if such a linguistic move (that is, relocating the human through the "post") is necessary in order to reveal different epiphanies, which could not be sustained within paradigms denoted and connoted by the historical notion of the human. The only way to achieve an answer to this question is by accessing the term archaeologically.

Let's start by reviewing its vocabulary definitions. For instance, the *Oxford Dictionary* describes the adjective "human," as "relating to or characteristic of humankind" (Oxford Dictionaries Online: entry "Human," n. pg.), further defining it as: "1. of or characteristic of people as opposed to God or animals or machines, especially in being susceptible to weaknesses; 2. showing the better qualities of humankind, such as kindness; 3. *Zoology* of or belonging to the genus *Homo*" (*ibidem*). The first denotation poses the human through three consecutive oppositions ("I am human because I am not God / animal / machine"). It thus relies on the technique of the concave mirror (that is, defining what is the human through what it is not), and so it does not answer our question, which is: *What* is *the human?* The second one defines it through moral characteristics. By choosing to affiliate the notion of the human with "the better qualities" of humankind, it reflects an anthropophilic preference; this bias does not allow us to account for it scientifically. The third one defines the human through its taxonomical classification, and it may operate as the closest apparatus of scientific significance to our archaeological goal. We will start from here to understand what contemporary society is reiterating as a supposedly "neutral" notion of the human—that is, what is often taken for granted when using the term "human." In order to do this, we will start by analyzing its etymology, which simultaneously covers the etymology of the taxonomical classification of the human as *Homo*. Before proceeding, we shall mention that, although this study will mostly focus on the limits and on the potentials of the term "human" in this particular linguistic outfit, different doors may open when addressing the notion of the "human" through different languages and cultural traditions.[7]

Where Does the Word "Human" Come From?

The word "human" is derived from Latin *humanus/a/um*, an adjective cognate to *humus*[1] meaning "earth,[2] ground, soil," on notion of "earthly beings" whose symbolic realm, according to ancient Romans, was marked through its oppositions to the divine, the bestial, and the barbarian. In other words, Gods or Goddesses[3] could not be accounted as "humans," and were neither nonhuman animals nor "barbarians"—that is, humans (according to our modern under-standing of the term) who were considered uncivilized. This aspect is emphasized by Martin Heidegger in his "Letter on Humanism," (1947), which is regarded as an important antecedent to the posthumanist approach, as he states:

> *Humanitas*, explicitly so called, was first considered and striven for in the age of the Roman Republic. *Homo humanus* was opposed to *homo barbarus. Homo humanus* here means the Romans, who exalted and honored Roman *virtus* through the "embodiment" of the *paideia* [education] taken over from the Greeks. (2001: 242)

Here, we have successfully identified the starting point of our inquiry: some humans began to refer to themselves as *homo humanus* in ancient Rome. This definition was posed through an opposition (from the barbarians) and through a recognition (in education). We will come back to these focal points after we contextualize the birth of the term by asking: *When and how did the Latin notion of* "humanus" *emerge?* In order to answer this question, we have to travel back in time to the age of the Roman Republican, and pay specific attention to a group of intellectuals who would be later called the Scipionic Circle, named after their patron, the politician Scipio Aemilianus (185–129 BCE). Although some scholars have problematized the actual existence of the Scipionic Circle (cf. Zetzel 1972), the ideals promoted by these intellectuals in their works reveal a shared sensitivity which is the key in understanding the birth of the term "*humanus.*" Involving philosophers such as Cicero and playwrights such as Terence, the thinkers connected to this Circle were greatly fascinated by Greek culture, which they studied and revered, in a philhellenic attitude, which was at the time criticized by Roman traditionalists[4] who considered the growing Hellenization of Rome a degeneration of traditional Roman values. The Scipionic Circle would bring about the blending of Greek and Roman culture, which would be defining in the birth of the notion of the human, merging *philantropia* (that is, the love and compassion for humanity) and *paideia* (that is, education and culture) with Roman values.

To fully understand these terms, we need to take a further step back and note that the Greek term for "human" is "*anthropos*" (which is the etymon of many contemporary words, such as "anthropocentrism" and "anthropology," among others). Although the Latin term "*humanus*" and the Greek term "*anthropos*" cannot be assimilated (Nishitani 2006), the Greek understanding of *anthropos* has had a deep influence throughout history on the reformulation of the notion of the human. It is worth approaching it, specifically, through Aristotle, who in *Politics*, Book 1, famously defined the human (*anthropos*) as a political animal (*zoon politikon*, in Greek), that is, connected to the "*polis*," meaning the city, which represents civilization: "Man is by nature a political animal, and a man that is by nature and not merely by fortune citiless is either low in the scale of humanity or above it" (Pol. 1.1253a). It is important to note that this "political man" is placed in a hierarchical scale through not only its external, and explicit, "citiless" people, but also its internal, and implicit, others: in Athens, for instance, women, slave, and resident aliens[5] were excluded from the political life. Following, Aristotle defines the human through "*logos*" (that is, speech, language, but also, reason): "Man alone of the animals possesses speech [*logos*]" (*ibidem*). It is important to stress the relation to language by noting that people who did not speak Greek were considered barbarians, such as the Persians, the Egyptians, and the Phoenicians, despite their remarkable civilizations. In classical Greek culture, *logos* and civilization were connected, in that, as Aristotle remarks: "speech is designed to indicate . . . the right and the wrong; for it is the special property of man in distinction from the other animals that he alone has perception of good and bad and right and wrong and the other moral qualities, and it is partnership in these things that makes a household and a city-state" (*ibidem*).

The primacy of the *logos*, marked by the preference for reason and rational thought, represents an important shift from the absolute supremacy of the "*moira*," that is, the unchangeable destiny or fate (personified in three Goddesses named together as *Moirai*, which is the Greek plural for *moira*). If reason allows for an ethical standing, it is the privilege of belonging to the city that gives access to "*paideia*," that is, the formal "education" of its members (although not everyone would have access to it[6]), and also the informal shared "culture" promoting a process of identification of the individual with the political ethos. "*Humanitas*" is the Roman revisitation of the Greek notion of "*paideia*," so that we can now see how the term "human" closely relates to other connected notions such as "culture," "reason," and "civilization."

The next question we shall address is: *If "humanus" was coined in the age of the Roman Republican, which writers started to employ this term?* The term can be found in early Latin comedy by playwrights such as Titus Maccius Plautus (c. 250 BCE–184 BCE), Statius Caecilius (c. 230 BCE–c. 168 BCE), and Publius Terentius Afer (c. 185 BC–159 BCE). For instance, in the play "Asinaria" (c. 211 BCE), Plautus famously wrote: "*Lupus est homo homini, non homo, quom qualis sit non novit*"[7] (a. II, sc. IV, v. 495), that is, "Man is a wolf to man, not a man, when he has not yet found out what he is like."[8] While Caecilius, probably in direct response, stated, "*Homo homini deus est si suum officium sciat*"[9] (Fragment VI), that is, "Man is to man a God when he recognizes his duty."[10] Here it is important to note that these translations are not fully accurate—this is why the original quotes in Latin are included in the main text. In fact, "*homo*" means "human" and it does not refer to a specific gender. In Latin "*vir*" means, specifically, "man" and "*mulier*" "woman," but it is also a fact that "*homo*" in Latin is regularly referred to and declined in the masculine form. Going back to our investigation, in his comedies, Terentius relocated the notion of the human from the abstract modes of the intellectual debate to the practical domain of everyday's life. He emphasized the human realm as self-defining, in a comprehensive approach which did not need the mechanisms of exclusion in order to function. His take could be summarized in the famous phrase to be found in his play "Heauton Timorumenos" (163 BCE): "*Homo sum: humani nihil a me alienum puto*"[11] (v.77): "I am a man; nothing that relates to man do I consider foreign to me."[12] It is interesting to note that Terentius, born in Carthage (North Africa), was brought to Rome as a slave by Terentius Lucanus, who later educated and freed by him. His life experience might have had a direct influence on his comprehensive take on *humanitas*, as Richard Bauman pointed out: Terentius "was well placed to preach the message of universalism, of the essential unity of the human race" (2000: 1).

If Terentius was one of the first authors to introduce the term, Marcus Tullius Cicero (106–43 BCE) was the intellectual who engaged in developing it more than anyone else,[13] and whose legacy has been most authoritative.[14] Greatly influenced by the work of Greek stoic philosopher Panaetius (c. 185–c. 110 BCE), Cicero's notion of *humanitas* provided a guide of ethical conduct and equanimity, not only in the daily practices of living, but also when exercising political power. His take on *humanitas* emphasized the interrelation between being moral, educated, and actively involved in public life, in a Latin revisitation of the Greek notion of *paideia*; his articulation of the concept will be crucial in the development of Renaissance Humanism (Nybakken 1939; Davies 1997: 15–20). And still, Cicero, in conformity with the views of his time, never opposed the institution of slavery or the subordinate condition of Roman women (Fraschetti 1999; Bauman 2000; Posner 2011: 23). His common *humanitas* did not challenge the hegemonic hierarchical sociopolitical configuration, as Vladimir Biti puts it: "Romans trusted that their gods destined them to rule and civilize the world, providing a 'human' unity to its ethnic, cultural and linguistic diversity" (2016: 332). To summarize, we can affirm that the Latin notion of *humanitas* was delimited through not only its explicit borders (for instance, the *homo barbarus* to civilize), but also its implicit ones, that is, the categories of humans who did not have access to the discussion (for instance, women, children, and slaves).[15] The roots of the word "humanity" have been mostly traced by free adult male intellectuals implicitly referring to other free adult male intellectuals. The values introduced by such a notion in the ancient world, if compared, for instance, to the *mos maiorum* (that is, the traditional Roman values), should be regarded as an important paradigm shift toward a comprehensive account on the human, by emphasizing, for instance, the universal human connection. And still its implicit and explicit restrictions, which would result in patronizing practices and colonizing policies, did not radically question the *status quo*, and should be equally accounted for in this archaeological enquiry. From a posthumanist perspective, exclusion may be perceived as a defining technique, which is traceable in the ways the notion of the human has been delineated and performed since the very origins of the coining of the term. We have successfully traced back the notion of the human to its etymological birth. Let's now go back to the third definition of the "human" by the dictionary, that is, "of or belonging to the genus *Homo*," and delve into its scientific classification.

Mammals or *Homo sapiens*?

How are humans classified in biology? The current biological understanding of the term "human" refers to the *Homo* genus, that is, a taxonomic rank which includes not only modern humans (*Homo sapiens*) but other species closely related and now extinct—for example, *Homo neanderthalensis,* which is also considered to be one of the last species to die out.[1] It is important to notice that such a classification has considerably changed over time, and its exact makeup is constantly under debate. Let's then ask the question: *When and how were humans first classified as* Homo sapiens? Once this point is filled, we will engage in a critical reflection on the constitution of this definition to see if the exclusivist techniques which characterized the linguistic birth of the human can also be traced in its scientific outfit. Let's start by pointing out a notable date in this genealogy, which is 1758,[2] when Swedish botanist Carl Linnaeus (1707–78)[3] coined the binomial name *Homo sapiens* (Latin for "knowing human"), referring to the only living species in the *Homo* genus. In order to properly understand such an event, let's first contextualize the religious and ideological coordinates in which science was located at the time.

Before the development of evolutionary studies, Western biology consisted primarily of taxonomy, the discipline of classifying and naming organisms,[4] which, considered to be creations of God, were thought to have remained unchanged since their genesis. Linnaeus also shared those beliefs. A deeply religious man and the son of a Lutheran pastor, he thought of himself as a second Adam. God charged Adam with the task of naming all living beings (Gen. 2: 19–20), and so the cover of Linnaeus's *magnum opus*, which was entitled *Systema Naturae* (1758), featured a man in the Garden of Eden completing his predecessor's task. On the frontispiece of his book, he placed the Latin motto: "*Deus creavit, Linnaeus disposuit,*" which means "God created, Linnaeus organized."[5] In "*Systema Naturae*" Linnaeus outlined his system for classifying all known and yet to be discovered organisms, according to the greater or lesser extent of their similarities, in a ranked hierarchy. Life, considered the superdomain, was divided into three kingdoms (plant, animal, and mineral), subsequently branched into: phyla, classes, orders, families, genera (plural for "genus"), and species. His classification, which replaced the Aristotelian system (which had been the main point of reference until then), strictly applied a binomial nomenclature, formed by two Latin names reflecting the categories of genus and species: for instance, in *Homo sapiens*, "Homo" refers to the genus, "sapiens" to the species. This approach brought much order and clarity to scientific nomenclature.[6] Furthermore, by arranging organisms according to physical characteristics, Linnaeus placed humans along with monkeys and apes into the order of *Primates*. His work scandalized religious authorities: for the first time in Western history, humans were located in a system of biological classification like any other animal or plant species. In doing this, Linnaeus's classification indirectly posed into question the accuracy of the Great Chain of Being (*Scala Naturae*). Rooted in Plato, Aristotle, and the Old Testament, the Great Chain of Being depicted a hierarchical structure of all matter and life (even in its hypothetical forms, such as angels and demons), starting from God: this model, with contextual differences and specificities, passed on, in its Christian interpretation, through the Middle Ages, the Renaissance, until the eighteenth century (cf. Lovejoy 1936). Linnaeus's classification brought along a paradigm shift which, although it did not imply evolutionary traits,[7] laid the groundwork for the theory of evolution as developed by Charles Darwin (1809–82). Yet, innovative on many levels, Linnaeus's system clearly reflected the social exclusions of his time.

In order to contextualize the scientific birth of the *Homo*, and thus offer a comprehensive perspective on the legacies of the human, we shall look more closely at the category of *Homo sapiens* and ask the question: *Are there any biased assumptions in Linnaeus's system? If so, do they allow for an impartial comprehension of all human beings under the notion of* Homo sapiens? Let's start with the racial connotations of his work. In the tenth edition of *Systema Naturae*, Linnaeus established five taxa (that is, taxonomic groups), for a further classification of the *Homo sapiens*, based on continent, skin color, and specific characteristics, plus the taxon *Homo monstrosus*, which embraced a variety of cases, such as dwarfs, giants, and people with congenital abnormalities.[8] His system of racial taxonomy described Europeans as white (*Europaeus albus*), Indian-Americans as red (*Americanus rubescens*), Asians as yellow[9] (*Asiaticus luridus*), Africans as black (*Africanus niger*). Characteristics were placed according to a Eurocentric perspective, so that Europeans were described, among other things, as "sanguine, brawny, gentle, and inventive"[10] (Vaughan 1982: 945); Indian-Americans as "choleric, obstinate, content, and free" (*ibidem*); Asians as "melancholy, rigid, haughty, and covetous" (*ibidem*); Africans as "phlegmatic, crafty, indolent, and negligent" (946); African women, "without shame" (Curran 2011: 158). Furthermore, while Europeans were considered to be "governed by laws" (Fluehr-Lobban 2006: 11), Africans were "governed by caprice" (*ibidem*), Asians were "ruled by opinion" (*ibidem*), and Americans "by customs" (*ibidem*), in a hierarchy which, in tune with the ideological paradigm of the Enlightenment, emphasized reason in contrast with tradition, superstition, or opinion, and so accorded the moral primacy to the government by law, characteristic of the Europeans. Linnaeus's taxonomical classification has had an enormous impact on the construction of racial theories till today.[11]

From a posthumanist approach, this Eurocentric partiality[12] undermines Linnaeus's taxonomical classification as a neutral and objective way to define the human. His racist and ethnocentric biases were combined with gender assumptions. In *Systema Naturae*, paralleling to *Homo Sapiens*, Linnaeus coined the term "Mammalia,"[13] as one of the six classes into which he divided animals, naming this specific group after their mammary glands. This preference does not necessarily seem to be grounded in scientific motivations, but in political ones. Apart from being a botanist, Linnaeus was also a physician, a father of seven children and a strong advocate of breastfeeding. In the eighteenth century, it became very popular in Europe for women of the upper and middle classes to employ wet-nurses,[14] who mostly belonged to the lowest classes; because of their challenging living conditions and poor health, this practice resulted in high infant mortality. The public debate became so heated that in 1794, Prussia, for instance, passed a law requiring healthy mothers to nurse their children. In her detailed article entitled "Taxonomy for Human Beings" (1993), Londa Schiebinger points out the classist outlines of this campaign, which did not problematize the poor living conditions of the wet-nurses or their babies, but mostly focused on the well-being of mothers and infants of the middle and upper classes. Schiebinger underlines how this "struggle against wet-nursing . . . emerged alongside and in step with political realignments undermining women's public power and attaching a new value to women's domestic roles" (1993: 383). Linnaeus was a strong advocate in this campaign; in 1752, he published the pamphlet "Nutrix Noverca" against wet-nursing, which promoted precious information about the virtues of breastfeeding, but also reiterated old sexist biases and superstitions.[15] We can now understand why the primacy given to the "*mammae*" (Latin for "breasts") in the constitution of the term "mammal" can be

interpreted as a "political act"—as Schiebinger puts it (1993: 382)[16]—more than
a scientific choice. As Schiebinger summarizes: "Within Linnean terminology,
a female characteristic (the lactating mamma) ties humans to brutes, while a
traditionally male characteristic (reason) marks our separateness" (*ivi*: 394). The
term "mammal," which is related to female biology and human specificities,[17]
is employed by Linnaeus to place the human species into the larger natural
system, stressing the role of the woman as a mother, and her relation to the
animal kingdom in her nursing nature. On the other side, Linnaeus coined the
term "*Homo sapiens*," which emphasized the human cognitive functions within
a male frame[18] and marked the distinction between humans and other primates,[19]
revealing the inner sexism and speciesism of both notions.

Let's now focus more clearly on the term "*Homo sapiens*" and notice that,
if taken not as an objective denotation, but as an autopoietic[20] connotation,
Homo sapiens appears like a somehow suiting definition of the human, at least,
from a philosophical perspective. In this sense, the human would stand as the
"knowledgable" species (that is, "*sapiens*") precisely because it is *that* species
which is postulating *that* specific knowledge. In other terms, the knowledge
of the *Homo sapiens* is created by the *Homo sapiens* to be comprehended and
of use to the *Homo sapiens,* in a self-referential way: nonhuman animals, for
instance, have no direct use of the knowledge generated by humans (it is worth
noting that this situation may change, for instance, with the rise of the machines,
as robots and artificial intelligence have already access to the human knowledge
that is shared and stored in the internet). This interpretation is somehow in tune
with Linneaus's motivations for choosing the term "*sapiens*." In fact, from the
first to the tenth edition of "Systema Naturae," the human is simply described
with the Latin maxim *Nosce te ipsum* (that is, "know yourself"). On this regard,
Agamben has stated:

> An analysis of the *Introitus* that opens the *Systema* leaves no doubts about the
> sense Linnaeus attributed to his maxim: man has no specific identity other than
> the *ability* to recognize himself. Yet to define the human not through any *nota
> characteristica*, but rather through his self-knowledge, means that *man is the
> animal that must recognize itself as human to be human.* (2004: 25–26)

Going back to our archaeological inquiry into the human, we can state that the
taxonomical classification of *Homo sapiens* defined the human through a self-
recognition ("*the animal that must recognize itself as human to be human*"); but
this self-recognition was still located in the hegemonic reflections of the concave

mirror, according to which some humans would be considered more human than others. This process of humanizing distorted the representation of the humans who did not have access to such postulation: for instance, Europeans were granted the human primacy, in comparison to Africans and Asians. In other words, *Homo sapiens* kept the biased assumptions of its Latin etymology intact, since such a self-recognition was still relying upon sexist, racist, and ethnocentric schemata (*humanus*, the plus, *barbarus*, the minus; male, the plus, female, the minus; able, the plus, differently abled, the minus, and so on). From a posthuman perspective, the coining of the term *"Homo sapiens"* marks an important attempt to relocate the human among all the other organisms; and still, considering that not all humans have been equally accounted for under this category, its inner hierarchical configuration undermines the presumed universality of its claim.

Interlude 2

In the second part of this book, we have addressed the question: *Of which human, is the posthuman a "post"?* We have enquired whether the notion of the human could be accounted, by itself, as a carrier for the exclusivism which historically developed through it. In our investigation, we have learned that nomenclatures are not neutral, but they are part of a wider apparatus of sociopolitical as well as economic and symbolic signification. A recollection of its etymological as well as taxonomical roots revealed that the ideological constraints embedded within the term "human" may partially account for its historical exclusivist legacies, which allowed for the dehumanization of the less-than-human others. In fact, both the Latin term "*humanus*" and the scientific category of *Homo sapiens* placed the human in a hierarchical scale, according to which some humans would be considered, explicitly or implicitly, more human than others. This information is functional in order to reflect upon the relevance of postulating a "post" to the notion of the human. Philosophical Posthumanism is a post-humanism, a post-anthropocentrism, and a post-dualism. As a post-humanism, it must be aware of its genealogical legacies and fully investigate what that might entail, acknowledging the limits and inferences of the historical constitution of the human, which, more than a static notion to be taken for granted, should be accessed as a process and as a verb (humanizing), for its dynamic, and also reiterative and performative, modes of proceeding.

From a post-anthropocentric perspective, we have learned that nonhuman animals have been repeatedly posed in a symbolic absence: their presence would be subservient to the hegemonic postulation of the human. They could not be dehumanized because, within these schemata, they had never been granted any ontological primacy. This speciesist symbolic monologue allowed for the inhuman treatment of "beasts" (to the point where this term came to signify "an animal as opposed to a human"[1]): they could be killed for leisure, confined in degrading conditions for human purposes and disposed of, calling for a new ethics in the treatment of nonhuman animals (Singer 1975). Here, we shall note that in most societies worldwide, anthropocentrism is still an undiscussed moral imperative. Philosophical Posthumanism is a radical response to the human primacy, and can be the turning point in epistemological beliefs by addressing the question "Who am I?" in conjunction with other related questions such as "What am I?" and "Where and when are we?" Rosi Braidotti, for instance, refers to the subject as a "transversal entity encompassing the human, our genetic neighbors the animals and the earth as a whole" (2013: 82). This shift in the social and individual perception of the human is one of the most important challenges we are currently facing as a species and requires a deeper analysis. Let's then explore the third signification of Philosophical Posthumanism, that is, post-dualism, in a comprehensive attitude which approaches the human as an open signifier, in its historical actualizations and also in its potentialities. In Part 2 we have mostly focused on the bio-discursive embodiments of the human; in Part 3 we will further proceed in this direction, and also, we will address more clearly the material, as well as spatiotemporal, embodiments of the human from the evolution of life in the Anthropocene, to the speculative reflection on posthumanities, to the multiverse. It is time to enter the post-anthropocentric and post-dualistic character of Philosophical Posthumanism, which successfully manifests its critical engagement and establishes its shift and theoretical outfit through the conditions of the "post." Now, we can ask the third question of our enquiry: *Have humans always been posthuman?*

Part Three

Have Humans Always
Been Posthuman?

Post-Anthropocentrism in the Anthropocene

In the first part of the book we have underlined the posthuman as an umbrella term which comprehends different movements and schools of thought, such as Transhumanism and Antihumanism. We have then immersed in the celebration of the birth of Philosophical Posthumanism, defined as a post-humanism, a post-anthropocentrism, and a post-dualism. In the second part, we have asked the question: Of which "human" is the posthuman a "post," and realized that not all human beings have been equally accounted for under the "human" label. The historical process of humanizing has emerged through, not only, the exclusions of the humans who were considered inferior, but also, a strict dichotomy with nonhuman animals and planet Earth. If post-humanism can be seen as the pluralistic symphony of the human voices who had been silenced in the historical developments of the notion of "humanity," post-anthropocentrism adds to this concert the nonhuman voices, or better, their silencing amid what is currently defined as the sixth mass extinction—the ongoing extinction of species caused, directly or indirectly, by human actions (cf. Wake and Vredenburg 2008). This book argues that an urgent answer to this scenario lays in philosophy, and specifically, in a theoretical and pragmatical post-anthropocentric shift in the current sociocultural perception of the human. Such a shift can only result by fully acknowledging the actual state of things, as Donna Haraway puts it, by "staying with the trouble" (2016: 1), to "stir potent response to devastating events" (*ibidem*). This chapter calls for an environmental and sustainable praxis by accessing the posthuman as a post-anthropocentrism (Braidotti 2013; Ferrando 2016b).

Why is anthropocentrism a problem? The centrality of the human implies a sense of separation and individuation of the human from the rest of beings. This epistemological approach has not only sociopolitical and ethical consequences, in the abuse that has been inflicted upon nonhuman others, but also geological implications. Anthropocentrism is inextricably connected to the rise of the

Anthropocene which, more than an isolated process, shall be addressed as one of the effects of an anthropocentric *Weltanschauung*, based on an autonomous view of the human as a self-defying agent. *Anthropo*-centrism and the *Anthropo*-cene share a common etymology, that is, the Greek term for "human" (*anthropos*),[1] whose centrality is pivotal in the coining of both terms. *When can we trace the beginning of the informal geological era of the Anthropocene?* There are different opinions on this matter (Zalasiewicz et al. 2008). From a historical perspective, Paul Crutzen and Eugene Stoermer, the scholars who have popularized the term (2000), locate the Anthropocene in the latter part of the eighteenth century, clarifying: "To assign a more specific date to the onset of the 'anthropocene' seems somewhat arbitrary, but . . . we choose this date because, during the past two centuries, the global effects of human activities have become clearly noticeable" (17). That date coincides with the invention of the steam machine by James Watts in 1784, which played a central role in the industrialization of modern society, and became iconic of the early Industrial Revolution during the age of the Enlightenment. Ever since, most human societies have increasingly adopted daily habits of living that are leading to a point of non-return in ecological and sustainable terms. In his article, "The Climate of History: Four Theses" (2009), historian Dipesh Chakrabarty explains: "In no discussion of freedom in the period since the Enlightenment was there ever any awareness of the geological agency that human beings were acquiring . . . . Geological time and the chronology of human histories remained unrelated" (208). In the era of the Anthropocene, this has changed. We are now aware that humans are geological forces, as Bruno Latour underlines: "The concept of Anthropocene introduces us to a third feature that has the potential to subvert the whole game: to claim that human agency has become the main geological force shaping the face of the earth, is to immediately raise the question of 'responsibility,' or as Donna Haraway is fond of saying, 'response ability'" (2017a: 38).

We can now understand the relevance of this proposed epoch to the current debate; we shall consequently ask the question: *Has the notion of the Anthropocene been contested?* It is important to note that the notion of the Anthropocene has been contested for different reasons.[2] From a posthumanist perspective, its generalization of the notion of the human ("*anthropos*") is problematic: for instance, does an indigenous tribe living a traditional life in the Amazon forest have the same environmental impact of people leading a regular life in an industrialized country, consuming groceries that come from far away and that are packaged in disposable plastic containers (etc.)? We should clarify that this reflection should not be simplified as a call for a return to a pre-industrialized way of living, even for the simple fact that such a move is an historical unfeasibility; we wish instead to contextualize the human experience, not to fall into imprecise generalizations. *What about the ecological impact of digital life?* Jussi Parikka, to underline the obscenities of the environmental damage across social, natural, and media ecologies, has renamed the Anthropocene as the "Anthrobscene" (2014). Furthermore, since this damage has been done in the name of capital (to make profit which would directly benefit a small fraction of humanity), some scholars have used the term "Capitalocene" (Moore 2016), including Donna Haraway, who has also referred to it as the "Plantationocene," and the "Chthulucene" (2016). If these different takes emphasize related aspects of the Anthropocene, all of them concord on the fact that it is time to enact a paradigm shift,[3] which we can define as post-anthropocentric.[4] This is one of the main goals of Philosophical Posthumanism, which can be approached as a post-humanism, as a post-anthropocentrism, and a post-dualism.

How can we achieve a post-anthropocentric paradigm shift? First of all, we need to acknowledge that this species-driven emphasis on the human as an autonomous entity stands on the psychotic speciesist perception, and on the related individual disconnect, of the human body as absolutely separated from planet Earth. Humans, like any other organism, have evolved and adapted in accord to their environments; such a relation has been mutually transformative and can be defined as an "intra-action" (Barad 2007). On one side, natural selection has been favoring those traits which would improve adaptability to surrounding environments (Darwin 1859); on the other side, with their actions and manipulations of their habitats, humans have had a pronounced impact on the environment. In post-darwinian terms, we can access the process of evolution as an intra-action, that is working both ways: humans are adapting to the environment and the environment is adapting to humans. Let's notice that the term "ecology" derives from Greek "*oikos*," meaning "home," that is, the discourse on the place we inhabit.

What is the Earth? Can a planet be considered an organism? Let's delve into this aspect more thoroughly. From a macro-perspective based on scale, human bodies live on the cosmic body of planet Earth, as much as, from a micro-perspective, bacteria live on, or inside, human bodies. Humans are in an essential relation to the planet: without it, humans would not be able to survive—think of the ground, producing the food which sustains our metabolism; or of the atmosphere containing oxygen, without which humans could neither breathe nor stay alive. *What is the Gaia hypothesis?* From a scientific perspective, the

Gaia hypothesis may come to mind, with its emphasis on the Earth as a self-regulating complex system (Lovelock 1995; Margulis 1998). James Lovelock, one of its main proponents, affirms: "Gaia theory sees the biota and the rocks, the air, and the oceans as existing as a tightly coupled entity. Its evolution is a single process and not several separate processes" (1988: 488). Although the emphasis on the interrelation of evolution has been criticized[5] and may not be the final answer, it bears important consequences in the era of the Anthropocene: "It affects even Darwin's great vision, for it may no longer be sufficient to say that organisms that leave the most progeny will succeed. It will be necessary to add the proviso that they can do so only so long as they do not adversely affect the environment" (*ibidem*). The relation to the environment becomes a drive in the course of evolution.

What kind of issues does the Gaia theory raise? The Gaia hypothesis has been criticized for different reasons, from scientific (cf. Schneider et al. 2004) to philosophical ones, including from a posthumanist perspective. For instance, Rosi Braidotti defines the Gaia theory as "geo-centered," since it proposes "a return to holism and to the notion of the whole as a single, sacred organism" (2013: 84). As she further explains, "What is problematic about it is less the holistic part than the fact that it is based on a social constructivist dualistic method. This means that it opposes the earth to industrialization, nature to culture, the environment to society and comes down firmly on the side of the natural order" (*ibidem*). And still, Gaia brings to the conversation something important: the cosmic embodiment that cannot be silenced. The current call for "naming Gaia" by Isabelle Stengers (2015) and "facing Gaia" by Bruno Latour (2017b) points in this direction, as Stengers affirms: "The intrusion of this type of transcendence, which I am calling Gaia, makes a major unknown, which is here to stay . . . : no future can be foreseen in which she will give back to us the liberty of ignoring her" (2015: 47). According to Stengers, the mere act of naming Gaia is political, standing as a subversive response to the scientific community which is still devoted to the "heritage of the Enlightenment," "to the grand narrative of human emancipation," who has blind faith in reason and who, "after hav[ing] contributed to skepticism with regard to climate change," "will devote all their energy to reminding" that we "must believe in the destiny of Man and in his capacity to triumph in the face of every challenge" (*ibidem*). But once a forest has been cut down, there is no going back. For instance, a giant sequoia can live to 3,000 years; from a human chronological standpoint, there is no replacement. The language of the age of the Enlightenment does no longer work in the age of the Anthropocene: the issues at stake are too high to be ignored.

Bruno Latour elaborates further on the epistemological implications of this condition, stating: "The point of living in the epoch of the Anthropocene is that all agents share the same shape-changing destiny. A destiny that cannot be followed, documented, told, and represented by using any of the older traits associated with subjectivity or objectivity" (2014: 17). In this sense, according to Latour: "the Earth is no longer 'objective'; it cannot be put at a distance and emptied of all Its humans. Human action is visible everywhere" (6). These onto-epistemological consequences radically undermine the subjective/objective trajectory. The posthuman approach destabilizes the limits and symbolic borders posed by strict dichotomies. Dualisms such as human/animal, human/machine, human/nonhuman, and, more in general, subject/object are re-investigated through a mediated perception which does not work on oppositions. The environmental turn, more than evoking an essentialization of the Earth, liquefies the relation between the Earth and the human; symbolically and materially, the Earth may turn into Gaia, the ancestral mother of all life; the human may acknowledge themselves as compost (Haraway 2015), eventually turning into *humus*, nourishing the Earth. Haraway is keen in emphasizing the "sym-chthonic forces and powers of which people are a part," although her referral of the human as a compost is posed in direct contrast to the posthuman: "I am a compost-ist, not a posthuman-ist: we are all compost, not posthuman" (2015: 161). From a philosophical posthumanist perspective, this polarization is unnecessary: I can be compost and posthuman, that is, posthuman compost.[6]

Let's address this point more clearly by asking the question: *Is the separation between life and death a strict dichotomy?* The posthuman deconstructs the clear division between life and death, which, more than strict categories, are seen as intra-acting processes. This perception is embraced by both Transhumanism and Posthumanism in different ways. Some transhumanists, for instance, maintain interest in cryonics, which is the practice of preserving at low temperature the body of people who have just died, in the hope that they could be revived in the future, once scientific and technological advances may allow to restore them to health. In this field, "death" is approached not as a final act or event, but as a process—the process of dying. Robert Ettinger (1918–2011), who introduced the concept of cryonics in his landmark book *The Prospect of Immortality* (1962), wrote: "Death is not absolute and final, but a matter of degree and reversible" (78). If Transhumanism follows Ettinger's take on approaching death as a process, Posthumanism takes a different route to come to similar conclusions. The idea of being compost, or better *com-post*,[7] underlines the never-ending nuanced passage between life and death, which are inevitably coexisting. *How can life and death coexist?* In order to answer this question, let's bring two simple examples, by mentioning that all the cells in the human body are constantly dying and regenerating—cells in the epidermis, for instance, last about a week. Another example can be found in our daily compost of vegetable scraps, which will decompose and break down into organic *humus* (that is, rich soil)—interestingly enough, *humus* is etymologically related to the term "human."[8] In this chapter we have underlined the inextricable bond between the human and planet Earth, and between the human and the soil, embracing the notion of posthuman compost. We have deconstructed a fixed notion of death from a transhumanist and posthumanist perspective; it is now time to address the notion of life.

Posthuman Life

Life is a pivotal notion in the social process of identity formation and requires a deeper reflection. According to the *Oxford Dictionary*, life is "the condition that distinguishes animals and plants from inorganic matter" (Entry: life, n. pg.). An investigation from a posthuman perspective may unravel different outcomes than the ones suggested by the dictionary. We shall ask more specifically: *Does the notion of "life" offer the ultimate border between animate and inanimate?* This is an important question which cannot be simply answered and needs to be broken up into coherent components; consequently, we will divide this chapter in two parts. In the first subsection, we will focus on the Western sub-categorization of the notion of life, which follows the Greek separation between *bios* and *zoē*. In the second subsection, we will focus on the fact that both the biological domain and ancient beliefs such as animism do not contemplate a fixed separation between what can be considered animate and inanimate. Following, we will present the notion of "artificial life," which, within the current scenario, is included in the comprehensive realm of posthuman life.[1]

a. *Bios* and *Zoē*

What is the scientific definition of life? Within the Western scientific context, the discipline which is specifically devolved to the study of life is biology. The recurrence of the prefix "bio" in Western disciplines related to life, further emphasized by the development of contemporary *bio*technologies and *bio*ethics, within the frame of *bio*politics,[2] needs a closer inspection since, as we will soon learn, it stands on a hierarchical dualism. As Giorgio Agamben reminds us in *Homo Sacer: Sovereign Power and Bare Life* (1995), *bios*, in its Greek etymology, is ontologically posed through its opposition with *zoē*: "The Greeks had no single term to express what we mean by the word 'life.' They used two terms that, although traceable to a common etymological root, are semantically and morphologically distinct" (*ivi:* 1). *Zoē* is common to all living beings, including "animals, men, or gods" (*ibidem*), and it can be defined as "bare life". *Bios*, on the other hand, is particular to the human because it is related to *logos*; it is the life that gives life meaning, and it recognizes humans as "human."[3] As Agamben notices:

> The fundamental categorial pair of Western politics is not that of friend/enemy but that of bare life/political existence, *zoē/bios*, exclusion/inclusion. There is politics because man is the living being who, in language [*logos*], separates and opposes himself to his own bare life and, at the same time, maintains himself in relation to the bare life in an inclusive exclusion. (8)

As we have noted in Part 2, the notions of *logos* (that is, language, but also reason) and *polis* (that is, city, but also, civilization) are structural to the Greek notion of *anthropos* (that is, human). By reminding these semiotic relations, we can better understand why Rosi Braidotti sharply underlines the political and social implications of the *zoē/bios* dualism, echoing the hierarchies enacted by other structural pairs, such as female/male or nature/culture. As she clarifies in *Transpositions: On Nomadic Ethics* (2006): "Life is half-animal, nonhuman (*zoe*) and half political and discursive (*bios*). *Zoe* is the poor half of a couple that foregrounds *bios* as the intelligent half; the relationship between them constitutes one of those qualitative distinctions on which Western culture built its discursive empire" (37). The primacy of *bios*, instead of *zoē*,[4] in the current constitution of terminology related to the notion of life in general, reveals its anthropocentric premises, demonstrating again[5] that nomenclature, more than a linguistic expression of scientific objectivity, reflects sociocultural norms and privileges. The anthropocentric choice of privileging *bios* is related to hierarchical assumptions which are deconstructed within the comprehensive approach of Philosophical Posthumanism.

b. Animate/Inanimate

What is life? In taxonomy, life is considered the highest rank comprehending all living beings; and still, as we will see, this notion is neither precise nor clearly delineated. The current understanding of life is merely descriptive, not definitive. In biology, life has been traditionally attributed to organisms which present most, or all, of these seven characteristics: organization, homeostasis, metabolism, reproduction, growth, adaptation/evolution, and sensitivity.[6] Yet, the border between animate/inanimate is difficult to mark and is often transgressed.[7] Viruses, for instance, exhibit some of the characteristics which are common to organic life, while they are missing others (for instance, metabolism, which is the reason why they depend on their host cell[8]); viruses are thus considered neither inanimate nor living, challenging the biological concept of life itself.[9] More in general, it can be stated that life is not a clearly defined notion. As Michel Foucault noted in *The Order of Things: An Archaeology of the Human Sciences* (1966), "Life does not constitute an obvious threshold beyond which entirely new forms of knowledge are required. It is a category of classification, relative, like all the other categories, to the criteria one adopts" (1970: 161). *What does it mean that life is a "relative" category of classification?* It means that "life" is a notion which is culture-specific and shall not be taken as an *a priori*. On one side, the notion of "life" exceeds the notion of the "human" (humans are included in it, but do not extinguish it); on the other, the notion of the human precedes the notion of life: "life" is a human notion, created by humans for the purpose of self-locating themselves in the larger picture; it is a species-specific notion based on shifting canons, and it greatly varies in different cultures and epochs. For instance, we can confidently affirm that many human adults currently living in New York City would confidently refer to a butterfly as a living being, and to a cell phone as an inanimate object. *But is this a definitive answer?* It is important to emphasize the specificity of the given example (characterizing it with terms such as "adults," "currently," and "glocalized"[10]) not to fall into a misleading generalization. Animism,[11] which is still practiced today in many different societies, refers to the vision of an animistic nature of matter, or to the presence of a soul or spirit in every entity, including objects, tracing no separation between the alive and the non-alive,[12] bringing precious perspectives to the posthuman reflection on "life."

Why is animism relevant? In order to answer to this question, we need to move from the Western hegemonic standpoint and embrace other genealogies. In fact, a posthumanist methodology should neither be sustained by exclusive traditions of thought nor indulged in hegemonic or resistant essentialist narratives (Ferrando 2012). It should be dynamic and shifting, engaging in pluralistic epistemological accounts to pursue more extensive perspectives, in tune with a posthuman ontology which radically challenges the taxonomical borders of "life." Let's then bring some examples to the discussion. For instance, in 2010, Japan hosted the first wedding conducted by a robot priest. Naho Kitano, in his article "Animism, Rinri, Modernization: The Base of Japanese Robotics" (2007), associates such an open-mindedness about the spiritual relevance of robots in Japan to the animist component of Shintoism. As early as 1974, Masahiro Mori, a Japanese pioneer of robotics who famously coined the notion of the "uncanny valley" (1970),[13] presented robots as spiritual beings eligible for attaining buddhahood in his book *The Buddha in the Robot*, stating (1974):

> From the Buddha's viewpoint, there is no master-slave relationship between human beings and machines. Man achieves dignity not by subjugating his mechanical inventions, but by recognizing in machines and robots the same buddha-nature that pervades his own inner self. When he does that, he acquires the ability to design good machines and to operate them for good and proper purposes. In this way harmony between humans and machines is achieved. (179–80)

In Mori's approach, there is no hierarchical relation between humans and robots: machines and humans are made of "the same buddha-nature." *Are machines animate?* Cultural beliefs play a crucial role in the reception and development of machines and advanced AI, so that, while in the West robots have been traditionally portrayed as the new "other" which might rebel and try to take over the world, like the golem in Jewish folklore or Mary Shelley's *Frankenstein* (1818), in Japan they partake of the spiritual quest. This tendency may be currently shifting, as we are witnessing an intimate perception of technological devices in countries which do not traditionally share animistic beliefs. In the United States, for example, the sensationalist debate on AI takeover in the media has polarized public opinion and sustained a growing fear toward robots, but the daily interaction with technology is telling a different story, bringing about a familiarity and a bond, which may gear toward "technological animism" (Richardson 2018). For instance, the attachment to cell phones has become so intimate that the neologism "nomophobia," as an abbreviation for "no-mobile-phone phobia" (cf. Yildirim 2014), has been proposed[14] to refer to the anxiety caused by the fear of being without a cell phone. If adults are partaking in this tendency of developing feelings of attachment toward technical objects,[15] children are already recognizing an existential dignity to machines that transcends the utilitarian perspective. As different studies have shown, "a significant proportion of children ascribe cognitive, behavioral, and especially affective, characteristics to robots" (Beran et al. 2011: 1). From a transcultural standpoint, animism is embedded in the perception of human infants on what to count as animate/inanimate: children often refer to objects as living entities—a tendency which has been famously pointed out by Jean Piaget in his pioneering work on child development (1929) and which has consequently been defined as "child animism" (Klingensmith 1953). Following these reflections, we can conclude that the strict border placed in the Western hegemonic tradition between organic/inorganic, biological/artificial, and physical/virtual has been radically challenged not only by different cultures and age perspectives but, more in general, by current developments in fields such as artificial intelligence, robotics, and virtual reality, among others.

What is the relationship between humans and robots? The relationship between humans and robots has attracted much attention. In respect to humans, robots are, at the same time, the other, the same, and the chimera. They can communicate in a human code without being human; they can hold a mechanical body and a biological brain;[16] they have been generated from human knowledge and categories and, still, they transcend them both. Cultural beliefs play a key role in the human reception of advanced AI, while political, social, and economic interests are crucial to its developments. Robots are going to evolve in unique and peculiar ways, which are hard to predict. The main risk run by humans consists in turning the robotic difference into a stigma for new forms of discrimination, based on how far such a difference can be placed from the human norm. To osmose with the robot ontology, humans have to undergo a radical deconstruction of the human as a fixed notion, emphasizing instead its dynamic and constantly evolving side, and celebrating the differences inhabiting the human species itself. For this reason, employing a critical posthumanist frame is crucial in the development of epistemologies informing the technological fields. Adopting such a standpoint will prevent humans from turning the robot into their new symbolic other and from falling into the dualistic paradigm that has historically characterized Western hegemonic accounts, articulated in opposites such as male/female, white/black, human/machine, and self/other. In the hypothetical cases of AI takeover scenarios, adopting post-humanist, post-anthropocentric, and post-dualistic social practices will also prevent advanced AI from dualizing, and eventually discriminating against, humans. A thorough reflection on this interaction among species relocates the discourse within a symbiotic paradigm, rather than a dualistic one. The difference becomes an evolutionary trait of existence; such a realization has not only scientific value but also social and political utility. The integral onto-epistemological approach of Philosophical Posthumanism may allow humans and robots to fully develop their interconnected potentials, eventually facilitating an original interspecies venture into the existential quest.

Are robots alive? Let's reflect on this point by presenting a cinematic tale which marked a shift in the understanding of inorganic life. The movie *Her* (Jonze 2013) portrays the intimate relationship between Theodore, a human male, and Samantha, an operating system (OS) with a female voice and heterosexual identity. The movie marked a new trend: the OS at first desires a human body to then realize that her own embodiment offers appealing possibilities, including an unlimited lifespan, not subordinated to biological death. She will leave a human in love, to embark in an existential quest with other OSs. In this movie, Samantha, on some level, is "more" alive than Theodore: not only does she have a longer lifespan, but her attitude toward life fully embraces the *joie de vivre*, the exultation of spirit proper of the Nietzschean *Übermensch*. The range of affects involved in the human/robotic interactions is a subject of ongoing research in different fields: from robopsychology (a specific form of psychology applied to robots), to affective computing, the branch of computer science focused on the development of artificial emotions. These fields of enquiry are related to the contemporary interest in the affective turn (Clough 2007) which, developed out of Spinozian reminiscences, focuses on how affects effect the social, political, cultural, and cybernetic realms. In Deleuzian and Guattarian terms (1980), one of the main consequences of the human/robotic interactions can be found in the becoming-machine of the human, and in the becoming-human of the machine. Let's delve into this aspect more thoroughly.

Artificial Life

Can life be artificial? The extensive redefinition of the notion of life developed within the field of cyborg studies is of key importance to the posthuman approach, which actually recognizes one of its genealogical sources in cyborg theory.[1] Life, within Posthuman studies, includes "artificial life,"[2] a notion which, in a circular way, invites for a revision of the concept of life itself. As Christopher Langton, the computer scientist who coined the term in his article "Studying Artificial Life with Cellular Automata" (1986), remarked:

> The study of artificial life . . . should not be seen solely as an attempt to simulate living systems as they occur in "nature" as we know it. Rather, it should be seen as an attempt to *"abstract from natural living systems their logical form."* In this sense, it should be seen as the study of not just organic life, but of life in principle. (147–48)

Following such an attempt to "abstract" a "logical form" from natural living systems, the notion of artificial life moves remarkably close to the notion of the human, which, as we have emphasized in the course of this book, is inexorably indebted to the legacy of the *logos*. Virtual reality marks an exponential shift in this direction: artificial life has been essentialized[3] in information patterns disjunct from any embodiment.

Does life need to be embodied? From a posthumanist epistemological perspective, the answer is: yes. Life, and more in general, existence is embodied. Although the notion of embodiment is crucial, as it informs the phenomenological perspective, the body that exists does not have to be biological or physical, it can be virtual;[4] it does not have to be singular or finite either. Let's proceed carefully, step by step, in this multifaceted topic, starting with a firm point, that is, the feminist reflection on artificial life. Sarah Kember, in her exhaustive book *Cyberfeminism and Artificial Life* (2003), takes note of the ontological move in the field of artificial life, and discredits a reductionist approach of life as disembodied information: "No stuff, no matter, no fleshy bodies, no experiences associated with physicality and nothing beyond the one-dimensional functionality of information processing" (3). She underlines the relevance of the genealogy of this reductionist approach by stating: "At the heart of Alife is the concept of life as information, and this is derived from molecular biology's notion of the genetic code, and its fetishisation of the gene as the fundamental unit of life" (*ibidem*). In fact, Christopher Langton's direct reference in the creation of the notion of "artificial life" (later shortened as "alife") was biochemistry and molecular structures. In Langton words: "There is a strong possibility that the 'molecular logic' of life can be embedded within cellular automata and that, therefore, artificial life is a distinct possibility within these highly parallel computer structures" (1986: 120).[5] In tune with this type of assumptions, a specific approach characterized by a disembodied perception of life developed within the field of cybernetics, mainly between the 1970s and the 1990s.[6] The critique of disembodiment[7] is at the core of Katherine Hayles's influential work *How We Became Posthuman* (1999), and has become one of the key points of debate in the feminist literature since then. Such a criticism touched upon a crucial deficiency in the development of AI and, directly or indirectly, had an impact on it: by the late 1990s, the notion of embodiment slowly gained centrality in the production of AI. As cyberneticists Kevin Warwick and Slawomir J. Nasuto affirm: "In the 1990s, researchers started to realize that pure, disembodied information processing is inadequate" (2006: 24). The notion of embodiment is currently informing the field for further research: "The area of embodied cognition has been born from a realization that a satisfactory theory of intelligence must entail a physically embodied agent, interacting in real time with its environment" (*ivi*: 24). Within this renewed interest for embodiment, the current development of Biological AI—that is, artificial intelligence constituted by a machinic body containing biological neurons (Warwick 2012)—further problematizes the notion of life.

Why is Biological AI a turning point? The creation of an artificial organism based on both biological and machinic components, such as Biological AI, undermines the Western dualistic mechanical/organic worldview and poses a symbolic threat to the polarized discussion on AI takeover and nonhuman personhood. For instance, shall a machine with biological neurons be granted rights, that is, robot rights? From a Western standpoint, the ontological impact of Biological AI is fundamentally disruptive. In his groundbreaking work *The Vital Machine: A Study of Technology and Organic Life* (1991), David Channell articulates the distinction between organic life and machines through the dualistic worldview which has defined Western civilization, and which has developed in two specific attitudes: the mechanical and the organic. While the mechanical view sees the universe itself as a machine, and so attempts to access it through a reductionist approach, the organic view is sustained through a vitalist approach and claims that the sum cannot be reduced to its smallest components: in this sense, machines should be considered organisms as well. According to Channell, the distinction between organic life and machines, which reflects the two worldviews that have defined Western civilization, is outmoded. Channell points to the emergence of a third worldview informed by genetics, quantum mechanics,[8] and computer intelligence, which he defines as "the vital machine." This shift in perspective is pivotal to the posthuman approach, according to which both the reductionist and the vitalist takes are unsatisfactory. And still, Channell's proposal is only partly in tune with a posthumanist sensibility.[9] First of all, after our recollection of the notion of "life," we can note that a vital approach is based on the assumption of a vital principle which, sustained by the notion of life (*vita* in Latin, from which: *vita-lism*), is hardly definable.[10] Furthermore, Channell's notion of "vital machine" bears some of the same problems that we have outlined reflecting on Agamben's proposal of the "anthropological machine"[11] (for instance, by undermining the process-ontological aspect of existence).

Is the interest on Artificial Life taking away from nonhuman animals? In other words, is Philosophical Posthumanism technocentric? This is a very important question, and this is why we shall clarify that Philosophical Posthumanism is neither a technocentric nor a luddite approach, and that its embracing of artificial life is neither absolute nor decontextualized. It is time to connect the post-anthropocentric response of Philosophical Posthumanism, to the discussion on artificial life. The destabilization of the border animate/inanimate through the comprehension of the field of "artificial life" within the notion of "posthuman life" is not posed in a hierarchical manner. Before we explain more clearly how these focuses of interest can successfully coexist and integrate, we shall acknowledge that some thinkers have been carrying this fallacy within the posthuman movement as well. Recently, Posthumanism is attracting a lot of attention and becoming mainstream. If this growing interest offers precious opportunities for dialogue and collaborations, one of the problems with Posthumanism entering fields which have been historically responsible for perpetrating traditional structures of power is evident in those thinkers who embrace the "exotic" difference, such as the robot, the biotechnological chimeras and the clone, without dealing with the differences embedded within the human realm[12] (the human "others," as emphasized by post-humanism) and planet Earth (the nonhuman "others," as emphasized by post-anthropocentrism). Philosophical Posthumanism does not rely on a hierarchical system; alterity (human and nonhuman) is embraced as an open and constantly evolving frame, not as the undisciplinable chaos to be normalized, otherized, or divinized. And still, at the moment, society is quick to hype technology. For instance, granting citizenship to Sophia the robot by Saudi Arabia in 2017 was an important achievement in the field of robot rights;[13] this news attracted major media attention. On the other side, minimum resonance was given to the ruling of the Amazon forest as "an entity subject of rights"[14] by Colombia's Supreme Court, granting the forest personhood (cf. Stubley 2018),[15] in a legal attempt to address the crucial problem of global deforestation and marking a precedent in climate change policies. From a posthuman perspective, this unbalance in media attention is symptomatic. Society is ready to be scared and fascinated by machines; the robot is considered the progenies that will eventually rebel and substitute the primacy of the human. Although this symbolic shift may seem radical, it keeps the hierarchical structure intact: the shift from Theocentrism to Anthropocentrism of the humanistic paradigm precedes the one from Anthropocentrism to Technocentrism of the current era. The centrality of the machine is not in tune with Philosophical Posthumanism, according to which the machine is part of evolution, but evolution is not approached as a vertical process: as Stephen Gould (1996) pointed out, in line with Charles Darwin (1859), evolution does not move toward complexity but toward diversification.

Does artificial life presume a new ontological primacy? From a philosophical posthumanist standpoint, the comprehension of artificial life in the realm of "posthuman life" does not bring along a new primacy over humans, nonhuman animals, or the environment. It does not imply an uncritical acceptance of dystopian futures in which "nature" will be replaced by artificial replicas. It is not a passage of the crown, from humans to robots. The radical movement of Philosophical Posthumanism deconstructs the center of the discourse, allowing for a multifocal approach and promoting a dynamic openness according to which a plurality of perspectives[16] can be accounted for. In the era of the Anthropocene, technology should be rethought as "eco-technology." *What does "eco-technology" mean?* It means that technology should be rethought not in separation from the environment, but as part of the environment. Let's clarify why. In the cycle of material existence, technological objects come from the Earth—for instance, in their embodiments made of mineral and metals, among other materials—and, once disposed of, will go back to it. *Is their material cycle separated from the notion of technology?* No, it is not. The notion of technology, from a posthumanist perspective, comprehends all of its implications, including the sociopolitical impact of its material and its disposal. For instance, the columbite-tantalite (coltan), a rare ore that is used in the production of electronics, including laptops and cell phones, is commonly found in the Democratic Republic of Congo (DRC) and mined in rebel-controlled territory, dramatically affecting civilians, wildlife, and national parks (Grespin 2010). We should also think of the toxicity of e-waste and its impact on human health and the environment (Widmer 2005). Furthermore, mainstream technologies such as cell phones and the internet increasingly require the presence of satellites in orbit, which are responsible for the growing amount of space debris (NASA Orbital Debris FAQs: n. year). To summarize, from a comprehensive posthumanist perspective, the notion of "technological development" should not be approached in a univocal manner (that is, bringing progress to a specific field only or to a specific species only), but they shall be regarded in a comprehensive way: the progress they bring to (some) humans, for instance, cannot be at the expenses of human, and nonhuman, "others."[17] Technological developments, from a post-humanist and post-anthropocentric perspective, require sustainable practices in their intentions and in their materializations. Philosophical Posthumanism invites us to proceed in relational and multilayered ways, in a post-dualistic, post-hierarchical praxis which sets a suitable way of departure to approach existence beyond the boundaries of humanism and anthropocentrism.

Evolving Species

What is "life" from an evolutionary standpoint? After acknowledging the living as a notion which fits specific human canons, let's now offer an overview of life[1] and of species from an evolutionary point of view. First of all, let's note that all life forms on Earth share the presence of deoxyribonucleic acid (DNA) to store genetic instructions; this molecule is only found in living matter although there are some exceptions, such as viruses and dead cells. To date, evidence suggests that life on planet Earth has existed for about 3.7 billion years.[2] There is no scientific consensus on how it originated, but the most credited hypothesis refers to this process as an abiogenesis, that is, biological life would have arisen from inorganic matter through natural processes.[3] Other hypotheses, such as exogenesis and panspermia,[4] claim that life did not originate on Earth, but somewhere else in space, and so they do not directly address the inquiry into the origins of life: the question of *where* life began does not answer the question of *how* it originated.[5] From a biological standpoint, all known life forms share fundamental molecular mechanisms, supporting the hypothesis of the last universal ancestor (LUA), a primordial single cell organism from which all life forms would have descended. Even though the hypothesis of one progenitor holds an older pedigree,[6] the first to formulate it within a satisfactory theory of evolution was Charles Darwin (1809–82). In *On the Origin of Species by Means of Natural Selection* (1859), he stated: "Therefore I should infer from analogy that probably all the organic beings which have ever lived on this earth have descended from some one primordial form, into which life was first breathed" (484). *Why is the discussion on the origin of life significant from a posthumanist perspective?* Although Posthumanism, in harmony with a cyborgian approach, does not urge a search for the "origins,"[7] the idea that all the living and extinct forms of life on Earth share a common ancestor[8] is an important point to reflect upon, because it poses a biological inextricability between the Self and the Others. We could come to the same conclusions by validating the hypothesis of a non-unitarian origin, which is gaining some traction in the scientific community, as one does not necessarily dismantle the other.[9] For instance, microbiologist Carl Woese (1928–2012) in the article "The Universal Ancestor" (1998) stated: "The universal ancestor is not a discrete entity. It is, rather, a diverse community of cells that survives and evolves as a biological unit. This communal ancestor has a physical history but not a genealogical one" (6854). In Woese's hypothesis, the genetic heritage of all modern organisms would have not derived through a vertical genetic transfer,[10] but through an horizontal gene transfer within a community of organisms. In Woese's words: "The universal ancestor is not an entity, not a thing. It is a process characteristic of a particular evolutionary stage" (6858). Both if we assume a single cell as the origin of an extremely diversified variety of life, as if we think of a community of cells evolving into a biological unit, we are witnessing the disruption of fundamental dichotomies: the one between the single and the multiple, the inner and the outer. According to the evolutionary history of life, which focuses on the evolution of living and fossil organisms, life has evolved from LUA—whether that be an entity or a process—to which every form of life on Earth, living or extinct, is related.

Since all known species have diverged through processes of evolution, *what does the notion of "species" mean from a genetic perspective?* When reflecting upon the notion of species from a genetic point of view, a kinship can be recognized, but not an assimilation. Let's take the example of modern humans. On one side, as author Victor K. McElheny notes: "Any two human beings on this earth are 99.9 percent identical at the DNA level" (2010: 196). On the other side, no two human beings are genetically identical to each other due to human genetic variation and epigenetics.[11] Another definition which is often proposed is that species may be described as a group of organisms that are capable of interbreeding; this generalization, though, may not apply to every species either (as in the case of organisms that reproduce asexually, among other cases). The notion of "species" is as challenging as the notion of life. Therefore, biological classification contemplates the "species problem," referring to the difficulties implied in defining such a term. For biologist Michael Ghiselin, "Much of the species problem has been the result of equivocal uses of species names as universal and proper" (1975: 537). In a mediation between the realist and the nominalist debate, we can affirm that species exist as long as none of their traits are essentialized: "species," in other words, is an immanent concept. Species are constantly changing and have no fixed boundaries. Modern humans, for instance, are still evolving, but the long-term dynamics of evolution take place over time periods which are inaccessible to human standards, such as one million years (Uyeda et al. 2011). Only short-term changes can be detected, as in the case of the genetic mutation which has resulted in lactose persistence in some human populations.[12] Specifically, a genetic mutation allowing lactose assimilation in adult humans developed out of the consumption of nonhuman milk and dairy products beyond infancy, a cultural practice related to animal domestication and dairying (cf. Gerbault et al. 2011: 863). This case is of particular interest from a posthumanist perspective because, rather than sustaining the Western dichotomy nature/culture, it emphasizes evolution as a naturalcultural process, through the continuity of biological adaptation and cultural practices.

From a post-anthropocentric perspective, *what does the notion of "species" infer? In other words, is the notion of "species" implicitly speciesist?* Although formulated within species-specific knowledge (that is, a system of knowledge developed by some humans for human purposes), the notion of "species" per se does not necessarily imply a speciesist engagement. Posthumanists have to situate their own embodied location. The fact that the hegemonic history of Western thought has been articulated through speciesist accounts, assuring the human species (generally essentialized as white, male, heterosexual, able, propertied, etc.) at the top of a hierarchical construct, should not hold as a consequence that the notion of the species becomes inherently discriminatory; it can actually be approached from an activist perspective. As scholar and environmentalist Vandana Shiva phrases it, in reflecting upon the biological and ecological consequences of crossing species boundaries in genetic engineering: "Boundaries have been an important construct for ecological restraint. 'Removing boundaries' has been an important metaphor for removing restraints on human actions, and allowing limitless exploitation of natural resources" (1995b: 281). In fact, the symbolic act of removing boundaries has only served the interests of (some members of) one species: the human.[13] Here we shall open a parenthesis and contextualize Shiva's remarks, as they stand in direct response to Haraway's cyborg, which we have embraced until now.

Why is Vandana Shiva critical of the notion of the cyborg? In the 1990s the postmodern notion of the cyborg, as proposed by Haraway, was mostly welcomed by feminism, as the disruption of traditional dualisms brought along by this notion allowed for a new space of reflection; but it also received some important criticisms. For instance, from an eco-feminist standpoint, Shiva affirms: "Post-modern feminists . . . see an increased degree of freedom not as the freedom of an organism to adapt, to grow, to shape itself from within but as the mechanistic addition of 'metal' to 'flesh' and the 'machine' to the 'body.' The inevitable consequence is to see the one without the other as incomplete" (278). This view, according to Shiva, is particularly problematic from an environmental standpoint, as we live "in an era where concern for preserving diverse forms of life, both biological and cultural, is emerging as a major challenge" (*ibidem*). In this sense, the biological act of hybridizing, which Shiva relates to genetic engineering and genetically modified organisms (GMOs), is not neutral, but is tied to political and economic powers, which leaves the capitalistic patriarchal paradigm intact by benefiting specific corporations and interests. For instance, Shiva highlights how the expensive GMOs seeds sold by Monsanto have aggravated the problem of farmer suicides in India.[14] This is also what Rosi Braidotti has defined as a "perverse" form of post-anthropocentrism" by advanced capitalism. *Why is advanced capitalism perversely post-anthropocentric?* Braidotti clearly explains it: "Because it is interested in the informational data, in the genetic code of all kind of species, some of whom are, in some respects, more advanced than we are" (Braidotti 2015: n. pg.). As an example, she refers to the robotic industry, which, for instance, "is cloning the smell of dogs, the radar of dolphins: capacities which the anthropomorphic body does not possess" (*ibidem*). We shall underline that, although the interest of advanced capitalism on life itself is post-anthropocentric (the human is not at the top of the hierarchy anymore), the anthropocentric paradigm is still left intact: this move only benefits (some) humans, and it certainly does not benefit the nonhuman animals who are studied and experimented upon. And that is why we can rephrase it as a perverse form of post-anthropocentric anthropocentrism. If the topics of GMOs and bioprospecting[15] (which may lead to biopiracy[16]) are ethically controversial, the possibility of human genetic engineering raises many ethical, social, and biological questions. Let's enter this discussion by addressing the notion of posthumanities.

Posthumanities

Will humans evolve into different species? The discussion on the future of humanity is of focal importance to the posthuman debate. In this context, the notion of "posthumanities" refers to hypothetical future species which would be genetically related to the human species (*Homo sapiens*), but no longer definable as such. In order to access this notion, we first need to understand more thoroughly how evolution works. It can be stated that evolution is constitutive of the notion of species: changes occur over time; populations may split into different branches, hybridize together, or terminate by extinction, so that no essentialism can be attributed to species in terms of fixity or purity. Evolutionary processes generate diversity at every level of biological organization; at the same time, diversity facilitates evolution. Evolution does not imply any type of hierarchy nor progression from inferior to superior organisms, nor does it support any essentialism or strict dualism; rather, it complies with a hybrid, processual perception of existence, which is in tune with Philosophical Posthumanism. *How does evolution work?* One of the main techniques of evolution has been defined by Charles Darwin (1859) as "natural selection," in opposition to "artificial selection."[1] While the latter refers to the processes by which certain traits are systematically favored by humans in breeding animals or plants, and which have been practiced since ancient times, natural selection recognizes a generative power to the environment, which represents a key element in the processes by which biological traits become either more or less common in a population, disrupting once again the inner/outer dichotomy. The environment is not an external entity in which organisms exist, but it is a constitutive element of their biological outfit. In this context, we shall touch upon space migration[2] and the consequences such a scenario might conceal, from an evolutionary perspective. Following the current activities of space exploration, space commercialization, and space tourism, NASA stated that the capability to send humans to an asteroid will be developed by 2025, and to Mars in the 2030s (NASA's journey to Mars, n.pg.). Private companies such as SpaceX are setting even closer deadlines, such as 2026: their mission is "making life multiplanetary" (SPACE X: n. pg.). If humans proceed to inhabit other planets (such as the Moon or Mars) or other habitats (such as asteroids), generation after generation their DNA may mutate, in order to adapt to those specific environments; at that point, if reproduction occurs in isolation, different human species may eventually evolve: such species might be referred to as "posthumanities." Here, we shall open a parenthesis on this notion—which, in Chapter 9, we have also attributed to a shift within the field of the humanities.

What does "posthumanities" mean? The term "posthumanities" exceeds the notion of the human, and it turns into an open framework, which is invoked to inclusively address future developments of humankind. The current reflection on this subject—which is undertaken by both transhumanist and posthumanist thinkers, with some differences—focuses on the increasing use of biotechnologies and genetic engineering, which can be revisited as forms of artificial selection. As we have mentioned in the previous paragraph, Darwin focused his interest on natural selection, but another naturalist, who has not been properly treated by history, did not make such a sharp separation between the natural and the artificial: he was the French biologist Jean-Baptiste Pierre Antoine de Monet, Chevalier de Lamarck (1744–1829), known as Lamarck. *Who was Lamarck and how is Lamarckism re-entering the conversation on evolution?* Lamarckism is a set of theories named after Lamarck, who believed in the inheritance of the acquired characteristics from an organism to its offspring. He first published his theories in his book *Philosophie Zoologique* in 1809, that is, fifty years before Darwin's *On the Origins of Species* (1859). Lamarck's idea of evolution (which he referred to as "transformism"—in French *transformisme*) is connected to the following notions:

1. the inheritance of acquired characteristics;
2. an internal force in organisms (Lamarck argued that individuals in a species "willed" themselves to change);
3. a linear pattern of evolution, according to which species change over time into new species and do not go extinct—this is a main point of difference with Darwin, who believed that species went extinct.[3]

Darwin was familiar with Lamarck's work, to which he refers mostly in the introductory section "Historical Sketch,"[4] where he also takes distance from him,[5] as Lamarck at the time had already been discredited by the scientific community (Ward 2018). Darwin's emphasis on adaptation and natural selection, or the survival of the fittest, did not leave space for the will of the organisms to change themselves, as Lamarck argued. Within the field of evolutionary studies, his theories had been mostly dismissed until the rise of genetic engineering and also the development of epigenetics.

What is epigenetics? Epigenetics[6] refers to the study of heritable changes in gene expression caused by mechanisms which are external to the underlying DNA sequence. The Greek prefix epi-, which can be translated as "over," "outside of," and "around," emphasizes the affect and effect of the environment, the diet or lifestyle, among other factors, demonstrating the irreducible intra-actions and intra-changes[7] between the genetic makeup of an organism and their "surroundings," presenting the genetic outcome as a process, more than a given. Let's bring to the discussion an example based on actual experiments, which were carried on agouti mice (cf. Dolinoy 2008). Two mice look very different: one has a clear coat and is obese; the other is much smaller and has a dark coat. *The two mice are genetically identical and are of the same age, so why do they look that different?* The answer lays in the diet of the mother during pregnancy; the mother was fed different dietary supplements which triggered different responses, showing how "nutritional and environmental factors affect . . . epigenetic gene regulation and subsequent adult phenotype" (*ivi*: S8). These experiments on agouti mice, among others, undermined the genetic determinist model,[8] demonstrating that genetics are not destiny. Epigenetics, in a broad sense, has been defined as a "link between nature and nurture" (Goldberg et al 2007: 635) and as "a bridge between genotype and phenotype—a phenomenon that changes the final outcome of a locus or chromosome without changing the underlying DNA sequence" (Dolinoy 2008: S10).

How does epigenetics occur? Let's offer a simple example to explain this mechanism. You are with a friend, who wants to understand how epigenetics work. You take a blank piece of paper and write "Hello!"; you show it to your friend and ask to read what it is written there; your friend will answer "Hello!." Then, you crumple up the paper into a ball and ask your friend to read what it is written on the paper. The instruction, that is, "hello," is still there, written on the paper, but now your friend will not be able to read it. On a similar way, the DNA is wrapped around special protein molecules called histones; the spacing between the histones, among other factors, can alter DNA accessibility, determining if the DNA can be read or not. As in our example, where the information was still on the piece of paper but your friend was no longer able to read it, the DNA instructions are still there, but they can no longer be accessed (and, consequently, processed).

Why is epigenetics relevant to Philosophical Posthumanism? Epigenetics plays a crucial role in the posthumanist deconstruction of the nature/culture divide, which turns into the more fluid "natureculture" proposal, such as in cyborg, and new materialist, feminist theory, according to which nature and culture are inherently entangled (cf. Haraway 2003; Barad 2007). Epigenetics also brings Lamarck back to the conversation. For instance, roboticist Rodney Brooks, in his book *Flesh and Machine: How Robots Will Change Us* (2002), has underlined the connection between the possibilities opened by contemporary biotechnologies and the Lamarckian will of individuals in a species to change themselves: "We will change ourselves from being purely the product of our genetic heritage to a more Lamarckian sort of species wherein we will be the product of our own technology" (232). Brooks, in tune with Transhumanism, is advocating for a switch in the evolution of the species for a direct and deliberate control; such a shift, which is a common theme within transhumanist literature, has also been individuated by bio-conservative philosophers and thinkers who do not necessarily endorse it. It is time to enter the fascinating and challenging arena of bioethics.

Posthuman Bioethics

To be or not to be genetically modified? The term "designer baby" is a controversial one. According to the *Oxford Dictionary*, a designer baby is "a baby whose genes have been chosen by its parents and doctors so that it has particular characteristics."[1] Currently, the genetic selection of embryos is carried in vitro, and may include choices related to gender, eye color, and to the preference of some parents to avoid genetic diseases that are life-threatening, by implanting embryos that do not carry a specific heredity. Emerging biotechnologies, such as CRISPR, are opening new potentials, including selecting different traits by adding, or removing, genetic material *via* gene editing. *What is CRISPR?* Emmanuelle Charpentier and Jennifer Doudna are the two main scientists who studied the mechanisms of the bacterial sequence CRISPR–Cas systems (commonly shortened as CRISPR); in 2012, they discovered its potentials for gene editing. They refer to CRISPR "as a simple and versatile tool for genomic editing" (2013: 50).[2] To further clarify it, Jennifer Doudna, one of the scientists involved in this groundbreaking discovery, defines CRISPR as "an efficient, effective tool for editing genomes—changing the code of life, the DNA in cells" (2018: 158). When asked what is the difference between CRISPR and more traditional techniques, she answered: "Instead of breeding creatures by trial and error over many generations to get the traits you want . . . now you can simply splice in a trait for a bigger nose, disease resistance, better nutrition, whatever. You can do it precisely in one generation and get exactly what you want. This is changing the way modern biology is being practiced, in everything from medicine to agriculture" (*ibidem*). Here, we should mention that, in order to use CRISPR technology, the DNA needs to be damaged first, so that the repair (carrying the new information) can be performed, with the possible risks that this may entail: some recent studies have shown that potential DNA damage, as a result of CRISPR technology, has been seriously underestimated (Kosicki et al. 2018).

Let's delve more thoroughly into CRISPR, since this technique offers a new twist to the prospect of designer babies: what until recently was considered pure science-fiction is now a real possibility.[3] In Doudna's words: "Does that mean somebody out there is actually making CRISPR babies? Probably not yet. But you could certainly envision that kind of work going on in parts of the world where there's less oversight and less regulation" (*ivi*: 163). Regulation, which is key in the actual developments of designer babies, is inextricably related to ethics and bioethics. It is time to ask the ethical question: *Should we further develop biotechnologies aimed at generating babies with "desirable" traits?* Before answering to this question, let's note that the field of bioethics focuses precisely on the question: "*Should* we do this?" and not "*Could* we do this?": the point is not if we can achieve these results scientifically, but if we should proceed in this path, ethically and morally speaking. An important antecedent to this type of approach is the history of eugenics.

What does eugenics mean? Coined in 1883 by Sir Francis Galton (1822–1911), a prominent English polymath who was also half-cousin of Charles Darwin, the term "eugenics" is formed by the words "*eu*" (in Greek "good" or "well") and "*genos*" (that is, "race, kind, offspring"). According to Kenneth Garver and Bettylee Garver, eugenics can be defined as "the science that deals with all influences that improve the inborn quality of the human race, particularly through the control of hereditary factors" (1991: 1109). A significant distinction, which first appeared in the article "Development of a Eugenic Philosophy" (1937) by American eugenicist Frederick Osborn (1889–1981), is sometimes traced between "negative eugenics" and "positive eugenics." According to this view, "negative eugenics" can be defined as "a systematic effort, whether decisional or programmatic, to minimize the transmission of genes that are considered deleterious" (Garver and Garver 1991: 1109); while "positive eugenics" can be defined as "a systematic effort, whether decisional or programmatic, to maximize the transmission of genes that are considered desirable" (*ibidem*). It is important to note that these two forms of eugenics cannot be easily separated, and that, historically, they have been often approached in conjunction. The history of negative eugenics is notably tainted with racism, ableism, and genocide. For instance, the eugenics movement was one of the leading sources of inspiration in the development of Nazi Germany[4] to the point that "to understand the German eugenic movement, it is necessary to trace the interrelationship of their race hygiene, euthanasia, involuntary-sterilization, and genocide programs" (*ivi*: 1112). But also the history of positive eugenics bears ableist outcomes, and some of widely accepted medical practices today can be regarded as negative eugenics.

Let's think, for instance, of prenatal diagnosis and the screening test for Down syndrome, which has led to a significant decrease of the number of babies born with Down syndrome in Europe and the United States. On one side, the expectant parents should have the right for Down syndrome fetal screening, if they wish so: knowing the results of the test can lead to a well-prepared and responsible decision to carry on with the pregnancy or to terminate it. The problem is that, according to many disabled activists, such as Marsha Saxton, "some medical professionals and public health officials are promoting prenatal diagnosis and abortion with the intention of eliminating categories of disabled people, people with Down's syndrome and my own disability, spina bifida, for example" (2006: 107). In other words, if the test comes out positive, the act of giving this information to the parents may turn into an invitation to terminate these pregnancies; and eventually, if the parents decide to continue with the pregnancy anyway, to a warning: *Are you really sure you want to proceed with it?* Meaning: you should not. This is when positive and negative eugenics meet, in a social and medical protocol which may implicitly support discriminatory practices. As feminist biologist Ruth Hubbard suggests, in her article "Abortion and Disability: Who Should and Should Not Inhabit the World?" (2006), on the topic of disability and reproductive rights: "No one these days openly suggests that certain kinds of people be killed; they just should not be born" (101). We should keep these problematic aspects in mind, when addressing the topic of designer babies.

Let's then go back to our discussion: *Should we, as a society, proceed in this path toward a future of designer babies?* Some say "yes," some say "no." For instance, German philosopher Jürgen Habermas (born 1929) has developed a critical reflection on the role of law in a social scenario in which genetic manipulation will bear increasing significance.[5] In *The Future of Human Nature*[6] (2001), he declared, "The human species might soon be able to take its biological evolution into his own hands" (2003: 21). As he further explained: "Partner in evolution" or even "playing God"[7] are the metaphors for an *auto-transformation of the species* which it seems will soon be within reach" (*ibidem*). Habermas thus stresses the urgency to develop legal strategies in order to protect personal identity, which may lead to the legal recognition and protection of the "right to a genetic inheritance immune from artificial intervention" (*ivi*: 7). According to this view, future generations of humans should have the right not to be genetically "enhanced." Habermas notes how the phenomenological distinction highlighted by philosopher Helmut Plessner (1892–1985) between "being a body" and "having a body" (*ivi:* 12) has become particularly relevant in the biotechnological era, when "the boundary between the nature that we 'are' and the organic endowments we 'give' to ourselves disappears" (*ibidem*). Here, we shall open a parenthesis and note that some schools of Transhumanism support a dualistic view in line with the idea that "I have a body"; according to this perspective, for instance, mind-uploading would result in technological immortality, since the continuity of the self would not be disrupted by the death of the biological body. On the other side, Posthumanism focuses on the importance of embodiment, thus stating: "I am my body," or better, to avoid any misunderstanding based on bodily looks or social constructions of the body: "I am being, in my body." According to this perspective, which emphasizes the phenomenological and existential relevance of embodiment,[8] the notion of the self is open and diffuse, and resides in the many processes, experiences, and relations that are dynamically co-constituting "my body," which is accessed as an open and evolving system in (relation to) other bodies such as, for instance, the human species as a social body, or the celestial body of planet Earth.[9]

Going back to Habermas, like most bio-conservatives, he makes a difference between therapy and enhancement, accepting the first but not the latter. In his words: "Only in the negative case of the prevention of extreme and highly generalized evils may we have good reasons to assume that the person concerned would consent to the eugenic goal" (*ivi:* 63). To fully understand Habermas's view, it is important to explain the difference between therapy and enhancement and, more in general, between bio-conservatives and bio-liberals. *What is the difference between bio-conservatives and bio-liberals?* First of all, let's observe that the notion of "bio-liberal" and "bio-conservative" should not be assimilated to the traditional divide, in political theory, between liberal and conservative or between radical and reactionary; nor, in US politics, between Democratic and Republican—for instance, someone can be a Republican and a bio-liberal, or a Democrat and a bio-conservative, and *vice versa*. Here, the prefix "bio-" is foundational, in the sense that it directs how each perspective access the realm of the "bios" (that is, human life, as presented in Chapter 20a). What the bio-conservative approach emphasizes is the conservation of the integrity of the "bio-" realm as much as possible and, consequently, of the biological body. This is why, the bio-conservative perspective may generate, for instance, out of the radical left (in a vindication of freedom from any external bio-technological authority or social control); and also, simultaneously, out of the religious right (since undermining God's creation would be considered irreverent). In general, we can state that most bio-conservative positions may accept therapy, but they do not support enhancement. On the other side, bio-liberals (under which label, we can place the transhumanist approach—although the two terms are not synonyms) most often support both therapy and enhancement. According to this position, in fact, the notion of "therapy" and "enhancement" are not easy to separate.

Why is the separation between "therapy" and "enhancement" slippery? Nick Bostrom and Rebecca Roache, in their article "Ethical Issues in Human Enhancement" (2008), offer a precise and interrelated definition of "therapy" and "enhancement," as they states, "In broad terms, therapy aims to fix something that has gone wrong, by curing specific diseases or injuries, while enhancement interventions aim to improve the state of an organism beyond its normal healthy state. However, the distinction between therapy and enhancement is problematic, for several reasons" (2008: 1). They thus present examples of standard contemporary medical practices which would be hard to classify, such as preventive medicine and vaccination, which "can be seen as an immune system enhancement or, alternatively, as a preventative therapeutic intervention" (*ibidem*). We can also think of plastic surgery: on one side, reconstructive procedures may be considered therapy; on the other, cosmetic procedures may be treated as enhancement. And still, what if someone had developed psychological issues because of their looks and thus decided to undergo cosmetic surgery: *Would this case be considered therapy or enhancement?* According to some ethicists, the separation between therapy and enhancement is liquid and hard to draw. Others disagree. According to Francis Fukuyama, for instance, the separation between therapy and enhancement is not that problematic: "While many people would argue that it is not theoretically possible to draw a clear distinction between therapy and enhancement, such distinctions are made all the time in the world of drug regulation, and are eminently something that a regulatory agency could be asked to do" (2012: 166). Once again, Fukuyama underlines the importance of regulations in approaching the possibilities offered within the field of emerging biotechnologies. Let's look into this aspects.

Human Enhancement

How to regulate human enhancement? In order to answer to this question, we shall go back to our distinction between the posthumanist and the transhumanist perspectives.[1] Even though the posthumanist attitude is not necessarily bio-conservative, it is generally characterized by a more cautious attitude, which begins by asking the primal question: *What is human enhancement?* Human enhancement refers to the attempt to overcome the biological limitations of the human body, and to challenge the borders of what the human species has historically been considered capable of, for instance, on a cognitive and physical level. It is a broad term to refer to a wide range of fields, such as radical life extension, brain-computer interface, and reproductive technologies, among others. Following on the discussion developed in Chapter 24, here we will only address prenatal genetic enhancement (that is, designer babies), a topic which is particularly challenging from an ethical perspective, as it raises many important aspects related to the future of humanity. Specifically, we will focus on three of them: the cultural specificity of values, the complexity of genes, and the sociopolitical implications of genetic discrimination. Starting with the first aspect, we may note that the notion of enhancement itself is relative and situated: for instance, enhancing attitudinal and/or physical characteristics, such as awareness or musculature, may be highly valued by some people and cultures, but not by others. To this sociocultural issue, we shall add the biological variable, as currently we do not know all that the genes are responsible for. According to bio-conservative ethicist Francis Fukuyama, for instance, the ambiguity as to what constitutes human "improvement" is based on the "failure to understand complexity in human evolution" (2012: 160).

Let's explain Fukuyama's important remark by asking the question: *Are the outcomes of genetic engineering fully predictable?* No, they are not. In order to further clarify this point, let's bring a vivid example to the discussion. "Schwarzenegger mice" are genetically modified mice which became known in the 1990s for their extraordinary musculature, a result of a genetic manipulation carried in the lab of molecular physiologist Lee Sweeney at the University of Pennsylvania. Rat genes that control muscle development were added at the embryonic level producing mice which grew very big: their musculature was almost double the one of mice which had not been genetically modified (cf. Barton et al. 2002). The media sensationalized the physical outcome of these mice, but a major effect of such manipulations was left in the shadow. In an interview for the documentary "Who is afraid of designer babies?" (Cook 2005), American geneticist Dean Hamer[2] reflects on the "Schwarzenegger mice" experiment, emphasizing an important, and often obscured, piece of information: "For some reason completely unexpected, this genetic change also altered the personality of the mice and made them very weak, passive, laid back; they would not even defend themselves" (40:27-40:39). What happened is that the gene responsible for muscle development in mice may have also affected behavior; as Hamer further explains, "One gene can do a lot of different things; we may think we know everything about a gene, but if we miss even one little aspect of what it does, we could really mess up some people" (40:51-41:01). Currently, we do not know all the functions of each gene; furthermore, genes do not work in isolation: their interaction with the other genes may also lead to unforeseen outcomes. To summarize this issue in relation to designer babies, we can state that adding or removing genes with the purpose of enhancing humans may have completely unexpected results.

Another risk to be taken into account when discussing designer babies is genetic discrimination. *What is genetic discrimination?* Genetic discrimination is a type of discrimination based on genetic information, for instance, in the case of someone being treated unfairly by their life insurance because they have a gene mutation that increases the risk of an inherited disorder.[3] The risk of genetic discrimination is potentially tied to the rise of designer babies. The process of enhancing "some" humans may most likely exacerbate social disparities based on biological primacies, which may be reinforced and dramatized by these emergent biotechnologies, leading to the "Gattaca argument." Based on the science-fiction film *Gattaca* (1997) by Andrew Niccol, this bioethical argument refers to a dystopian society based on genetic manipulation, selection, and profiling. It is important to note that, in the movie, genetic discrimination is illegal; and still, every aspect of that society is based upon it. As Stefan Lorenz Sorgner puts it, "There is the risk that beings with different capacities will receive a different moral status, which is the reason why we have to take the *Gattaca* argument serious. . . . [O]ne has to progress with great care, so that both human beings, as well as trans- and posthumans can be judged on the basis of the same dignity"

(2013: 154). By proceeding with great care calls into action the precautionary principle, which is at the core of the European ethical and bioethical tradition, among others.

What is the precautionary principle? The precautionary principle proceeds by emphasizing the context of uncertainty and by taking into consideration possible seen and unseen risks; in popular wisdom, it can be summarized in the ancient proverb: "better safe than sorry." Not everyone agrees with that. Currently, there are different laws enforcing different agendas, depending on each country. China, for instance, is at the very front of the research on genetic engineering. In his article "Striking a Balance: Policy Considerations for Human Germline Modification" (2018), Joshua Seitz notes how China, which was the first country to report the editing of the human germline,[4] currently has a regulation that results in guidelines more than strict rules: "In China, HGM [Human Germline Modification] is regulated by a detailed regulatory framework. . . . Nevertheless, the current law in China amounts to non-binding guidelines and as a result, development of HGM might continue in the future" (79-80). This reflection opens some legal questions regarding regulation. In fact, if some countries proceed in this path, soon we will have babies whose genetic code may have been manipulated at the embryonic level.[5] This is the case, for instance, of our fictional character Kim, who was born in a country favorable to HGM, and whose DNA was genetically engineered. As a young adult, Kim decides to travel around the world. While traveling, Kim meets Andrea, who was born in a country where HGM was, and still is, illegal. They fall in love and move to Andrea's country; some years later, they have a child, Ananda, whose DNA carries Kim's genetic modification, in a country where HGM is prohibited. *What kind of legal, social, and psychological consequences will this situation cause, to Ananda, Kim, and Andrea?* This fictional case clearly shows that in the case of human enhancement, reflecting on regulation just from a national standpoint may not be effective. This type of discussion should be addressed from a species perspective, creating an intra-cultural bioethical dialogue that may open new possibilities for peace politics and collaborations, as it clearly highlights that we are connected as a species, and that "'we' are in this together, but we are not all the same" (2012: 120), as Rosi Braidotti states in relation to the human condition.

Precautionary or proactionary? If the posthumanist approach may underline the precautionary principle, when addressing these topics, the transhumanist reflection engages upon them through the "proactionary principle." *What is the proactionary principle?* Formulated by Max More (2004) in opposition to the precautionary principle, the proactionary principle emphasizes people's freedom in actively innovating technology: in this sense, the transhumanist approach is a bio-liberal approach, as it accesses the re-definition of the "bio-" realm in a way that is less precautionary and more proactionary.[6] One limit of this approach is that with the exception of Democratic Transhumanism, which particularly stresses the importance of a democratic access to these biotechnologies,[7] most transhumanist accounts on the evolution of the human species are not complying with a comprehensive acknowledgment of the social, political, and environmental consequences of human enhancement. Transhumanist reflections on these topics are often characterized by a progressivist techno-centric approach based on anthropocentrism; and still, precisely because of their enthusiastic support and committed research on this subject, their inputs greatly expand the horizon of reflection on the possible scenarios of the future of humanity.[8]

What is the bioethical[9] standpoint of Posthumanism in relation to human enhancement? We have already noted how a post-humanist understanding of human enhancement (here to be intended in an extensive way) problematizes who would have access to these technologies, bringing the sociopolitical aspects into consideration. We have also underlined how this notion is not absolute, but relative and culturally situated: what can be regarded as human enhancement by someone, or by some societies, may not be regarded as such by someone else, or by some other societies. To this, we can add a post-anthropocentric critique, underlining the fact that anthropocentrism is inherent to the proposal and discussion on human enhancement. In fact, most of the ethical and bioethical dilemmas related to cloning or enhancing humans beings are mostly absent when relating to other species. Let's think, for instance, of the widespread presence of GMOs ingredients in the global market, or of the fact that already in 1992 Dolly the sheep became the first mammal to be cloned, followed soon after by the transgenic sheep Polly and Molly, which were the first mammals to be cloned and genetically modified at the same time (a human gene was added to their genome). On one side, a posthumanist approach calls for a bioethical standing that exceeds the realm of human exceptionalism. In this sense, the precautionary principle shall be implemented also when dealing with nonhuman life and with the bio-sphere, for instance, by taking seriously the hazards of GMO crops contaminating non-GMO and organic crops through cross-pollination, and the incidence of abnormalities in cloned animal,[10] among other issues. From a post-dualistic perspective, human enhancement is not just about the human condition. The evolution of the human species shall be reflected upon in relation to the evolution of planet Earth. In fact, the development of genetic enhancement technologies may have major effects not only from a sociopolitical standpoint but also from a biological and environmental one.

Is Posthumanism against human enhancement? Not necessarily. The possibilities opened by the prospect of human enhancement are so wide and varied that dismissing them completely to avoid possible risks may also preclude some important opportunities for the human species and for planet Earth. For instance, if the research on CRISPR genome editing eventually developed a safe way to modify, at the embryonic level, germline mutations that predispose to cancer, *would you ban this procedure?* This is also an interesting case where the line between therapy and enhancement may be disputed: on one side, eliminating the risk of cancer can be seen as a form of preventive medicine, that is, therapy; on the other, since evidence of cancer in humans is found throughout recorded history, eradicating it can be regarded as a form of enhancement. A further point to consider is that if you were willing to embrace this technology, would you also be open to other prenatal genetic manipulations aimed at eliminating, for instance, diseases such as Alzheimer and schizophrenia? What about genetic engineering to expand life expectancy and maximize cognitive abilities? These are just some examples, among many other possible applications that could appeal to a considerable number of prospective parents. The potential of these technologies is so significant that some people see human enhancement as inevitable, although they do not support it.[11] We may be in favor or against: in either case, we need to reflect on these technologies seriously and wisely.

Following, we will attempt to envision a safe path to bridge the precautionary principle with the proactionary one, in a mediated tone which may suit the praxis of Philosophical Posthumanism. The first step would be to proceed with great caution, learning more about these technologies before starting to experiment with them. We should also take into consideration that the current techniques of genetic manipulation rely on assisted reproductive technologies (ART), for example, in procedures such as in vitro fertilization (IVF), which can be invasive to the body of the prospective mother, and preimplantation genetic diagnosis (PGD), which may be invasive to the growing embryo. We should also keep in mind that technologies are not performed in a vacuum, but they reflect, and sometimes exacerbate, social problems that already exist in the world. For instance, in India,[12] prenatal sex determination—which is still practiced, although it is illegal—is a direct cause for the sex-selective abortion of female fetuses, exposing a cultural context where sons are favored due to patriarchal customs and gender biases (Hassan 2012). All these precautions are mentioned here not to defer the prospect of human enhancement, but to enable the flourishing of responsible research that may bring important contributions to human and nonhuman life. In general, when addressing the topic of human enhancement, we can state that adopting a precautionary approach to allow for a proactionary goal may be the way to go: all these steps should be taken in conjunction, moving toward a society that may eventually be ready—socially, politically, environmentally, and scientifically—to sustain the multilayered occurrence of human enhancement.

Is this take on human enhancement valid for all the thinkers who define themselves as posthumanists? Not at all. Some posthumanists are completely against human enhancement, for some of the reasons exposed above (this position is particularly popular in Southern Europe, for instance, in Italy). Some posthumanists are in between (this text can be seen as an example of this position); others lean, with caution, toward a favorable take which is close to the one of Democratic Transhumanism—for instance, the position of Stefan Lorenz Sorgner (2016) can be located here. Furthermore, envisioning forthcoming posthumanities is a subject which not every area of thought related to Posthumanism is willing to engage upon. For example, Karen Barad has stated: "My interest is in thinking about the limits of humanism, and hence I use the term 'posthumanism' to indicate this critical engagement; this should not be taken to mean that I advocate positions that use the notion of the posthuman as the next stage of the human, as if it no longer makes sense to talk about the human" (2007: 428). From the comprehensive standpoint of Philosophical Posthumanism, one position does not have to exclude the other. The deconstruction of the human, as well as the re-elaboration of the nonhuman realm, is not in conflict with a posthumanist reflection on future evolutions of the human species. One area of reflection which does engage with the future of humanity is Speculative Posthumanism.

What is Speculative Posthumanism? In his article "Deconstruction and Excision in Philosophical Posthumanism" (2010), David Roden, one of the main proponents, has defined it as such:

> Speculative posthumanists claim *that descendants of current humans could cease to be human by virtue of a history of technical alteration.*[13] The notion of descent is "wide" insofar as the entities that might qualify could include our biological descendants or beings resulting from purely technological activities (e.g., artificial intelligences, synthetic life-forms, or uploaded minds) (2010: 28).

Note the non-hierarchical way in which Roden locates human and posthuman evolutionary possibilities: "It does not imply that the posthuman would improve upon the human state or that there would exist a scale of values by which the human and posthuman lives could be compared" (*ibidem*). In his monograph *Posthuman Life* (2015), Roden further clarifies this point: "Posthumans in this sense are hypothetical wide 'descendants' of current humans that are *no longer human* in consequence of some history of technological alteration" (22). In his writings, Roden uses the neologism "wide descent" in order to underline that "exclusive consideration of biological descendants of humanity as candidates of posthumanity would be excessively restrictive" (*ibidem*). According to this position, the species-specific experience of humans and posthumans would be radically different. Remarking on the significance of the species may actually facilitate a posthumanist epistemological approach that stands on a hybrid perception of life. As we are going to see in the next chapter, humans share a species-specific cognitive organization: even though each and every human being has a different and unique way to form their own phenomenological experience, their cognitive apparatuses are similar, while they physiologically differ from the ones of other nonhuman animals, and possibly, from the ones of future posthumans. This reflection on posthumanities and the speculative history of technological alteration brings us back to our archaeological endeavor: *Is "life" an adequate term to refer to these hypothetical evolutionary scenarios?* Let's answer to this question by delving into the epistemology of Philosophical Posthumanism.

Cognitive Autopoiesis

Are there alternatives to the notion of "life"? The answer is yes, there are other terms that have been proposed by scientists and thinkers who have felt compelled to employ different concepts to the notion of life. *Why?* Because its cultural and scientific limitations do not necessarily allow for a comprehension of the set of onto-epistemological possibilities opened by the current developments in the field of artificial intelligence, which are raising challenging questions such as: *Is the internet alive? Are robots nonhuman persons?* The *MIT Encyclopedia of Cognitive Science*, under the entry "artificial life," explains, "The claim that even virtual creatures in cyberspace could be genuinely alive is called Strong A-Life. . . . [M]ost reject the view that such creatures can be alive in just the same sense that biological organisms are, but allow that they are, or could be, alive to a lesser degree" (Wilson and Keil 1999: 37). A notion which has received considerable attention in this context is autopoiesis: "Whether life does require material embodiment, and whether it is a matter of degree, are philosophically controversial questions. Proponents of autopoiesis (the continual self-production of an autonomous entity) for example, answer 'Yes' to the first and 'No' to the second" (*ibidem*). The notion of autopoiesis has had a significant impact on the development of second-order cybernetics[1] in the 1970s and, to a lesser degree, on posthuman theory in the 1990s and early 2000s, as we will soon see. With its focus on the self-organizational peculiarity of living beings, the autopoietic proposal offers the possibility to go beyond bio-centrism, opening the notion of life to non-biological beings as well, such as artificial intelligence.

In order to understand the terms of the debate more thoroughly, let's start by asking: *What does "autopoiesis" mean?* Coined from Greek "auto-" meaning "self" and *"poiesis"* meaning "creation, production,"[2] the notion of autopoiesis was developed in the 1970s by biologists Humberto Maturana (1928–) and Francisco Varela (1946–2001), who were originally attempting to define living systems, by emphasizing a system's capacity to reproduce and maintain itself. The notion of autopoiesis can be accessed from different perspectives, such as biology, technology, and cognitive sciences. *Where did the concept of autopoiesis first appear?* The concept of autopoiesis first appeared in Maturana and Varela's influential article "Autopoiesis and Cognition: The Realization of the Living" (1972),[3] where Maturana states: "I understood for the first time the power of the word 'poiesis' and invented the word that we needed: *autopoiesis*. This was a word without a history, a word that could directly mean what takes place in the dynamics of the autonomy proper to living systems" (*ivi*: xvii). By the time they published their book *The Tree of Knowledge: The Biological Roots of Human Understanding* (1987a), their take on the notion of autopoiesis[4] had become more explicitly cognitive, that is, related to the process of acquiring knowledge.

Is the notion of autopoiesis exhaustive from a posthuman perspective? The notion of autopoiesis bears special relevance to Philosophical Posthumanism from an archeological perspective. In fact, it was very influential in the 1990s and early 2000s, discussed in books that can now be considered milestones within posthuman theory, such as *How We Became Posthuman* (1999), in which Katherine Hayles engages with it in the frame of the history of Cybernetics. It is also embraced in *What is Posthumanism?* (2010), where Cary Wolfe develops, in posthuman terms, Niklas Luhmann's[5] social theory (2002), which was built on Maturana and Varela's notion of autopoiesis. More recently, the autopoietic approach has been radically criticized, as Donna Haraway succinctly puts it: "Nothing makes itself; nothing is really autopoietic or self-organizing" (2016: 58). In tune with the work of biologist Lynn Margulis (1938–2011) and her emphasis on the role of symbiosis in evolution (cf. Margulis 1991; Margulis 1998, among others), Haraway proposes the term "sympoiesis" instead of "autopoiesis." *What does sympoiesis mean?* Formed by the union of two Greek words—"sún" (which means "together") and "poiesis" (which means "creation, production")—"sympoiesis," according to Haraway, means "making-with" (2016: 58). As she further explains: "It is a word proper to complex, dynamic, responsive, situated, historical systems. . . . Sympoiesis enfolds autopoiesis and generatively unfurls and extends it" (*ibidem*). The criticisms that brought Haraway to coin the term "sympoiesis" partially coincide with the reasons why, in this study, we will not rely on autopoiesis as the ultimate way to define life. In fact, its emphasis on the autonomy of the organism[6] does not seem to take enough into account all the necessary relations and exchanges that occur between the organism and the environment,[7] for instance, in the processes of self-maintenance, such as food providing[8] and waste releasing, among others.

We will still engage with the notion of "autopoieis," focusing, instead, on the cognitive value of the autopoietic proposal.

What is Maturana and Varela's cognitive approach? In the work of Maturana and Varela, the notion of cognition is specifically revisited according to their autopoietic view. As Francisco Varela explains: "Biological cognition in general [is] not to be understood as a representation of the world out there but rather as an ongoing bringing-forth of a world, through the very process of living itself" (1995: 211). Before proceeding, let's briefly clarify some nomenclature, asking the question: *What is the difference between cognitive science and epistemology?* While the field of epistemology addresses the philosophical question: "*How do we acquire knowledge?*," cognitive science studies the actual process of acquiring knowledge (that is, cognition), which can be addressed from a physiological as well as a technological standpoint. For instance, philosopher Frederick F. Schmitt differentiates epistemology from the cognitive science by describing epistemology as "the conceptual and normative study of knowledge" (2004: 841), while defining the cognitive science as "the interdisciplinary empirical study of cognition in human beings, animals, and machines" (*ibidem*). Autopoiesis offers a unique light on the notion of cognition,[9] by addressing it as a technology of biological revealing: there is no world "out there," and there is no ultimate separation between the subject and the object, which are ontologically co-constituting each other. In order to understand this point more clearly, we have to take a further step back and refer to the origins of Maturana and Varela's reflection.

Where does the notion of autopoiesis come from? The origins of Maturana and Varela's reflection shall be found in physiology, and specifically, in the experiment described in the article "What the Frog's Eye Tells the Frog's Brain" (Lettvin et al. 1959). The experiment was set to observe how the frog's eye communicates information to the frog's brain. Maturana was one of the contributors, along with other scientists connected to the Macy Conferences,[10] such as Warren McCulloch (1898–1969) and Walter Pitts (1923–69).[11] Their findings were groundbreaking within the field of cognitive theory. They realized that "the frog does not seem to see or, at any rate, is not concerned with the detail of stationary parts of the world around him. He will starve to death surrounded by food if it is not moving. . . . He will leap to capture any object the size of an insect or worm, providing it moves like one" (1968: 234). In other words, the frog perceives "food" only as something which is moving and will starve to death even if surrounded by food, if such food is not moving. These results carried significant cognitive as well as epistemological consequences, pointing out the species-specific language through which one species (in particular, frogs) processes information. In the voice of the authors, "Fundamentally, it shows that the eye speaks to the brain in a language already highly organized and interpreted, instead of transmitting some more or less accurate copy of the distribution of light on the receptors" (254–55). We will come back to autopoiesis soon. First, though, we shall open a post-anthropocentric parenthesis about the frog experiment, and note that, although it carried valuable information to refute anthropocentrism on cognitive grounds—as we will see soon— its premises were still based on fundamental speciesist assumptions, which inherently justified animal experimentation.

What about animal testing? Rather than objecting on the specific practices employed in the frog's experiment by the researches, who were actually careful in trying not to be invasive to the frog body,[12] the foundational ethical issue here exceeds the one of the animal's pain, and refers directly to the use of animals in labs. In this book, we have referred to a number of different examples from animal research, such as the agouti mice (in Chapter 23) and the "Schwarzenegger mice"(in Chapter 25). It is time to address animal ethics, underlying with philosopher Raymond G. Frey (1941–2012), that the issue is not about "what justifies the painful use of animals in science, whether for our own or for their benefit," but about "what justifies their use at all, painful or otherwise" (*ivi*: 13–14). By pointing out this foundational problem in the field of applied ethics in animal research, we shall offer a more comprehensive reflection on Lettvin's experiment, displaying not only its explicit but also its implicit legacies, in tune with a posthumanist methodology which does not take any assumptions for granted, not even from a meta-theorical perspective. This allows for self-critique: *Is a post-anthropocentric reading of the frog experiment ahistorical?*

The contrast between the views of science as a self-affirming context which elicits the use of animals under the purpose of scientific advancement had long been under scrutiny before Lettvin's experiment. For instance, the Brown Dog Affair—a political controversy over vivisection in England (1903–10)—was based on the publishing of the book *The Shambles of Science: Extracts from the Diary of Two Students of Physiology* (1903), where animal rights advocates Lizzy Lind af Hageby (1878–1963) and Leisa Katherina Schartau (1876–1962) recalled the animal experiments they had witnessed at the medical lectures held at the University of London. Their motivations were not only ethical but epistemological. In Lind af Hageby and Schartau's perspective, methodology could not be separated from the knowledge it produced, as they sharply phrased it:

> Our object in taking up the study of physiology has been twofold: first, to investigate the *modus operandi* of experiments on animals, and then to study deeply the principle and theories which underlie modern physiology. / The two are closely related, for the rapid strides on the way of progress, which physiology claims to have made within the last fifty years, have passed over the bodies of uncountable long-suffering animals. (1903: vii–viii)

According to Lind af Hageby and Schartau, the operational modes of the scientific inquiry cannot be separated from their results. This approach clearly resonates with posthumanism as a praxis, according to which a posthuman methodology shall be in tune with its onto-epistemological endeavors (Ferrando 2012).

What are the explicit and implicit assumptions of the frog experiment? The speciesist assumptions of the frog experiment become obvious in the language utilized in the article. As Katherine Hayles[13] has subtly noticed: "To produce scientific knowledge . . . the frog's brain had ceased to belong to the frog alone" (1999: 134), symbolized by the linguistic choice of the authors to drop the possessive, "referring to the frog's brain simply as 'the brain' " (*ibidem*). Before proceeding, we shall note that this textual analysis is not intended as a direct criticism toward Lettvin et al., but as a posthumanist invitation toward a comprehensive perception of the article, in all of its significations, both written and implied. In "What the Frog's Eye Tells the Frog's Brain," for instance, the description of the frog is established in the very first paragraph of the article, through a standpoint which is gender non-neutral[14] and anthropocentric. This is how the article begins: "A frog hunts on land by vision. He escapes enemies mainly by seeing them. His eyes do not move, as do ours" (1968: 233). The frog, which is referred grammatically as a "he,"[15] is epistemologically presented through an anthropocentric dualism: "ours" refers to the human eyes, while the frog's implicitly become the eye of the "other." Such premises are followed by humanistic assumptions throughout the text, according to which some ways to perceive "reality" are portrayed as more objective than others.[16] Maturana later realized the conflicting framework of the frog experiment stating, "The epistemology that guided our thinking and writing was that of an objective reality independent of the observer" (1980: xiv); note that the observers, in the case of the frog experiment, were also the authors of the article, so their implicit biases were explicitly reflected in their way of writing. By then, Maturana and Varela were directly addressing the question: *How is knowledge constructed?*

They concluded, on epistemological grounds, that "no description of an absolute reality is possible" (1980: 121).[17]

Which kind of criticisms did Maturana and Varela's theories receive? Maturana and Varela's cognitive theories have been regarded as relativist[18] and radical constructivist.[19] Their views have been criticized for giving too much emphasis to autonomy, self-referentiality, and, eventually, solipsism. *What is solipsism?* Solipsism is the epistemological approach according to which any knowledge which resides outside of the knower's mind, and/or experience, is not fully knowledgeable. It can be summarized in this example. Two people are talking to each other. One asks the other, "Do you understand what I am saying?". The other says: "Yes." The problem generates here: how can the person who is asking *really* know if the person who is answering "yes," *really* understand what she, or he, is saying? A solution to this dilemma is offered by Alan Turing (1912–54) in his groundbreaking article "Computing Machinery and Intelligence" (1950), where he notably proposes a test, later defined as the Turing test, to determine a machine's ability to think, addressing the question: "Can machines think?" (1950: 433). In this article, Turing addresses the solipsistic paradox through the pragmatic option of the "polite convention," which he explains this way: "A is liable to believe 'A thinks but B does not' while B believes 'B thinks but A does not.' Instead of arguing continually over this point it is usual to have the polite convention that everyone thinks" (ivi: 446). *What is the polite convention, according to Alan Turing?* In our daily interactions, we comply with the polite convention to communicate with others, assuming that they can think, as they assume that we can think. According to Turing, if a machine acts as intelligently as a human being, we should apply the polite convention to machines as well, and politely convene: yes, machines can think.

Here, we should play a thought experiment and ask the question: What if, after one year of interacting with a friend you met online and with whom you became very close, you find out that this friend is not human, but is the latest development of a humanoid robot? You never asked your friend if they were human, so your friend was not lying to you; you were just assuming that you were developing a friendship with a human, and this was not the case. *Would you still cultivate your friendship, after realizing that your friend is a robot?* This thought experiment wishes to clarify the notion of the polite convention. Specifically, if your answer was "no," then we may ask: If for one year you developed a precious friendship with your friend, why, knowing that your friend is a humanoid robot would change the perception of your friend? This was scenario A. Let's go on with this thought experiment and play scenario B, according to which, after knowing that you were a human, your friend became really upset; they thought that you were a humanoid robot, and now, that they have found out you are a human, they feel deceived and want to end this friendship.[20] *Do you think it is right for your friend to judge you for being human and decide to end this friendship?* On an individual level, scenario B adds perspective from the other side of the power relationship. On a social level, this scenario may be revealing for the (unlikely, but still possible) case of AI takeover: how would humans feel if, let's say eighty years from now, in same parts of planet Earth, superintelligent AI do take over and decide that humans are not as intelligent as them, and so they want to deprive humans of some basic rights, such as voting and reproductive autonomy? The role of embodiment is crucial in Turing's article, according to which most of the objections regarding the question "Can machines think?" come from human-centric beliefs and fears. As he critically remarks, "We like to believe that Man is in some subtle way superior to the rest of creation. It is best if he can be shown to be *necessarily* superior, for then there is no danger of him losing his commanding position" (*ivi*: 444). On another side, the Turing test can be regarded as human-centric, since the referential point of machine intelligence, according to this view, is human intelligence: this comparison could be limiting and unnecessary. And still, we shall contextualize Turing's proposal—which was developed in the 1950s—as a pioneer attempt to seriously address the possibility of machine learning, and to destabilize cognitive anthropocentrism.

What is cognitive anthropocentrism? Cognitive anthropocentrism is the view according to which humans are cognitively superior to other species. To support this view from an epistemological perspective, we need to assume that there is only one reality, which can be represented, more adequately, in how humans perceive the world; according to these premises, human cognition would be the most adequate to perceive the world. But, as we have learned through the frog experiment, each species processes reality in a different way; this cognitive difference does not imply a hierarchy, as each perception of the world is adequate to the correspondent species. Let's bring an example to the discussion and visualize some humans and some ants who, independently from each other, are exploring a room; both groups eventually find themselves in front of a wall. The humans cannot proceed further and, most likely, will stop there, try to find a way out (through a door or a window, for instance), or go back. The ants, on the other side, will simply walk on the wall, and then on, upside down, to the ceiling—in fact, what looks like a smooth surface to a human eye, may reveal itself as an uneven surface full of toeholds to an ant, perfect to crawl on. In other words, for the ants the wall is not a wall, as it does not limit their trajectory in any way.

Is one perception of the "wall" more accurate than the other? No, they are simply different, as both comply with the embodied situatedness of each actant. More than relativism, we should rather develop Maturana and Varela's insights within the frame of perspectivism, which better emphasizes the role of embodiment and plurality. In so doing, we shall bring the cognitive notion of autopoiesis to the posthuman epistemological arena and, through it, present Posthumanism as a perspectivism.

Posthumanist Perspectivism

What is the difference between relativism and perspectivism? The *Oxford Dictionary* defines "relative" as "considered in relation or in proportion to something else"; the second definition is: "existing or possessing a specified characteristic only in comparison to something else; not absolute."[1] But *what is that "something else" which is presupposed by the notion of "relative"?* Semantically, "relative" requires another term of comparison; its counterpart is the notion of "absolute."[2] "Relative," in other words, is part of a dualism, so that a paradigmatic shift toward relativism, structurally, can be seen as the reverse side of the coin of what is trying to relativize. For instance, the relativist turn which characterized some of the most radical Western philosophies of the twentieth century can be seen, from a historical and meta-historical perspective, as a direct response to the absolutist and universalist approaches of the previous eras. The dichotomy absolute/relative can be successfully approached as oppositional poles, but one pole cannot be accounted without the other: they sustain one another in a necessary relation. The classic criticism: "The statement that there is no absolute truth is an absolute truth per se" emphasizes the co-constitutive inextricability of the dichotomy absolute/relative. Instead of partaking for one side or the other, we shall rather dismiss such a dualism itself, and consider perspectivism as a more suited notion to depict what is at stake in Maturana and Varela's work, not to mention Posthumanism itself.

Where does perspectivism come from? Perspectivism can be found in many different worldviews and continents, from the Amerindian perspectivism of Amazonian cosmologies (Viveiros de Castro 1998) to the Indian subcontinent. In this section, we will explore some common ground. Let's start by noting that Philosophical Posthumanism shares a striking point in common with the ancient spiritual tradition of Jainism and the doctrine of *anēkāntavāda* (non-absolutism), that is, the principles of pluralism and multiplicity of viewpoints (cf. Sethia 2004). Reality is perceived differently from diverse points of view; no single point of view can be regarded as the complete one, as John M. Koller underlines: "This ability to see the other person as no longer the 'other' . . . , underlies the capacity for empathy and sympathy with the other that operationalizes *ahimsā*" (2004: 86–87). *Ahimsā* is a Sanskrit word which literally means "not to harm"; it is the principle of non-violence toward all living beings, which is foundational in different religious traditions, such as Hinduism, Buddhism, and Jainism. *What are the roots of perspectivism in Western philosophy?* The term "perspectivism" etymologically bears a phenomenological, embodied legacy, coming from Latin, in the formula: *per* (prefix meaning "through") plus the verb *specere*,[3] which means "to look at."[4] Within the history of Western philosophy, the roots of Perspectivism shall be found, more specifically, in the thought of Friedrich Nietzsche, who famously stated in *On the Genealogy of Morals* (1887):[5] "Let us be on guard against the dangerous old conceptual fiction that posited a 'pure, will-less, painless, timeless knowing subject' . . . . There is *only* a perspective seeing, *only* a perspective 'knowing'" (2000: 555). Over the years, Nietzsche's perspectivism has aroused perplexity in many commentators (cf. Seipel 2015). And still, even though we may not fully embrace his proposal, Nietzsche's shift is of key relevance to our understanding of a posthumanist epistemology. In fact, on one side, he stressed the importance of situating the act of knowing in a specific perspective, instead of adopting a universalized, homogenized, and fit-for-all stand (which, as we have previously seen in Part 2, would most likely reflect specific biases and power structures); on the other, he valued the plurality of gazes to offer a more comprehensive picture, as we will soon see.

Is Nietzsche's perspectivism human-centric? Here, we shall remark that the perspectives Nietzsche is referring to, do not have to be human, although he is aware of the fact that his own investigation stands on specific human standpoints, is communicated in human terms, and it may better fit the gaze of future humans, rather than of his contemporaries, as repeatedly affirmed in his work, for instance, in *The Will to Power* (1906[6]).[7] This collection, posthumously assembled and published by his sister, Elizabeth Förster-Nietzsche (1846–35), is particularly relevant to our current discussion. For instance, in book three, section 481 (1883–88), Nietzsche takes a clear distance from a static notion of the subject stating, "'Everything is subjective,' you say; but even this is interpretation. The 'subject' is not something given" (1967: 267). The process of acquiring knowledge corresponds to the process of acquiring self-knowledge, that is, knowledge of the self. In autopoietic terms, getting to know the "other" reflects the process of getting to know the "self." In posthuman terms: the subject and the object are not separated. Nietzsche thus explains his perspectivism: "In so far as the word 'knowledge' has any meaning, the world is knowable; but it is *interpretable* otherwise, it has no meaning behind it, but countless meanings—'Perspectivism'" (*ibidem*). For Nietzsche, there are no absolute truths which can be attained, only situated perspectives.[8] Nietzsche develops the hermeneutical significance of his perspectivism, affirming:[9] "Against positivism, which halts at phenomena—'There are only facts'—I would say: No, facts is precisely what there is not, only interpretations" (1967: 267). Following, he adds: "It is our needs that interpret the world; our drives and their For and Against" (*ibidem*). In using the first-person plural pronoun ("it is *our* needs that interpret the world"), and in comparing his proposal to two specific philosophical approaches, positivism and subjectivism, Nietzsche is implying that the eyes behind his own approach are human. This is not always the case, as he states:[10] "There are many kinds of eye. Even the sphinx has eyes—and consequently there are many kinds of "truths," and consequently there is no truth" (291). The statement that "there is no truth" needs additional explanation in the context of this book and, more in general, Posthumanism. Let's address this point by analyzing it in conjunction with the notion of "fact."

Does Posthumanism sustain the notion of "fact"? In the post-truth era in which we are arguably situated, we should clarify that Nietzsche's undermining of notions such as "facts" and "truth" does not support the current post-factual approach to politics; more than erasing the possibility of knowledge, it erases the possibility of universalizing one standpoint as the absolutely objective one.[11] And still, his critique of facts (as quoted above: "Facts is precisely what there is not, only interpretations") may lead toward a slippery path. This is why, here, we will not discard the notion of "fact," but we will re-access it from a posthumanist perspectivist standpoint, according to which facts can be seen as the integrated landscape of all the material perspectives related to a specific factual node. For instance, the fact that I exist can be approached as the choral symphony of my phenomenological experiences, together with the experiences of all the human and nonhuman agents I interact with. In other words, the fact that I exist is not only posed from the self—"I know that I exist"—or from the others—"I know that I exist because others know that I exist," but shall be accessed as a process constantly sustained by all of these intra-related flows. Eyes are everywhere, in a multiplication of perspectives that enriches our posthumanist understanding of epistemology and ontology, eventually bringing our reflection to the multiverse, as we will see in Chapter 30.

Plurality is of key importance to the understanding of Posthumanism, as well as of Nietzsche's perspectivism. In *On the Genealogy of Morals*, for instance, Nietzsche states, "The *more* eyes, different eyes, we can use to observe one thing, the more complete will our 'concept' of this thing, our 'objectivity,' be" (2000: 555). This passage bears particular significance to posthuman epistemologies and ethics, as they both embrace the perspectivist critique to absolute universalism and, within the contemporary debate, support the shift from generalized multiculturalism—which has been criticized from many different perspectives, notably by feminism[12]—to situated pluralism and diversity. *What does pluralism imply from a philosophical posthumanist perspective?* Pluralism, with its emphasis on the respectful co-existence of different perspectives, individuals, groups, and systems, is at the core of Philosophical Posthumanism. Feminist Epistemology, with its onto-epistemological understanding of embodiment and situatedness, has most contributed to its development. Let's explain why by asking the question: *What is feminist epistemology?* In the 1990s, the feminist debate on science produced original epistemological approaches, eventually labeled under the encompassing term of Feminist Epistemology. Among these, the standpoint theory, which was developed by theorists such as Sandra Harding, Patricia Hill Collins, Dorothy Smith, and Donna Haraway (cf. Harding 1991; Haraway 1996b, among others), is particularly relevant to our discussion.

What is the standpoint theory? The standpoint theory focuses on a key aspect, that is: the starting point of knowledge production. Each human being views the world from a specific standpoint, which is informed by their embodiments, individual experiences, social and cultural structures, religious beliefs and political choices, among other factors. Within this frame, the pursuit of disembodied neutral objectivity, traditionally claimed by scientific practice, is seen as a rhetorical move which has historically benefited those who claimed it—more specifically, the same subjectivities who had explicit access to positions of power, in the hierarchy established through the implicit processes of humanizing, as we have seen in the Part 2. Objectivity, on the other end, is situated and embodied; in Haraway's words, "Feminist objectivity means quite simply *situated knowledges*" (1996b: 188). Since marginalized and/or oppressed individuals and groups must learn the views of those who belong to the privileged hegemonic positions, they can be considered bicultural; therefore, their perspectives may be seen as more objective than the views of the people located at the center of the hegemonic discourse, who are not required to learn about the margins. For instance, women born and raised in a patriarchal society will eventually become familiar both with patriarchal standards and codes and also with knowledges and values, which are not accessible from the hegemonic patriarchal perspective (such as the female embodied experience; the realization of the pervasiveness and normalization of sexism and heterosexism, among other discriminatory frames; the feminist critique; and so on). This specific claim developed into the notion of "strong objectivity" (Harding 1993), which is skeptical of the traditional "value-free" models, since they often maintain, under the disguise of neutrality, biases and values which ultimately reflect the researchers' mindsets and goals. On the contrary, "strong objectivity" is aware of its own location: with its emphasis on situated knowledges, Feminist Epistemology sets the grounds for the development of a posthumanist epistemology, based on embodied perspectivist accounts.

What about nonhuman perspectives? Here, we shall ask if the perspectivist approach complies with all three of the main analytical layers that we have identified in Philosophical Posthumanism, specifically: post-humanism, post-anthropocentrism, and post-dualism. From a post-humanistic standpoint, valuing different human perspectives is an important step toward the comprehensive approach of Philosophical Posthumanism. And still, from a post-anthropocentric standpoint, if all the perspectives taken into consideration were only coming from human embodied beings, we would still be working within a cognitive anthropocentric schema. Accessing nonhuman perspectives means taking into consideration the existence of other species, their needs, their habits, and their co-evolution, in relation to our species and all the other species. It means hearing their messages, which may not be verbal or intellective, but they are still very clear. For instance, the massive sound of nonhuman animals displaced by deforestation and industrialization should be heard and fully acknowledged. At this point in time, human societies shall not cut any more forest down.[13] Instead of erecting new buildings, humans should focus on restoring abandoned structures and rehabilitating the numerous sites that have been heavily polluted by human actions, implementing ecosystem management and ecological engineering, until the dynamic balance has been re-established, to later diminish human intervention in order to sustain multispecies co-habitation and co-existence. This approach resonates with the notion of "multispecies justice" (Haraway 2016) and "the cultivation of viral response-ability," which Haraway defines as "carrying meanings and materials across kinds in order to infect processes and practices that might yet ignite epidemics of multispecies recuperation" (2016: 114). From a political and economic perspective, we shall bring into the conversation the worldview of "earth democracy" proposed by Vandana Shiva: to be a part of a healthy planet, humans must take into account peace and sovereignty for all living beings. As Shiva states: "Earth democracy evolves from the consciousness that while we are rooted locally we are also connected to the world as a whole, and in fact, to the entire universe" (2005: 5). More specifically, she explains, "Ecological security is our most basic security; ecological identities are our most fundamental identities. We are the food we eat, the water we drink, the air we breathe" (*ibidem*). On one side, Shiva's calling for "fundamental identities" might not fully suit the posthumanist narrative, which moves in the direction of coalition and affinity (attitudes that may suggest openness and bridging: "I" in relation to "others"), instead of essentialist identities (attitudes that may lead toward closeness and separation: "I" in distinction from "others"), as reflected upon by Donna Haraway in "A Manifesto for Cyborgs" (1985). Let's open a parenthesis and clarify this point.

Affinity or Identity? The debate on this topic, which flourished in the 1990s as a result of Haraway's suggestion, is still relevant today, as a generative critique of the possible risks that an uncritical acceptance of the essentialist premises of some type of identity politics may entail. As Haraway phrased it, "The recent history of US left and US feminism has been a response to this kind of crisis by endless splitting and searches for a new essential unity. But there has also been a growing recognition of another response through coalition-affinity, not identity" (1989: 196–97). The premises of this discussion lie in the personal and political ramifications of such tactics. To simply put it, on the one hand, the notion of "woman" is a plural notion: every woman is different (that is, "women"). Following, any generalization about women cannot acknowledge all the differences among women and, consequently, may create misunderstanding and frustration. On the other hand, how can we talk of sexism, for instance, without a clear definition of the notion of "women," since this bio-cultural construction is the reason why women have been systematically discriminated against? A possible solution to this problem lies in the notion of "strategic essentialism."

What is "strategic essentialism"? Feminist theorist Gayatri Spivak proposed the notion of "strategic essentialism" (1984) within the frame of postcolonial theory; according to this view, minorities could opt for a strategic use of essentialism. In this sense, for instance, we can talk of violence by men against women, using two concepts "women" and "men" that, far from defining every woman and man on Earth, are used strategically, to express a social problem which needs to be addressed now. In Spivak's words: "I felt that rather than define myself as repudiating universality . . .—rather than define myself as specific rather than universal—I should see what in the universalizing discourse could be useful and then go on to see where that discourse meets its limits. . . . I think we have to choose again strategically, not universal discourse but essentialist discourse" (1984: 183). Many have criticized this approach, including Spivak herself, who would eventually distantiate herself from strategic essentialism, claiming that "my notion just simply became the union ticket for essentialism" (Danius et al. 1993: 35). And still, strategic essentialism represents a precious resource when the limits of language, and/or sociopolitical projections, have become such impediments that they are actually holding back the discussion on urgent issues. Going back to Vandana Shiva, her calling for "ecological identities" as "our most fundamental identities" can be read in strategic political terms, as well as material ones, to emphasize the human as ecologically situated. This point is of key importance from a posthumanist perspective, because it combines the relevance of human well-being with multispecies justice. Being posthumanist does not mean being anti-human (that is, against the human or in favor of human extinction).[14] The post-dualistic perspective of Philosophical Posthumanism brings us to the understanding that an ecological balance is reflected in the prosperity of humans as well. For instance, psychologists Kirk Warren Brown and Tim Kasser have tested the relation between subjective well-being and ecologically responsible behavior in adults and adolescents; their findings demonstrated that "a sustainable way of life . . . enhances both personal and collective well-being" (2005). Here, we shall note that biodiversity is a measure for the health of ecosystems: "health" etymologically derives from proto-Germanic *hælþ*, which means "whole."

What is the relation between perspectivism and embodiment? From a posthumanist perspective, the relation between perspectivism and embodiment is a *sine qua non*, that is, an indispensable condition. On this regard, Rosi Braidotti states: "The posthuman knowing subject has to be understood as a relational embodied and embedded, affective and accountable entity and not only as a transcendental consciousness" (2018: 1). To which, she adds, "Two related notions emerge from this claim: firstly, the mind-body continuum—i.e. the embrainment of the body and embodiment of the mind—and secondly, the nature-culture continuum—i.e. 'naturecultural' and 'humanimal' transversal bonding" (*ibidem*). Here, we will emphasize the "embrainment of the body" and the "embodiment of the mind" in relation to Nietzsche's perspectivism and Maturana and Varela's cognitive theories, embracing a materialist approach that deconstructs the dualistic mind/body separation; following, we will move our attention to the "nature-culture continuum" and reflect on matter and nonhuman agency. As far as Nietzsche goes, his perspectivism, and more in general, his whole philosophy, is corporeal;[15] the gaze which allows for an act of knowing is not a disembodied one. For these reasons, more than relativism, Nietzsche's perspectivism stands as a suited theoretical reference to Maturana and Varela's theories.[16]

Do embodiments have to be physical and/or biological? The rejection of the frontal dichotomy physical/non-physical is in tune with Nietzsche's perspectivism, which is necessarily embodied,[17] although such embodiments do not have to be strictly physical. As Sorgner puts it: "Nietzsche later in his work did reject the thesis that the body was physical, because then he held that everything is the will to power" (2007: 34). *What is the will to power*[18]? The will to power is a prominent doctrine in the philosophy of Nietzsche. It can be summarized as a main driving force in all living beings, but it cannot be limited to the living, since it is not reducible. As Nietzsche underlines, "There is no will: there are treaty drafts of will[19] that are constantly increasing or losing their power" (1967: 381). This non-reducibility of the will to power[20]—which was influenced by Nietzsche's reading of Ruđer Josip Bošković (1711–87) and his theory of forces[21]—resonates with the posthuman relational ontology proposed by Karen Barad (2007), and her agential turn, as we will see in Chapter 28. In this pluralistic scenario, agency does not have to be confined to biological organisms, but can be extended to the inorganic[22] realm, contemplating social bodies and systems as well (Luhmann 2002).

What about alternative types of embodiments? According to a posthumanist perspectivist standpoint, we can state that every perspective is embodied, but such embodiments do not have to be physical: they can be digital, virtual, or even oneiric. Let's bring some insights to the discussion. In cybernetics, an avatar indicates one (of many) graphic representation of a user, while its etymology suggests a transcendental nexus: in Sanskrit "avatar" refers to the appearance or manifestation of a deity from heaven to earth, and it is widely translated into English as "incarnation." Alternative embodiments are contemplated in psychological, spiritual, and religious domains (Ferrando 2016a). Altered states of consciousness, trance rituals, and psychoactive substances form part of shamanic practices in different traditions, and are aimed to achieve spiritual elaborations of the self through a mediated perception of the physical body. Ontological and epistemological perspectivist worldviews are recurrently found in Amerindian mythologies and cosmologies. As anthropologist Eduardo Viveiro de Castro, in his groundbreaking article "Cosmological Deixis and Amerindian Perspectivism" (1998), states: "Myth speaks of a state of being where bodies and names, souls and affects, the I and the Other interpenetrate, submerged in the same pre-subjective and pre-objective milieu" (483). According to Viveiro de Castro, Amerindian perspectivism does not support any strict dichotomy; on the contrary, it actually "implies a redistribution of the predicates subsumed within the two paradigmatic sets that traditionally oppose one another under the headings of 'Nature' and 'Culture': universal and particular, objective and subjective, physical and social, fact and value, the given and the instituted, necessity and spontaneity, immanence and transcendence, body and mind, animality and humanity, among many more" (*ivi:* 469–70). In this pre-dualistic worldview, for instance, shamans are "trans-specific beings" (*ivi:* 471), that is, beings who can transcend their species-specific cognitive organization and perceive consciousness beyond a particular bodily appearance or manifestation, adding another critical layer of understanding to our previous discussion on autopoiesis, as reflected upon in Chapter 26.

What about dream embodiments? The dreamworld is another interesting topic for reflection. Islam, for instance, has a foundation in dream initiation: the Isra and Mi'raj—the Night Journey during which Mohammed ascends to heaven and speaks to God—has been described as both a physical and spiritual journey (cf. Colby 2008). Another revealing example can be found in the teaching tradition of Advaita Vedanta, which is one of the main schools of Indian philosophy. According to Advaita, which literary means "non-two," "non-dual" (Rambachan 2006; Timalsina 2009), the inner essence of an individual (Ātman) corresponds to the transcendent existence (Brahman): no frontal dualism between immanence and transcendence can be established. Following this understanding, Advaita complies with a distention of the dualistic perception between being awake and being asleep (cf. Sharma 2004), individuating, instead, three related states of consciousness: waking, dreaming, and deep sleep. The individual awareness is presented as a continuum between the awake and the asleep phases. Anantanand Rambachan, in *The Advaita Worldview* (2006), underlines: "In all three states, Advaita contends, *ātman* as awareness is common and constant" (40). Although Advaita shares many points in common with Philosophical Posthumanism, one of the main differences can be found in the monistic ways the Advaita doctrine of "awareness only" has historically developed such an understanding. As Rambachan explains, "The rejection of duality can be interpreted in terms of the ontological perspective that there is ultimately no essential plurality in what exists" (*ivi:* 3). By some schools of Advaita, plurality is seen as an "illusion" (*ivi:* 9). Differently, Philosophical Posthumanism recognizes diversity as one of the main technologies of evolution, and sees pluralism as the necessary complement to monism: in this sense, Philosophical Posthumanism is both a monistic pluralism and a pluralistic monism.[23] A posthumanist epistemological perspectivism, situated in a mediated plurality of embodied perspectives, sets the conditions for the development of Philosophical Posthumanism as a process relational ontology. We will conclude here our epistemological reflection to address, more specifically, the realm of ontology: the two fields, as we will see, are closely related.

From New Materialisms to
Object-Oriented Ontology

The movement which has delved more thoroughly into the ontological aspects of the posthuman is New Materialism. *What is New Materialism?* In order to answer this question, let's go back to our archaeological investigation. If life cannot be fully described without a self-referential starting point, matter, on some level, precedes such a notion: anything which is considered alive within Western scientific canons is constituted of matter. Here, we are trying to neither reduce biology to physics (Canguilhem 1952) nor attribute any primacy to matter. What we shall offer is a complete overview of the posthumanist theoretical scenario. In order to do so, we will investigate matter and the ways through which matter materializes; we will approach such a reflection through New Materialism,[1] another specific movement which we have not presented yet. First of all, let's clarify that the term "materialism" may create some confusion, since it may also refer to historical materialism, that is, the historiographical approach developed by Karl Marx (1818–83), which emphasizes the relevance of material conditions to the development of human relations, societies and, consequently, history. *Does New Materialism come from historical materialism?* As Diana Coole and Samantha Frost point out, "The renewed critical materialisms are not synonyms with a revival of Marxism" (2010: 30); more literally, they reinscribe matter as a process of materialization, in the feminist critical debate. *Who coined the term "New Materialism"?* The term was coined independently by Rosi Braidotti and Manuel DeLanda in the mid-1990s (Dolphijn and van der Tuin 2010: 48). Already traceable in the focus given to the body by corporeal feminism (Grosz 1994; Braidotti 1994; Kirby 1997), which developed in the mid- to late 1990s, such a rediscovered feminist interest became more extensively matter-oriented by the first decade of the twenty-first century.

Where does New Materialism come from? New Materialisms philosophically arose as a reaction to the representationalist and constructivist radicalizations of late Postmodernity, which somehow lost track of the material, with the consequent risks of postulating an inner dualism between what was perceived as manipulated by the act of observing and describing pursued by the observers, and an external "reality" which thus would become unapproachable.[2] Even though the roots of New Materialisms can be located within Postmodernism, New Materialisms point out that the postmodern annihilation of the dualism nature/culture resulted in a clear preference for the nurtural aspects of it, in a multiplication of genealogical accounts investigating the constructivist implications of any natural presumptions,[3] in what can be seen as a wave of radical constructivist feminist literature related to the success and major influence of Judith Butler's works[4] (1990, 1993). Such a literature exhibited an unbalanced result: if "culture" did not need to be bracketed, "nature" for sure did. In an ironic tone, Karen Barad, one of the main theorists of New Materialisms, implicitly referring to Butler's book *Bodies that Matter* (1993), has stated: "Language matters. Discourse matters. Culture matters. There is an important sense in which the only thing that does not seem to matter anymore is matter" (2003: 801). New Materialisms pose no division between language and matter: biology is culturally mediated as much as culture is materialistically constructed. New Materialisms perceive matter as an ongoing process of materialization, elegantly reconciling science and critical theories: quantum physics with a post-structuralist and postmodern sensitivity. Matter is not viewed in any way as something static, fixed or passive, awaiting to be molded by some external force; rather, it is emphasized as "a process of materialization" (Butler 1993: 9). Such a process (which is dynamic, shifting, inherently entangled, diffractional, and performative) has neither any primacy over the materialization, nor can the materialization be reduced to its processual terms.[5]

What is agential realism? In her influential book *Meeting the Universe Halfway: Quantum Physics and the Entanglement of Matter and Meaning* (2007), Karen Barad, combining her expertise in theoretical physics with feminist theory, proposes an agential realism, which reworks the concept of phenomena as "the ontological inseparability of intra-acting agencies" (206), recognizing agency to the nonhuman realm. This agential realism is based on a relational ontology, as she states: "This relational ontology is the basis for my posthumanist performative account of material bodies (both human and nonhuman)" (139). As Barad clarifies, agential realism takes a distance from the representationalist approach: "This account refuses the representationalist fixation on words and things and the problematic of the nature of their relationship, advocating instead *a relationality between specific (re)configurings of the world through which boundaries, properties, and meanings are differentially enacted* (i.e., discursive practices, in my posthumanist sense) *and specific material phenomena* (i.e., differentiating patterns of mattering)" (*ibidem*). Here, we shall stress the fact that Barad locates her agential realism within a posthumanist frame, instead of an antihumanist or a transhumanist[6] one, even though she keeps a critical stand from Posthumanism as well:[7] "Posthumanism, as I intend it here, is not calibrated to the human; on the contrary, it is about taking issue with human exceptionalism" (136). What Barad opts for is "a *posthumanist performative* approach to understanding technoscientific and other naturalcultural practices that specifically acknowledges and takes account of matter's dynamism" (135). We will follow Barad's suggestion, and investigate matter from a scientific perspective, to address the relevance of contemporary physics to the posthuman debate. Before doing that, we shall note some of the risks run by new materialist thinkers.

What are some of the risks run by new materialist thinkers? One of the risks run by some new materialist thinkers is vitalism.[8] *What is vitalism?* According to the *Routledge Encyclopedia of Philosophy*, vitalism is the belief that "living organisms are fundamentally different from non-living entities because they contain some non-physical element or are governed by different principles than are inanimate things" (entry "Vitalism", Bechtel and Richardson 1998: n. pg.). This idea can be found transhistorically, from antiquity to modern science, in different forms: "In its simplest form, vitalism holds that living entities contain some fluid, or a distinctive 'spirit'. In more sophisticated forms, the vital spirit becomes a substance infusing bodies and giving life to them; or vitalism becomes the view that there is a distinctive organization among living things" (*ibidem*). From a posthumanist perspective, vitalism is a problematic approach because it relies upon the notion of life ("vita" in Latin), which, as we have seen in Part 2, carries a series of pre-scientific assumptions and is ultimately undefinable[9]. For a lack of a better word, some new materialist thinkers feel comfortable using the term "vitalism" by addressing it from a Spinozian-Deleuzian genealogy[10]. *What is Spinoza's conatus?* The philosophy of Baruch Spinoza (1632–77) features as a central theme the notion of the *conatus*, which he defines, in the *Ethics*, Book II, Prop.VI, as the tendency or impulse according to which: "Everything, in so far as it is in itself, endeavours to persist in its own being." Gilles Deleuze (1925–95), who was greatly influenced by Spinoza to the point of dedicating to him an entire book *Spinoza: Practical Philosophy* (1970; Engl. Trans. 1988), defines the *conatus* as such: "Not a tendency to pass into existence, but to maintain and affirm existence" (99). The vitalist emphasis on an irreducible self-organizing force can be found in some new materialists thinkers. Let's consider, for instance, this quotation from Diane Coole and Samantha Frost: "Perhaps most significant here is the way new materialist ontologies are abandoning the terminology of matter as an inert substance subject to predictable causal forces. According to the new materialisms, if everything is material inasmuch as it is composed of physicochemical processes, nothing is reducible to such processes, at least as conventionally understood" (2010: 9). Coole and Frost are promoting a comprehensive perspective which destabilizes the view of matter as "inert substance," but their proposal is still based on a hierarchical dualism, which is clearly posed in the following passage: "For materiality is always something more than 'mere' matter: an excess, force, vitality, relationality, or difference that renders matter active, self-creative, productive, unpredictable" (*ibidem*). Materiality, which now becomes a "vitality" among other terms, turns into "something *more* than 'mere' matter." The consequent risk is creating a dichotomy between materiality and matter, where materiality constitutes the positive pole due to that indescribable element which, under a deeper scrutiny, can be identified in the principle of life itself.

What is "vital materiality"? The reference to vitalism is explicit in Jane Bennett's *Vibrant Matter: A Political Ecology of Things* (2010). Here, Bennett proposes her notion of "vital materiality," which aims to emphasize nonhuman matter over the ontological privilege of the human, as she states: "Vital materialists will thus try to linger in those moments during which they find themselves fascinated by objects, taking them as clues to the material vitality that they share with them" (17–18). This perception, according to Bennett, bears ethical consequences: "This sense of a strange and incomplete commonality with the outside may induce vital materialists to treat nonhumans—animals, plants, earth, even artifacts and commodities—more carefully, more strategically, more ecologically" (*ibidem*). Although her tactics might prove successful on an ecological and ethical level, from a philosophical posthumanist perspective, they can be still regarded as humanistic. Let's see why. Bennett's proposal is an important step away from the self-glorified human exceptionalism that characterizes most philosophical trends. Her theoretical development of the understanding of nonhuman agency has seriously contributed to the reflection on posthuman agency. *Why is Bennett's notion of nonhuman agency relevant to Philosophical Posthumanism?* Her focus on the idea that "non-human things and forces actively shape the bodies they encounter, including the humans" (2017: 447), suggesting that "in many cases, human intentions, strivings or deliberate activities are not the key operators" (*ibidem*), is an important step toward the comprehension of a posthuman type of agency where not only the human and nonhuman realms bear signification, but also the modalities of existence, as we will see in Chapter 30. And still, not all of Bennett's proposals can be easily embraced by Philosophical Posthumanism. *What are some of the differences of Bennett's proposal from Philosophical Posthumanism?* Two of the main differences are vitalism and anthropomorphism. For instance, Bennett concludes her book with what she defines as a "Nicene Creed for would-be vital materialists" (122), which is aimed at summarizing her view in an evocative and agential prose, calling for action. This is the complete passage:

> I believe in one matter-energy, the maker of things seen and unseen. I believe that this pluriverse is traversed by heterogeneities that are continually *doing things*. I believe it is wrong to deny vitality to nonhuman bodies, forces, and forms, and that a careful course of anthropomorphization can help reveal that vitality, even though it resists full translation and exceeds my comprehensive grasp. I believe that encounters with lively matter can chasten my fantasies of human mastery, highlight the common materiality of all that is, expose a wider distribution of agency, and reshape the self and its interests. (122)

Although appealing, her suggestion of a strategic anthropomorphization and a recognition of vitality to nonhuman agents runs the risk of turning their existence into a humanistic assimilation, which dissolves the original encounter with alterity, in a homogenization and reduction of the difference to the same. From a historical perspective, Bennett's profession of vital materialism results in a *mea culpa* of the humanistic subject, which echoes religious and moral rhetorics. The "one matter-energy, the maker of things seen and unseen" sounds like a reformulation of the Abrahamic God; the Christian notion of the original sin is redesigned as human-centrism and its "fantasies of human mastery"; a right and a "wrong" are empirically located in self-imposed hermeneutical practices. Bennett's subject is, more specifically, the good willing and well-educated human, portrayed in their effort to engage with an existence which, to use Bennett's words, "exceeds" their "comprehensive grasp." We can certainly appreciate her effort to destitute the sovereignty of the humanistic subject; and still, Bennett's proposal of anthropomorphization can be seen as the reverse side of that specific humanistic privilege she wishes to destabilize (this inclusion of the nonhuman implicitly reconfirms human primacy). For this reason, Philosophical Posthumanism can be aligned, more specifically, with Barad's agential realism. Let's see why.

How does vitalism differ from Barad's agential realism? Barad's notion of agential realism emphasizes the intra-constitution of existence without employing mediated terms: "Rather than giving humans privileged status in the theory, agential realism calls on the theory to account for the intra-active emergence of 'humans' as a specifically differentiated phenomena. . . . Intra-actions are not the result of human interventions; rather, 'humans' themselves emerge through specific intra-actions" (2007: 352). Barad's theoretical investigation on matter is beyond good and evil. Barad does not fall into the illusion of the origins: humans themselves are intra-actions, and so they cannot be reduced to a material or a moral foundation. Differently, Bennett individuates her ontological starting point, as well as her ethical strategies, in an undefined vital principle. Let's reflect on this point further. In doing this, we will introduce another movement to which Jane Bennett has been partially associated with,[11] and which is not always included under the umbrella term of the posthuman, although it shares some points in common: Object-Oriented Ontology.

What is Object-Oriented Ontology (OOO)? Object-Oriented Ontology is a philosophical movement which arose more clearly at the beginning of the second decade of the twenty-first century, in order to bring back the attention to the object, or, more specifically, to the independency and autonomy of the object—to be considered not in dependence from the subject, nor in relation to other objects. Although there are different takes and approaches within this movement, Peter Wolfendale identifies two essential components in OOO: "First, that every object exceeds the ways in which it is presented to other objects; and second, that every object is independent of every other object" (2017: 297). Wolfendale underlines how this "prioritizing individuality and discreteness over relationality and continuity" (2017: 298) is "in opposition to many strands of contemporary metaphysics (e.g., actor network theory, process philosophy and related new materialisms)" (*ibidem*). This prioritizing also sets OOO apart from Philosophical Posthumanism. This is why the field of OOO is not always included in the posthuman discussion, with some exceptions.[12] And still, a generative exchange between the two movements should develop, as OOO brings some important questions to the posthumanist reflection, by calling for a deeper reflection on the ontological significance of relationality, as we will see in the following sections.

What are the main similarities between OOO and Philosophical Posthumanism? Both Philosophical Posthumanism and OOO can be located in the ontological turn.[13] Although Posthumanism and OOO cannot be assimilated, they do share some important points in common, such as the rejection of the Cartesian mind/body dualism and a post-anthropocentric sensitivity. As Graham Harman, one of the founders of the movement, states, "OOO rejects the Cartesian dualism that treats the thinking human being as one sort of entity (*res cogitans*) and the nonhuman animals, inanimate beings and the human body itself as another sort (*res extensa*)" (2015: 404). This rejection brings OOO to a type of post-anthropocentrism which, as in the case of Philosophical Posthumanism, does not comply with an antihuman[14] stand. In Harman's words: "Although some critics of OOO hold that its removal of human beings from the centre of the universe entails a further claim that 'humans are worthless,' this is not the case" (2015: 404). And still, this type of post-anthropocentrism cannot be fully assimilated to the post-anthropocentric approach of Philosophical Posthumanism.

Let's delve into this aspect asking the question: *What are the main differences between OOO and Philosophical Posthumanism?* Although there are some important similarities between the two movements, they differ greatly. Let's starts by tracing a genealogy of OOO, which, according to Harman (2015), can be located in the phenomenological tradition, passing through Martin Heidegger and Bruno Latour. The acknowledgment of these sources is shared with Philosophical Posthumanism, but OOO skips a crucial contribution: the studies of the differences (such as feminism, postcolonialism, critical race theory, etc.) within the postmodern frame. This omission comes with some serious consequences: the notion of the human in OOO is still based on the assumption of a "neutral" and generalized human subject. The human is not approached as a plural notion. The first analytical frame of Philosophical Posthumanism, that is, post-humanism, is missing in OOO: the composite symphony of plural voices which are necessary to give rise to a comprehensive account on the human is silenced again in this generalized post-anthropocentric move. Harman, in a post-anthropocentric critical tone, states, "The human remains 50 per cent of every philosophical situation." And still, this "human"—which, according to Harman, should leave space to the nonhuman—has not been deconstructed: *Of which human are we talking about?* We are missing one of the main components of the post-humanist approach, that is, the understanding of the human as a term which cannot be taken for granted. This inaccuracy resolves in a multiplication of presumptions which are not shared by Philosophical Posthumanism.

What are flat ontologies? The main characteristic of OOO is its primacy toward the object, here considered in an extensive way: from objects to hyperobjects (Morton 2013), in a formation of objects within objects, based on scale. This approach welcomes the ongoing debate on flat ontology[15], a term adopted by philosopher Manuel DeLanda[16] to define an ontology "made exclusively of unique, singular individuals, differing in spatio-temporal scale but not in ontological status" (2002: 47). The notion of flat ontology, which has been further developed within the frame of OOO, allows for a strategic post-anthropocentric turn by recognizing that the human has no privileged status. And still, although DeLanda developed this notion in Deleuzian terms[17], a flat ontology does not exhaust the philosophical posthumanist ontological enquiry. The problem starts with language: to simply put it, the term is misleading as no ontology can be "flat." In process philosophical terms, to be aware of existence implies existing. Following, to go back to our perspectivist approach: *How can we have flat ontologies if there are always perspectives*[18]? Please note that we are not talking about the perspective of the "subject." Posthumanism offers a generative critique to the subject/object dualism not by prioritizing one instead of the other, or assimilating one to the other, but by embracing both relationally, as intra-connected actants in an open and respondent context, which is also constantly shifting. To reply to OOO's criticism of correlationism[19]—and specifically, Quentin Meillassoux's critique of "this belief in the primacy of the relation over the related terms" (2008: 5)—we should clarify that such relations do not hold any primacy either. We can thus re-access Barad's agential realism,[20] expanding on her notable affirmation "Relata[21] do not precede relations" (33), by adding that relations do not precede relata either. In fact, relata and relations generate out of co-constitutive, embodied, agential processes, situated in specific spatio-temporal environments. In other words, the questions of "who" and "what" cannot be approached in disjunction from "when," "where," and "how." To understand this point more thoroughly, we need to enter the enchanting realm of physics, in the name of philosophical posthumanist ontology.

Philosophical Posthumanist Ontology

What is matter? From a physics perspective, anything which has mass and volume is considered matter: humans, for instance, are made out of matter, as well as robots, jellyfish, and roses. The way matter appears on the large scale might be misleading, if taken as its ultimate state. Matter, on a subatomic level, is not static or fixed, but is constantly vibrating. Matter is relational and irreducible to a single determined entity: any reductionist approach has historically and scientifically failed.[1] According to the string theory,[2] an active research framework[3] in quantum physics,[4] matter, at a subatomic level, may be composed by tiny vibrating loops of energy, defined as strings. *What is string theory, and why is it relevant to Philosophical Posthumanism?* We will delve into this theory more in detail, because it offers valuable insights for an ontological development of Philosophical Posthumanism. Let's start by reflecting on how the materialization of matter occurs, according to string theory. In order to do this, we will offer an example which is commonly employed within the field, and compare these strings to those of a musical instrument. Musical strings, depending on how they vibrate, produce different sounds; in a similar way, the vibrations of these strings of energy would be responsible for matter to exhibit different properties, consequently producing different kinds of particles, and eventually, different modes of existence.

Theoretical physicist Lisa Randall, whose work addresses our current understanding of the properties and interactions of matter, explains it so: "String theory's view of the fundamental nature of matter differs significantly from that of traditional particle physics. According to string theory, the most basic indivisible objects underlying all matter are strings—vibrating, one dimensional loops or segments of energy" (2005: 283). Following, she undermines any reductionist approach, explaining that these strings "are not made up of atoms which are in turn made up of electrons and nucleons which are in turn made up of quarks. In fact, exactly the opposite is true. These are fundamental strings, which means that everything, including electrons and quarks, consists of their oscillations" (*ibidem*). According to Randall, "String theory's radical hypothesis is that particles arise from the resonant oscillation modes of strings" (*ibidem*). This is a big step away from any previous theories within Western science. By referring to our previous example of musical strings, we can understand Randall's explanation: "Each and every particle corresponds to the vibrations of an underlying string, and the character of those vibrations determines the particle's properties. Because of the many ways in which strings can vibrate, a single string can give rise to many types of particle" (*ibidem*). The ontological agential relationality postulated by string theory is non-redeemable: matter is in relation to, and, at the same time, manifesting as, its vibrations. In other words, the strings (that is, matter at a subatomic level) are, in relation to these oscillations, being (they are vibrating) and also being with (the vibration constitutes them in their specific and differential characteristics).

Monism or pluralism? In ontological terms, Philosophical Posthumanism can be addressed as a pluralistic monism or a monistic pluralism. Neither monism nor pluralism by themselves could be feasible to sustain an ontology of the posthuman; both should be listed in order to disrupt the dualism one/many and thus avoid turning this discussion into the problem of the origins (which can be summarized in the question: is it a monism before being a pluralism, or a pluralism before being a monism?). The one is necessarily and constantly differentiating, and so it (they) is (are), at the same time, many. To understand this proposition, quantum notions such as the wave-particle duality, and the quantum entanglement, may be of help. *What is quantum entanglement?* The term "quantum entanglement" was coined by Schrödinger (1935b) to describe a specific connection between quantum systems, which occurs when particles that were interacting become separated, resulting in a pair which has to be described with reference to each other, as manifesting the same quantum mechanical description. *What is the wave-particle duality?* First proposed by Louis de Broglie (1892–1987) in 1924, the wave-particle duality[5] can be defined, in the words of physicist Lee Smolin, as "a principle of quantum theory according to which one can describe elementary particles as both particles and waves, depending on the context" (2001: 234). In other words, the context becomes crucial in the ways particles manifest; this behavior resonates with the dissolution of the strict division between subject and object, as well as between the human and the environment, as we have seen in Chapter 19. Such a scenario is in line with Karen Barad's relational ontology, which she considers the *conditio sine qua non* of her agential realism.[6] In Barad's words, "Agential realism resolves these issues in a way that is consistent with recent theoretical and experimental developments. Like other recent interpretations of the quantum theory, it is based on a relational ontology" (2007: 352).

Let's further explain this point by asking: *What kind of ontology does quantum physics suggest?* Quantum physics suggests a relational ontology. An interesting example of such a relationality can be seen in the observer effect, also known as the measurement problem,[7] which refers to the changes that the act of observing produces on a phenomenon, and which has demonstrated the inextricable relation between the "subject" and the "object," as well as the dynamic and pluralistic natureculture of matter. In the words of physicist Alastair Rae:

> Quantum physics leads to a rejection of determinism . . . so that we have to come to terms with a universe whose present state is not simply "the effect of its past" or "the cause of its future." Quantum theory tells us that nothing can be measured or observed without disturbing it, so that the role of the observer is crucial in understanding any physical process. (1986: 3)

Quantum physics annihilates the possibility of a strict dualism between the subject and the object, presenting them as relational and reciprocally constituting one another, in line with cognitive autopoiesis and perspectivism, as presented in Chapters 17 and 18.

What is reductionism? Before proceeding, let's clarify what we mean by reductionism. We can define reductionism as "the belief that phenomena and organisms are best understood by breaking them into smaller parts," as Vandana Shiva and Ingunn Moser put it in their anthology *Biopolitics* (1995: 286). *What is the problem with reductionism?* This view has many limits. As Shiva summarizes in the book's epilogue (which is entitled "Beyond Reductionism," as a statement of her position): "By reductionism we mean the belief that the world is made up of atomized fragments, which associate mechanistically to make larger systems: the fragments determine the system" (*ivi:* 267). A main downfall of this view is that "the internal relations are ignored in determining properties and processes" (*ibidem*). In fact, the intrinsic relationality of matter delegitimates any reductionist approach. When dealing with matter at a subatomic level, asking if these strings are its final foundational bits is not a feasible point, given that such a question is formulated on the assumption that matter can be actually reduced to a single entity. Theoretical physicist Leonard Susskind, one of the main proponents of string theory, goes straight to the point: "We seem to be dealing with a new kind of mathematical theory in which the traditional ideas of fundamental versus derived concepts is maddeningly elusive" (2005: 379). *What kind of posthumanist philosophical insights emerge out of string theory?* Such a view offers an alternative perspective on ancient human dilemmas, such as the search for the origins or the terms of causality: the fundamental and the derived can be reversed, in a materialist undoing of any fixed identity. We can thus understand why Posthumanism comfortably generates out of the hybrid, out of the cyborg: in the origin which has no origin (as we have previously seen, the cyborg is an hybrid term itself[8]). String theory, on one side, fully resonates with the posthumanist post-dualistic approach; on the other, it offers exciting and challenging inputs for a posthuman ontological reflection. In fact, Susskind locates such a non-derivable scenario in the "Landscape," which he describes as "a dreamscape in which, as we move about, bricks and houses gradually exchange their role. *Everything is fundamental, and nothing is fundamental.*[9] The answer depends on the region of the Landscape we are momentarily interested in" (*ibidem*). *What does Susskind mean by the "landscape"?* The notion of "Landscape" refers to all the possible configurations entailed by the physics hypothesis of the string theory, as Susskind explains it: "The Landscape is not a real place. Think of it as a list of all the possible designs of hypothetical universes" (381). We can think of the landscape as all the potential outcomes which may arise out of the generative power of the strings—here "power" should be understood in its Latin etymology as *potentia,* meaning both "power" and "possibility."

How is string theory related to the hypothesis of the multiverse? Ultimately, string theory asserts the hypothesis of a multiverse.[10] On one side, the math of string theory, in order to function, requires a distinct feature, which is extra-dimensions of space (Randall 2005; Bars et al. 2010), consequently advancing the hypothesis that this specific dimension is only one of the many occurring. On the other, scientific investigations on matter from the micro to the macro level of materialization, from quantum physics to the fields of cosmology and astrophysics, have recently arrived to the same hypothetical conclusion: this universe might be one of many. The hypothesis of the multiverse is inherently posthuman; it not only stretches any universe-centric perspective (problematizing the inclusive, but still centric, notion of a universe), but it materializes the dissolution of strict binaries, dualistic modes, and exclusivist approaches. This is why we shall conclude our historical and theoretical recollection on the posthuman with a reflection on the multiverse, which invites for a renegotiation of the border between the possible and the potential. Let's consider, for instance, how many crucial scientific theories and discoveries were at first considered impossible, and thus rejected, at the time they were first proposed. As biologist Thomas Henry Huxley[11] (1825–1895) stated, "History warns us, however, that it is the customary fate of new truths to begin as heresies and to end as superstitions" (1880: 549). A posthumanist perspective, to fully comply with a comprehensive approach, shall address the possibility of the possible, of the potential, and even of the "impossible,"[12] within its epistemological and ontological realms of inquiry.

The Multiverse

What is the multiverse? The multiverse is one of the most challenging hypothesis formulated by cosmologists and physicists in the last decades; it is the next step in the human revision of the cosmos, which historically first posed the Earth at its center (in the geocentric Ptolemaic system), then the Sun (with the heliocentric model of the Copernican revolution), to later realize that our solar system is part of a galaxy, and such a galaxy is one among millions of other galaxies. The multiverse represents both the ultimate decentralization of the human and the final deconstruction on any strict dualisms; this is why it needs a thorough inspection. We will divide this section in three parts. In the first part, we will present the notion of the multiverse as developed within the field of Western science; in the second part, we will analyze it from a philosophical perspective; in the third part, we will develop it into an original thought experiment, which may expand our ontological as well as existential understanding of Philosophical Posthumanism.

a. The Multiverse in Science

Before delving into its scientific implications, we shall note that, since the hypothesis of the multiverse is not supported by experimental evidence yet, it has been criticized for its lack of empirical testability and falsifiability (cf. Woit 2006, among others). Here, we should also clarify that the multiverse is not a homogeneous hypothesis, and it may apply to different types of proposals. To be more precise, as cosmologist Max Tegmark stated in the article "Many Worlds in Context" (2010), the multiverse "is not a theory, but a prediction of certain theories" (558). In this influential text, Tegmark incorporated the different views on the multiverse in four main levels.[1] We are going to present each of them following Tegmarks's original categorization in levels,[2] to then provide our own philosophical argument. We should also note that the references Tegmark uses for each level are strictly drawn from Western science, while other possible sources could be evaluated, such as the pluriversal (that is, worlds within worlds) worldviews of the shamanist and animistic traditions of East and South Asia,[3] among others. *What are the four main views of the multiverse?* Staying within Western science, these are the four levels proposed by Tegmark to summarize the history and the different meanings of the notion of the multiverse:

Level I: Regions Beyond Cosmic Horizon[4]

This level refers to the scientific evidence for the expansion of the universe, based on Edwin Hubble's discovery (1929),[5] which demonstrated that distant galaxies are moving away from ours at very high speeds. If this universe is infinitely expanding, there may exist another portion of it where, for instance, an exact duplicate of this world might have formed. (These types of multiverses would be characterized by the same laws of physics sustaining our world.)

Level II: Other Post-Inflation Bubbles[6]

This second level is based on the inflationary theory (Guth and Steinhardt 1984; Linde 1994), and specifically on eternal inflation (Linde 1986), according to which our Big Bang would be one of many: separate universes may spring up as bubbles of spacetime in an infinite and random formation of "bubble universes." (These types of multiverses could be characterized by very different laws of physics from the ones sustaining our universe, as by different manifestations of the same laws.)

Level III: The Many Worlds of Quantum Physics[7]

Within the field of quantum physics, the hypothesis of many-worlds[8] interpretation was first proposed by Hugh Everett (1930–82) in his PhD dissertation *Theory of the Universal Wave Function* (1956). In this scenario, every event is a branch point, and reality itself is seen as a branched tree; every possible quantum outcome is realized in parallel worlds, in a reinterpretation of Schrödinger's cat thought experiment. *What is Schrödinger's cat thought experiment?* Austrian physicist Erwin Schrödinger (1887–61) illustrated with this thought experiment (1935a) what he saw as the problematic application of quantum mechanics to everyday scenarios, presenting the case of an imaginary cat which may be both alive and dead, depending on a random event. According to Schrödinger, this was a paradox: a cat could not be both dead and alive at the same time. According to Everett, this was possible: a cat could be both dead and alive. In his hypothesis of many-worlds, a specific event could create a branch point and the consequent formation of different quantum outcomes: in one world, the cat would be dead; in another parallel world, the cat would be alive. (These types of multiverses would be characterized by the same laws of physics sustaining our world.)

Level IV: Other Mathematical Structures[9]

This type of multiverse includes all the mathematical structures which can be conceived, but not observed as physical realities, in our universe. (These types of multiverses would be characterized by entirely different sets of laws of physics than the ones sustaining our universe).

Is the notion of the multiverse posthuman? Even if the notion of the multiverse is inherently posthuman, all four levels in which Tegmark presents the current scientific perceptions of the multiverse are conceived through the Self/Others, here/there paradigm, in an approach which resonates with humanistic dualisms, based on the necessity of the Others as reverse mirrors of the Self. Let's analyze such aspects more in detail. On one side, these other universes are depicted to be so far that they will never be reached; on the other, they are investigated through the anthropocentric desire of postulating different worlds with "people with the same appearance, name and memories as you," to use Tegmark's words when describing Level I (as reported in note 4). Of all the possibilities which may be investigated, and among all the possible evolutionary outcomes which might take place in other universes, *why focus on the narcissistic projection that the human realm is flourishing somewhere?* This type of hope seems to resonate with the humanistic fascination for the uncanny,[10] defined by Sigmund Freud (1856–39) in his essay "The Uncanny" (1919), as "something which is secretly familiar" (245); in this text, he also reflects upon the notion of the double as "an insurance against the destruction of the ego" (235). The double is often contemplated as a possibility within the scientific literature related to the multiverse, and is at the very core of Everett's proposal (Level III), which focuses on the human-centric fascination with the idea of universes in which there might be other versions of "me," in a reinscription of the multiverse within the frame of assimilation, instead of the difference. Furthermore, Everett's branch-tree quantum scenario results in an overabundance of universes in which every single event which could have possibly happened did happen in some world. Such an approach introduces what we will define as the problem of overabundance, which is present in many scientific, as well as philosophical, views on the multiverse. In his article, Tegmark addresses this issue, which he defines as "the wastefulness worry"; his answers, though are not fully exhaustive from a posthumanist perspective as he states:

> Why should nature be so wasteful and indulge in such opulence as an infinity of different worlds? Yet this argument can be turned around to argue for a multiverse. What precisely would nature be wasting? Certainly not space, mass or atoms—the uncontroversial Level I multiverse already contains an infinite amount of all three, so who cares if nature wastes some more? (2010: 576)

To which, he adds, "The real issue here is the apparent reduction in simplicity. A skeptic worries about all the information necessary to specify all those unseen worlds. But an entire ensemble is often much simpler than one of its members" (*ibidem*). There are different problems with this kind of approach. Let's take a close look.

Why "the wastefulness worry," in the hypothesis of the multiverse, cannot be easily dismissed? First of all, Tegmark refers to "nature" as something separate and unrelated to humans ("*who cares* if *nature* wastes some more [space/mass/ atoms]"), while, as we have previously seen, precisely the opposite is accurate.[11] Furthermore, his approach toward an unlimited overabundance of matter, energy, and spacetime resonates with the wasteful approach of capitalistic societies toward goods and products, located in a sociopolitical perspective which does not perceive nature as relational and integrated, but as separated and endlessly resourceful, no matter what. This type of attitude can be seen as a projection, an extension, and an expansion of the anthropocenic[12] paradigm. The theoretical hypothesis of the unlimited resources of nature, and its wasteful opulence, in creating an infinity of worlds, is in tune with the current management, and actual (ab)use, of non-sustainable resources by some economically advantaged human societies, leading planet Earth to an ecological collapse. In the era of the Anthropocene, we have learned that natural resources are not unlimited, and that human actions have a direct impact on the environment: this is why humans are now recognized as "geological forces" (Chakrabarty 2009), as we have seen in Chapter 19. Going back to our critical reading of Tegmark's classification, both the problem of overabundance and the ego-driven desire for the double are present in Level IV, according to which any conceivable mathematical structure would be related to an actual universe, as Tegmark states: "The level IV universes are completely disconnected and need to be considered together only for predicting your future, since 'you' may exist in more than one of them" (576). The peculiarity of Level II, for instance, is characterized by the impossibility of any type of relation between the other universes and this universe: they would be located so far that, in Tegmark's words, "you would never get there even if you traveled at the speed of light forever" (the full passage is reported in note 6). Even if this level may describe actual modes of existence, it stands as an unreachable domain. More in general, we can state that all four levels of the multiverse re-propose the strict dichotomies: this world/the other worlds; this universe/the other universes; here/there, where "there" is usually considered as far as we can imagine, and so ultimately unreachable. The hypothesis of the multiverse is very promising from a posthuman standpoint; and still, the current scientific discussion may benefit from a post-humanist, post-anthropocentric, and post-dualistic critique.

b. The Multiverse in Philosophy

What about the notion of the multiverse in the field of philosophy? We will now present a philosophical overview on the notion of the multiverse,[13] which will show how, on many levels, this set of reflections share many points in common with the scientific perspective previously presented, such as the tendency to fall into humanistic assimilations. *Who coined the term?* The term "multiverse" was coined by philosopher William James (1842–1910) in his essay "Is Life Worth Living?" (1896) where he stated: "Visible nature is all plasticity and indifference, a moral *multiverse*,[14] as one might call it, and not a moral universe" (26). Within the domain of philosophical inquiry, the notion of possible worlds is traceable in the work of Gottfried Wilhelm von Leibniz (1646–1716), and specifically in his "Essays of Theodicy on the Goodness of God, the Freedom of Man and the Origin of Evil" (1710), where he claimed that the actual world is the best of all possible worlds.[15] Such a view, which does not necessarily imply the actual existence of other worlds, has antecedents in the reflection on possible worlds found in medieval[16] theories of modality (Knuuttila 1993): within this frame, the idea of possible worlds can be found in the works of Al-Ghazali[17] (1058–1111), Averroes[18] (1126–98), Fakhr al-Din al-Razi[19] (1149–1209), and John Duns Scotus[20] (1267–1308).

What about contemporary philosophy? Within contemporary philosophy, the first thinker to fully revisit such a subject was David Lewis (1941–2001) who in

On the Plurality of Worlds (1986) advocated for a modal realism, as he claimed: "I advocate a thesis of plurality of worlds, or *modal realism*, which holds that our world is but one world among many. . . . There are so many other worlds, in fact, that absolutely *every* way that a world could possibly be is a way that some world *is*" (2). Modal realism does not solve the issues we have detected in the scientific hypothesis of the multiverse, more specifically, the problem of overabundance and the ontological dichotomy: this world/other worlds. In Lewis's view, not only "*every* way that a world could possibly be is a way that some world *is*"—we will come back to this point—but these different worlds have no relation with each other, neither spatial, temporal nor causal. As he states, "The worlds are something like remote planets; except that most of them are much bigger than mere planets, and they are not remote. Neither are they nearby. They are not at any spatial distance whatever from here. They are not at any temporal distance whatever from now" (*ibidem*). The following passage is particularly expressive of such a polarized approach, as Lewis emphasizes: "They are isolated: there are no spatiotemporal relations at all between things that belong to different worlds. Nor does anything that happens in one world cause anything to happen at another. Nor do they overlap" (*ibidem*). Lewis's proposition of a series of unrelated worlds that have no influence on each other[21]—which can be seen as a strict form of modal essentialism[22]—brings this question to mind: *If these worlds do not share anything in common, why should we even bother with them?* Instead, we shall ask the opposite question: *If other words exist, do these worlds share something in common?* We are going to reflect on this question through a thought experiment, which we can refer to as the "posthuman multiverse."

What is the posthuman multiverse? In this thought experiment, we will propose a posthuman interpretation of the multiverse genealogically located in the wave opened by the notion of the rhizome (Deleuze and Guattari 1987). This view, as we will see in the next subsection, does not consider any possible world as an actual one, simply because any "possible" world means, more specifically, any possible world which humans can postulate (through their imagination, mathematics and so on), and it would resolve into a form of ontological anthropocentric solipsism.[23] The main differences we are stressing from Lewis's are the following: (1) An *indefinite number* of possible words does not imply *any* possible worlds. 2) All these possible worlds are not completely separated from each other, but are in a *material relation with each other*. We have already argued on point 1, in what we have previously defined as the problem of overabundance. Let's thus delve into point 2. Strictly speaking, the notion of a posthuman multiverse proposes the hypothesis of a multiverse in which the same energy/matter constituting our dimension would be also constituting other dimensions. A specific vibrational domain would be keeping each dimension intact. For instance, a radio can simultaneously tune to many different channels, because each cable is transmitting at a different frequency; similarly, our dimension would be materializing at a specific range of vibrations, in the larger frame of the multiverse, where, speculatively, different vibrations of matter could give rise to an indefinite number of material dimensions.

c. A Thought Experiment: The Posthuman Multiverse

Editorial Note. Please note that in this section we are going to switch the authorial perspective from the first plural ("we") to the first person ("I"). The reason is that, while this thought experiment is not necessarily representative for the posthumanist community as a whole, the posthuman multiverse is a promising notion which may spark original insights to the posthuman debate.

Why a thought experiment? The multiverse, although intrinsically nonhuman-centric, is often reduced to another arena where one projects human-centric wishes and assumptions. Instead, I asked myself what would a posthumanist approach to the multiverse bring to the discussion. I thus reflected on it by not counting on any essentialism, polarity, or strict dualism, but relying on a hybrid, mediated, and process-ontological perspective. I will now present this interpretation both as a thought experiment, which may expand a speculative perception of the self, and a material hypothesis, which may conceal a possible physics outfit of the multiverse. Within Tegmark's classification, what I am proposing shares some aspects with Level III but with some crucial differences. I will call it a posthuman multiverse, by referring to the philosophical inputs which inspired this reflection.

What does this thought experiment entail? The thought experiment of the posthuman multiverse is based on the deconstruction of the Self/Others paradigm. It entails that matter, while constituting this universe, would also be actualizing an indefinite number of other universes, in a process of both relationality and autonomy. What I am suggesting is that if we radically deconstruct the separation of the Self and the Others, we can think of the multiverse as happening right now, here, through our own bodies, through the same matter which is composing this universe. The difference which would allow us, for instance, to perceive a similar mode of existence, could be seen, in physics terms, as a specific vibrational range. More than parallel dimensions, ontically separated from each other, the posthuman understanding of the multiverse would be envisioned as generative nets of material possibilities simultaneously happening and coexisting, corresponding to specific vibrations of the strings,[24] in a material understanding of the dissolution of the strict dualism one/many. The identity of one dimension would be maintained under the conditions of a specific vibrational range, and by the material relations to other dimensions, in a multiplication of situated affinities and convergences.

What does this thought experiment mean in relation to "you"? In the speculative frame of the posthuman multiverse, the strings would be simultaneously establishing different universes related to specific vibrational properties. In such a scenario, the self would be constituting the self by constituting (and by being constituted by) an indefinite number of "others." Let's think of this through a radical thought experiment. Before we do so, let's ease into the conversation by asking the question: *Who am I?* If we think of ourselves some years ago, we can recognize some patterns and some differences: we probably look somehow different, but we may still like some of the same food, or we may still have some of the same dreams and aspirations. We can mostly agree that I am who I am right now; I am also related to whom I was yesterday and to who I am going to be tomorrow: all these "me" cannot be approached in separation. Now let's enter our thought experiment by adding another layer. *What if the matter that constitutes "you" is constituting "others" in different dimensions?* What if this co-generating was not random, but connected to specific energetic fields that were trans-dimensional, that is, they exceeded this specific dimension? In other words, *what if our way of existing had multidimensional ripple effects?* If quantum strings can manifest different properties depending on different vibrations, they could manifest different properties "simultaneously", given that time, according to the theory of general relativity (Einstein 1916), cannot be accounted independently, but as a dimension of spacetime.[25] Different from many of the scientific and philosophical proposals previously presented, such a view does not support the hypothesis of many versions of "you" existing in different dimensions, since "you" would be a distinct combination of this specific vibrational domain which would be constantly changing, manifesting new symbiotic energetic alliances. This type of scenario does not entail a dualism between the strings and their vibrations; the two terms are inseparable: the strings are manifesting in a specific mode because they are tuned to a definite vibration, as much as definite vibrations are manifesting through the specific tuning of the strings. Every dimension can be seen as an autopoietic mode of existence which, even though it may perceive itself as autonomous, is intrinsically connected to many other modes of existences, but again, not necessarily directly related to all modes, since, within a rhizomatic perspective, such a relationality may be established indirectly, as we will see in the next section. Matter is relational; we can think of different modes of existence as relating through specific nodes—to use a terminology developed within the Network Theory,[26] and to refer, more in general, to the Actor/Network Theory (Latour 1987, 2005; Law and Hassard 1999). The question of how relationality is established is of key importance to posthumanist ontology. In this regard, a philosophical notion which is of help, is the rhizome.

What is a rhizome? This term, which originates in botany, refers to "a continuously growing horizontal underground stem which puts out lateral shoots and adventitious roots at intervals," as defined by the *Oxford Dictionary*.[27] To bring some vivid examples, we can think of the ginger roots, the turmeric roots, or the roots of the lotus. One specific characteristic of the rhizome is its horizontality: any part of it may generate new plants, as the rhizome is the horizontal stem of a plant which may branch out roots, and shoots, from its nodes. *Why is notion of the rhizome relevant to Philosophical Posthumanism?* The botanical rhizome was elaborated into a philosophical concept by Gilles Deleuze (1925–95) and Félix Guattari (1930–92). Their pivotal text *A Thousand Plateaus: Capitalism and Schizophrenia* (1987), which is of great relevance to the development of a philosophical posthumanist ontology, brought to the discussion not only the concept of the rhizome, but also other relevant notions such as, just to mention a few: multiplicity,[28] assemblage, connection, nomadicity, and heterogeneity.[29] One passage which is particularly inspiring in this respect can be found in Section 8 "1874: Three Novellas, or 'What Happened?'". In this quote, each becoming is conceived as a rhizome of lines; some lines are specific to a species, some are pressed "from outside"; others can be deliberately invented:

> Individual or group, we are traversed by lines, meridians, geodesics, tropics, and zones marching to different beats and differing in nature. We said that we are composed of lines, three kinds of lines. Or rather, of bundles of lines, for each kind is multiple. . . . For some of these lines are imposed on us from outside, at least in part. Others sprout up somewhat by chance, from a trifle, why we will never know. Others can be invented, drawn, without a model and without chance: we must invent our lines of flight. . . . There are different animal lines of flight: each species, each individual, has its own. . . . The lines are constantly

crossing, intersecting for a moment, following one another. . . . It is an affair of cartography. They compose us, as they compose our map. They transform themselves and may even cross over into one another. Rhizome. (202–03)

The notion of the rhizome, as delineated by Deleuze and Guattari, was particularly significant with the rise of the internet and the development of linkability. We can now understand why.[30] Think, for instance, when surfing the net. You may start by googling something specific, such as "habitable planets in our solar system," and ending up two hours later reading on something which seems completely unrelated, such as biodegradable glitter, or how to make kombucha. If you wonder how that could have possibly happened, you now have the answer. This is the power of the rhizome and the significance of all the lines that are passing through it, such as: the algorithms used in Google search engine, your stream of consciousness, advertisements, which country, and what machine, you are connecting from, and so on.

What is the difference between the metaphor of the rhizome and metaphor of the multiverse? Even though the rhizome can be traced as an important antecedent for a posthuman approach to the multiverse, philosophically, the two notions cannot be assimilated. In the view of Deleuze and Guattari, for instance, the rhizome does not support the presence of a structure. They state, "It is certain that they [the lines] have nothing to do with a structure, which is never occupied by anything more than points and positions, by arborescences, and which always form a closed system, precisely in order to prevent escape" (203). A posthuman multiverse does not necessarily exclude the co-presence of a structure, but approaches it in a process-ontological non-hierarchical way. For instance, if we think about the material possibility of interpermeating dimensions[31] constituted by quantum strings, the specific vibrational range which would allow the coherence of each dimension could be seen as a type of vibrational structure, even if not a definitive nor an essential one. Such vibrations, according to the string theory, constitute and are constituted by the strings, so that the vibrational structure itself is in a mode of becoming: the structure is what is constituted by the structure, with no separation. In theoretical terms, philosophical posthumanist ontology can be approached as a pluralistic monism or a monistic pluralism.

What are humans, within a posthumanist multiverse? Humans, and any other manifestations of being, in the frame of the multiverse revisited through the rhizome, can be perceived as nodes of becoming in a material network; such becomings operate as technologies of the multiverse, as modes of revealing, to go back to Heidegger, thus re-accessing the ontological and existential significations of technology itself. The technologies of the self are also significant here, and can be related to those lines that we are inventing, to re-access Deleuze and Guattari through Foucault.[32] Such technologies become crucial when postulating posthuman normative ethics and pragmatics, which, within the frame of a posthuman multiverse, cannot be separated from ontology. On some level, we are already talking in ethical terms when we are conceiving humanity (and, more in general, existence) as a material network: the way we inhabit our dimension, what we eat, what we think, how we behave, who we relate to, creates part of the network of who and what we are; this is not a disembodied network, but a material one, whose agency exceeds the political, social, and biological human realms. In such a frame, the multiverse can be perceived not only as an ontology, but also as a path of self-discovery, once the self has been recognized as the others within, ultimately turning into a relational intra-activity of ontic manifestations, in agreement with Barad. The recognition of the self in such an extended network of pluri-dimensional magnitude bears ethical, social, and political implications, not to mention existential ones. In order to understand this point more vividly, let's play a game of imagination. Imagine that one day you realize that every single action you have ever taken, every thought you have ever had; every dream you have ever dreamed; every word you have ever spoken, have been affecting and effecting the materialization of existence, in the multiverse. In light of this thought experiment *How did you perceive your life performance, by approaching it extensively, with all of its multidimensional ramifications exposed?* It is time to talk about posthuman agency.

What is posthuman agency? Posthuman agency can be envisioned in modalities of existence which employ strategies of encounter and relationality, rather than assimilation. This complies with a posthuman type of agency where not only the human and nonhuman realms bear signification, but also the modalities of existence. A posthuman agency, which is necessarily related to the understanding of Posthumanism as a praxis, can be perceived as an existential awareness which exceeds the notion of a one-dimensional becoming. The human, within this type of framework, turns into a network of energies, alliances, matter, and perspectives, relating to any other forms of existence, allied through different material outcomes, and possibly, in different quantum dimensions, in a radical onto-existential re-signification of being. In this type of scenario, the final deconstruction between immanence and transcendence takes place, inviting the situated actors to envision their own network of both alliances and filiations beyond, and at the same time including, any specific space-time complexion. The posthuman has thus reached the final deconstruction, revealing an approach on existence which, although situated in the recognition of its own autopoietic modes, does not comply with any ontological dualism, assimilation, centralization, or presumption, relationally expanding its own material and semiotic network of alliances and significations, and ultimately, recognizing itself as a monistic pluralist (or a pluralistic monist) form of becoming.

Interlude 3

In the third part of this book, we have addressed two main questions related to Philosophical Posthumanism: *What is post-anthropocentrism? And, what is post-dualism?* To understand the notion of post-anthropocentrism, we have reflected upon the current geological era of the Anthropocene. In our research on the posthuman, we have first presented the deconstructive project, relating it to its necessary inquiry into the notion of the human. Then, we have moved toward the "bio" realm, investigating life from a biological perspective and addressing important concepts to the posthuman debate, such as: speciesism, autopoiesis, and sympoiesis. Our reflection on bioethics has led us to a discussion on future evolutions of posthumanities; in this type of inquiry, evolution itself has been investigated as a technology of existence. Following, we have accessed the third level of reflection. To understand post-dualism thoroughly, we have entered the realm of ontology, which comprehends the human as a question as well as life as a question, but exceeds them both. In this part, we have delved more specifically into the processes of materialization, asking the question: *How does matter materialize?* We have introduced the scientific and philosophical notion of the multiverse, which we have further expanded into an original thought experiment on the posthuman multiverse, to emphasize posthumanist ontology as a monistic pluralism and a pluralistic monism. We have thus accessed the final boundary, the one between the Self and the Others, taking the posthumanist post-dualistic approach to the domain of ontological existentialism.

It is time to turn this historical, genealogical, and theoretical journey into pluralistic envisioning; it is time to celebrate the end of this book and the blooming of the posthuman community. Let's cheer with a glass of kombucha, if you wish. *Why may kombucha be a suited option for a posthumanist celebration?* The SCOBY is the symbiotic culture of bacteria and yeast which is used for brewing kombucha. Also referred to as a "mother," this mixed culture grows syntrophically, that is, one species lives off the products of another species. In this process of interdependence, the nutritional habitat (which is sweetened black, or green, tea), once fermented, turns into kombucha. This beverage is fun (it can be sparkling and flavored), healthy (it contains probiotics), and affordable (it can be easily made at home). This trivial example is not that trivial. Existing as a post-humanist implies an ethical attitude which may include a personal reflection on dietary habits, for instance. *What does "ethics" mean?* In order to understand this point more clearly, it is important to reflect upon the term "ethics," which derives from ancient Greek *"ethos"*:[1] originally meaning "accustomed place,"[2] it refers more generally to "habits, customs." In this sense, we can reflect upon the ethical spaces we inhabit, both from an individual and from a species perspective, which manifest in our daily habits of existence, with their diffuse consequences and ethical implications. Let's then ask the question: *How can we exist, as posthumanists?*

Concluding Celebration

Existing, as a Posthumanist

It is time to celebrate Philosophical Posthumanism as a regenerating wave of critical thinking, an emergent philosophical approach which is contributing to a radical revision of social norms and existential habits. It is time to ask the focal question: *How can we exist, as posthumanists?* Let's stage the celebration of Philosophical Posthumanism by asking a series of urgent questions which will bring about exciting answers. First of all, *can we be posthuman now?* Yes. According to Philosophical Posthumanism, we can already be posthuman now.[1] In the philosophical posthumanist debate, the posthuman not only is addressed as a potential evolutionary step (or leap) of the human,[2] but is approached, more specifically, as a shift in perspectives, which touches upon many levels of inquiry: from the onto-epistemological level to the ethical and the sociopolitical, the biotechnological, and the existential ones. *How can we become posthuman?* According to Philosophical Posthumanism, in order to become posthuman, we need to reflect on our location in this material, dynamic, and responsive process, that is, existence. In so doing, a key move is becoming aware of our implicit and explicit biases and privileges, as they can only limit our existential perception. To reaccess our location as open networks requires undergoing a radical deconstruction of closed identities, including the human identity.

Can humans be posthuman? Yes, indeed. Belonging to the human species does not necessarily entail an anthropocentric standpoint. Philosophical Posthumanism, in fact, can be approached as a post-humanism, a post-anthropocentrism, and a post-dualism. In this book, we have followed a gradual process, dismantling the hypotheses of human supremacy and human exceptionality across three levels. We have first deconstructed the historical, social, and linguistic notion of the human, coming to the conclusion that the human is not one, but many. As a *post-humanism*, Philosophical Posthumanism invites for an epistemological move: from generalized universalism to situated perspectivism. From a sociopolitical standpoint, it sustains a shift from categorical multiculturalism (based on the dualism "us"/"them") to pluralism and diversity, by emphasizing the human as a plural notion: from human to humans, with an "-s" (all humans are different, and still, related).

What does it mean to be posthuman, in relation to other species? We have then expanded the analysis to a second level of deconstruction, investigating the bio-domain from a post-anthropocentric perspective, highlighting that the line between human animals and nonhuman animals is not definitive; for instance, humans share much of their DNA with nonhuman animals. Furthermore, the great diversity of nonhuman animals cannot be classified, and simplified, under one category "nonhuman," which only suits the necessity of the hierarchical dichotomy: human/nonhuman, according to which the human is exceptional and superior to the nonhuman. As a *post-anthropocentrism*, Philosophical Posthumanism allows for a relocation which is aware of speciesism and of the devastating effects of anthropocentric habits, thus marking a passage from technology to eco-technology; from justice to multispecies justice; from the generalized self-denomination as "humans" to the more precise biological nomenclature of "human animals." This book highlights the urgency to develop the posthuman turn into practices of existence which fully embrace a post-anthropocentric sensitivity, alongside a post-humanistic perception of the human species, in the broader frame of post-dualism.

Lastly, we have reflected on the physical structure of matter, destabilizing any reductionist approach by accessing existence from a non-universe-centric perspective; we have thus embraced the physics hypothesis of the multiverse as a thought experiment which expands our ontological awareness. As a *post-dualism*, Philosophical Posthumanism reveals a necessary move from individuality to relationality, marking the passage from "human animals" to embodied posthuman networks, performing as nomadic sites of potentialities and actualizations. Philosophical Posthumanism can be counted as a theoretical philosophy of the difference, which demystifies any ontological polarization through the postmodern practice of deconstruction. Therefore, we have defined it, at the modal level, as a post-centrism and a post-exclusivism: a "post" which is constantly opening possibilities and does not comply with stationary hierarchical views. This epistemic opening does not rely on assimilations to the same, but on acknowledgments of diversity, in tune with evolutionary processes, which manifest in dynamics of diversification. In this sense, evolution can be addressed as a technology of existence: *"physis"* ("nature" in Greek) and *"techne"* are co-constitutive domains.

Why is technology relevant to the discussion on Philosophical Posthumanism? The ontological dimension of technology is a crucial node when it comes to a correct understanding of the posthuman. While the transhumanist emphasis on the technological domain risks creating a new exceptionalism (that of the artificial, virtual, or robotic element), the opening of the posthuman, according to Philosophical Posthumanism, is not hierarchical: the dualism human/machine is not simply altered, but rather structurally deconstructed. Feminist and post-colonial studies, among others, have shown the racist and sexist framework in which the discourse on "techne" has been historically articulated. One of the main risks run by humans in approaching artificial intelligence through the anthropomorphic paradigm consists in turning the robotic difference into a stigma for new forms of exclusions, based on how far this difference can be positioned with respect to the hegemonic norm of the human, which is based on antropocentric values. To osmose with the robo-ontology, humans have to first perform a radical deconstruction of the human as a fixed notion, emphasizing instead its dynamic and constantly evolving side and celebrating the differences that inhabit the human species itself.

Is this the era of Philosophical Posthumanism? Philosophical Posthumanism is the philosophy of our age. The posthumanization of society is happening. Even if anthropocentric and dichotomic tendencies are still regarded as the norm, a growing number of beings are becoming aware for the need of a paradigm shift, and are thus revisiting old concepts and new values from a different perspective, bringing together post-humanist, post-anthropocentric, and post-dualistic insights. In this sense, Philosophical Posthumanism can be understood as a philosophical approach which suits the geological time of the Anthropocene: in the posthumanist perspective, the ecological dimension is not separated from the technological one, and technology is not reduced to its technical endeavors, opening the discussion to the technologies of existence. *What are the fields of investigation of Philosophical Posthumanism?* The fields of investigation of Philosophical Posthumanism are broad; they include bioethics and futures studies, but do not resolve in them. In the context of contemporary thought, Philosophical Posthumanism represents a promising approach to reflect on the present, on the past, and on possible futures without techno-centric or linear presumptions; this is reconciled with a vision of the posthuman in which not only human, ahuman, and nonhuman actants are characterized by agency,[3] but also modes of existence. Posthuman agency is extensive and diffuse; it can be traced in the modes of existence that employ strategies of encounter, recognition, and relationality, rather than hierarchical attitudes, rigid dualistic models, and assimilative techniques. This level of awareness sparks the posthuman in our daily practices of living. Once we access ourselves as open networks, we can perceive, more clearly, how our impact, effects, and affects on this planet are broad and extensive, manifesting in entangled, subtle, and diffuse ways; this is a crucial step toward the intention of existing as a posthumanist, because, in this understanding, the separation between theory and practice is no longer sustainable.

Is Philosophical Posthumanism a praxis? Yes, Philosophical Posthumanism is praxis: acting is, also, intra-acting; thinking is, also, "intra-thinking."[4] This approach expands our perception of existence beyond the self-imposed limits of the human in the strict sense of the term. Humans, in this scenario, recognize themselves as embodied networks of energies, alliances, and filiations, situated, and at the same time, beyond their spatio-temporal specificity, intra-connected to other forms of existence through an indefinite number of material synergies and possible dimensions. In this radical re-signification of being, the final deconstruction between immanence and transcendence takes place. Philosophical Posthumanism offers precious insights to relate not only to the singularitarian openness of the possibilities contemplated within the contemporary developments of science and biotechnologies, but also to the ontological potentials following the discoveries and hypotheses postulated within the field of physics. Posthumanism is an empirical philosophy of mediation, which offers a reconciliation of existence in its broadest sense: matter is vibrating energy. Posthumanism can be perceived as an existential awareness that exceeds the notion of flat ontologies, by accepting the challenge of the physics hypothesis of the multiverse. Humans, and any other manifestation of being, are approached as nodes of multiversal becoming in material networks; such becomings function as modes of biological, technological, and existential revealing. In the posthuman ontic framework of pluralistic monism, or monistic pluralism, any manifestation of existence is connected to (some form of) alterity (*monistic character*), but cannot be assimilated or reduced to it (*pluralistic character*). In this kind of scenario, every sort of exceptionalist presumption or centric prejudice represents an irredeemable obstacle to the material fluidity, and semiotic possibilities, of these networks. The posthuman thus tunes in with the "pre-"human: in this broad sense of multiversal rhizomacies, we have always been posthuman.

Why Philosophical Posthumanism? After this radical deconstruction of the human, the proposal could be to abandon the term in its entirety. *Is it time to say goodbye to the human?* Not yet. On some level, it is a matter of negotiating the sentimental field with regard to a known term, a familiar concept: an effect and an affect—in short, a recognition. Currently, most humans would recognize themselves under the "human" label. It seems that the era of the "post" without "human" is not ripe yet. This is the historical era of the "posthuman," which is not (just) a cultural revolution nor a natural evolution; rather, a naturalcultural co-evolution that may bring the posthuman era to an eventual integral *epoché*, sustained by a socio-physiological lightening from the weighty baggage of prevaricating strategies and non-acknowledging identity tactics. Philosophical Posthumanism must be rooted in an extensive critical account of what it means to be human, providing a strategic *terminus a quo* from which imagining posthumanities which call into question the traditional hegemonic discourse, which has historically dismissed the value of the difference, in consequent processes of discrimination and homogenization.

It is time to bring the three aspects of Philosophical Posthumanism together and clarify why we do need them all. Even if post-humanistic and post-anthropocentric social performances may eventually overcome some forms of discrimination, such as racism, sexism, and speciesism, if we do not embrace post-dualism and critically address, and deconstruct, rigid forms of dualistic identity-formation practices, other forms of discrimination will consistently continue to arise. We can think, for instance, of discrimination against future posthumanities, as in the case of the progenies of those humans who may migrate to space in the near future, and whose biology, and technology, may adapt, generation after generation, to conditions in space, eventually evolving into different species. We can think of discrimination against "designer babies"; and *vice versa*, we can think of discrimination against humans who were not genetically "enhanced"—for instance, a society based on genetic discrimination is portrayed in the sci-fi movie *Gattaca* (1997). We can think of discrimination against intelligent machines by (some) humans; and also, *vice versa*, we can think of discrimination against humans by (some) intelligent machines, as in the case of AI takeover scenarios. This is why it is extremely important to take into account post-dualism as part of the philosophical posthumanist approach. According to post-dualism, the posthumanist radical deconstruction shall not assert any type of absolute dualism, assimilation, or centralization. More specifically, post-dualism emphasizes how traditional strategies of identity-formation, routinely based on essentialist dichotomies, must be addressed, deconstructed, and constantly revised. Philosophical Posthumanism criticizes the need to establish symbolic essentialized "Others"; instead, it recognizes the human as the others within.

How can alterity be within the self? Let's answer this question by providing some evocative examples. In fact, "we" are constantly changing; we are processes; we are like oceans in their vast comprehensiveness. For instance, think of yourself one day ago: how did you look, what were your dreams and perspectives; who were your friends? Let's step back five years ago: how did you look, what were your dreams and perspectives; who were your friends? And if you were to go back fifteen years ago, can you still remember how you looked, what your dreams and perspectives were, and who your friends were? These three versions of "you" (one day ago, five years ago, and fifteen years ago) are different on many levels, and still, they all constitute who you are now. The ways "we" think and communicate is the result of unlimited interactions with other human and nonhuman beings. "We" are (also) our gut microbiota, but "we" do not think of "them" as such, most of the times. The food "we" eat literally becomes part of our bodies. The environment "we" inhabit has a direct impact on the epigenetic regulation of our gene expression, and so on. We are like oceans, but we often do not think of us in these extended and dynamic ways. Philosophical Posthumanism offers a theoretical invitation to think openly, in a genealogical relocation of humanity within multiversality and alterity within the self. Philosophical Posthumanism brings a radical shift which can apply to many different levels of comprehension, from the personal outlook to the prospect of the species. Its contribution to the planetary vision is urgent, critical, and, at the same time, regenerative—an anomalous wave[5] in the history of philosophy.

Notes

Introduction

1 This book is an expansion on the topics first elaborated in my article
"Posthumanism, Transhumanism, Antihumanism, Metahumanism, and
New Materialisms: Differences and Relations" (2014c).

2 The term "cyborg," coined in 1960 by Manfred Clynes and Nathan Kline, refers to a
being constituted by both biological and artificial parts (Clynes and Kline 1960).

3 The cyborg does not stand in an original myth, as Haraway affirms: "In a sense, the
cyborg has no origin story in the Western sense. . . . An origin story in the 'Western,'
humanist sense depends on the myth of original unity" (1985: 51). We will come
back to this point in Chapter 22.

4 Note that the term "nature-culture" as an hybrid of both natural and cultural
characteristics can be already found, for instance, in Latour 1991. Here, I am using
the neologism "natureculture" (without the hyphen) as specifically developed by
Donna Haraway (2003), to express that nature is already cultural, and *vice versa*,
thus avoiding the simplification or essentialization of each term.

Chapter 1

1 The term "cyborg" was coined in 1960 by Manfred Clynes and Nathan Kline, and refers
to a being constituted by both biological and artificial parts (Clynes and Kline 1960).

2 Yet, there is no enough data available to determine the long-term side effects of such
implants on humans.

3 On the relation between identity and technology, it is interesting to observe the
development of the thought of Sherry Turkle, one of the pioneers in focusing on the
sociology and psychology of the growing impact of virtuality on the constitution
of human identity. We can note this development in her published work. In *The
Second Self: Computers and the Human Spirit* (1984), she pointed out how computers
cannot be seen as external tools, but are part of the social and personal life of their
users. In *Life on the Screen: Identity in the Age of the Internet* (1995), she debated that
computers affect the ways humans see themselves as humans. Lastly, in her work
Alone Together: Why We Expect More from Technology and Less from Each Other
(2011), she argues that social media represent more of an illusion of companionship
rather than authentic communication.

4 The technologies of the self, that is, the methods and techniques through which human beings constitute themselves (Foucault 1988), are a crucial notion for the posthuman; we will delve into this aspect in Chapter 12.

5 As Katherine Hayles, in her influential book *How We Became Posthuman: Virtual Bodies in Cybernetics, Literature and Informatics* (1999), has stated:

> The thirty million Americans who are plugged into the Internet increasingly engage in virtual experiences enacting a division between the material body that exits on one side of the screen and the computer simulacra that seem to create a space inside the screen. Yet for millions more, virtuality is not even a cloud on the horizon of their everyday worlds. Within a global context, the experience of virtuality becomes more exotic by several orders of magnitude. It is a useful corrective to remember that 70 percent of the world's population has never made a phone call. (20)

6 Some interesting points in common can be traced with the path of the middle way (the path of moderation between extremes), as taught by Buddhism.

7 Vandana Shiva's environmental activism, for instance, is supported by a body of thoughts which shares a lot in common with a posthumanist approach. In *Monocultures of the Mind: Perspectives on Biodiversity and Biotechnology* (1993), Shiva presents traditional knowledge systems as major contributions to the understanding of biodiversity, ecological sustainability, and naturalcultural diversity, as she states:

> The main threat to living with diversity comes from the habit of thinking in terms of monocultures; from what I have called "Monocultures of the Mind." Monocultures of the mind make diversity disappear from perception, and consequently from the world. The disappearance of diversity is also a disappearance of alternatives .... Alternatives exist, but are excluded. Their inclusion requires a context of diversity. Shifting to diversity as a mode of thought, a context of action, allows multiple choices to emerge. (5)

8 Think, for instance, of the assemblage as an ontological framework, as developed by Deleuze and Guattari (1980).

9 As Michel Foucault has clearly underlined in *The Order of Things: An Archeology of the Human Sciences* (1966; Engl. Transl. 1970): "[the human science] appeared when man constituted himself in Western culture as both that which must be conceived of and what is to be known" (345).

10 To be intended, specifically, in a nomadic way (Braidotti 1994).

11 Hannah Arendt (1906–75), in *The Human Condition* (1958), evocatively wrote: "It is highly unlikely that we, who can know, determine, and define the natural essences of all things surrounding us, which we are not, should ever be able to do the same for ourselves—this would be like jumping over our own shadows (10)." Consequently, we could define this self-awareness as a recognition of the unredeemable presence of the "shadows," to use Arendt's expression.

12 We are going to come back to this point in Chapter 26.
13 This practice cannot be done once and for all, but it should be constantly
     re-enacted. We will come back to this aspect, specifically in Chapters 6 and 12.

Chapter 2

1 The term was coined by Jacques Derrida (1930–2004) in *Of Grammatology* (1967),
    as a personalized translation of *Destruktion*, to be found in Martin Heidegger's
    Being and Time (1927). Derrida's semiotic deconstruction of the binary oppositions
    which sustain the constitution of the text can be traced as one of the genealogical
    sources of Posthumanism, as will be noted in Chapter 6.
2 We will come back to this point in Part 2, where the notion of the human will be
    explained, more specifically, in its Western, white, male, ableist, and hegemonic
    connotations.
3 That is, the human at the top—think, for instance, of the Great Chain of Beings, as
    we will see in Chapter 18.
4 Such a genealogical location of the posthuman is already pointed out by William
    Spanos in his pioneer text *End Of Education: Toward Posthumanism*, published in
    1993.
5 The subject historically formulating the Discourse was supposed to be objective
    and universal, but it finally appeared in its embodied vestiges as Western, white,
    male, heterosexual, propertied, and abled, among other specific terms. Note that the
    notion of "Discourse" is intended here not only in the Foucaultian use of the term—
    as a way of constituting knowledge, social practices, and power relations (Foucault
    1976)—but also as the phallogocentric *logos* (Irigaray 1974) and the symbolic order
    (Kristeva 1974).
6 "For the time being, we cannot, must not, choose between the One and the Many,
    Humanism and Deconstruction, Community and Dissemination. We can only
    reopen them to constant negotiations" (Hassan 1987: XVII).
7 I am grateful to the philosophical community of Naples, connected to Prof. Simona
    Marino and Prof. Giuseppe Ferraro (University of Naples "Federico II"), for helping
    me identifying the inner conflicts embedded in the notion of "inclusion." Mindful
    of this conversation, I have embraced the term "com-prehensiveness," whose
    dynamics work on a paradigm of connection (com-) and understanding, rather
    than separation (in-/ex-) and *otherizing*.
8 It has to be noted, though, that in Hayles's writing, the term "posthuman" refers to
    both a posthumanist and a transhumanist position, as she states:

    If my nightmare is a culture inhabited by posthumans who regard their bodies
    as fashion accessories rather than the ground of being, my dream is a version

of the posthuman that embraces the possibilities of information technologies without being seduced by fantasies of unlimited power and disembodied immortality, that recognizes and celebrates finitude as a condition of human being, and that understands human life is embedded in a material world of great complexity. (1999: 5)

9 For a historical and theoretical account on Cultural Posthumanism, see Halberstam and Livingston 1995; Badmington 2000; Miah 2008, Section 2. "Posthumanism in Cultural Theory" (81–5).

10 To quote Cary Wolfe,

Just because we direct our attention to the study of nonhuman animals, and even if we do so with the aim of exposing how they have been misunderstood and exploited, that does not mean that we are not continuing to be humanist— and therefore, by definition, anthropocentric. Indeed, one of the hallmarks of humanism—and even more specifically that kind of humanism called liberalism—is its penchant for that kind of pluralism, in which the sphere of attention and consideration (intellectual or ethical) is broadened and extended to previously marginalized groups, but without in the least destabilizing or throwing into radical question the schema of the human who undertake such pluralization. In that event, pluralism becomes *incorporation*. (99)

Chapter 3

1 On the differences between the two movements, see, among others, Ferrando 2013; Ranisch and Sorgner 2014.

2 Also defined as "whole brain emulation," mind uploading describes the hypothetical process of transferring or copying a conscious mind from a brain to a non-biological substrate (Moravec 1988), with the onto-epistemological risks of dualism and mechanism that such a view entails.

3 It is interesting to note that transhumanists value the human body and advocate self-responsibility in maintaining health and well-being, in order to live longer and keep the biological body alive until other options might become available—I thank Natasha Vita-More for her input and clarification on this point.

4 Note that Francis Fukuyama's *Our Posthuman Future: Consequences of the Biotechnology Revolution* (2002), which gained mainstream attention because of its emphatic critique of what he called a "posthuman future," is based on the assimilation of Transhumanism and Posthumanism, and so Fukuyama's use of the term "posthuman" mostly refers to the transhuman perspective.

5 We will reflect on the differences and similarities between Posthumanism and OOO in Part 3, Chapter 28.

Chapter 4

1 For a historical overview on ideas which have contributed to the formation of Transhumanism, see "A History of Transhumanist thought" (2005) by Nick Bostrom.

2 Specifically, Dante uses this verb in "Paradiso," Canto I, when he sees Beatrice and, through her eyes, perceives the divine:

> Trasumanar significar per verba
> non si poría; però l'esempio basti
> a cui esperienza grazia serba. (v. 70–73, 1896: 524)

Translated by Henry Cary as: "Words may not tell of that trans-human change; and therefore let the example serve" (1909: 289).

3 Specifically, in the dialogue between two secondary characters (Julia and Reilly), as the former states,

> You and I don't know the process by which the human is
> Transhumanized: what do we know
> Of the kind of suffering they must undergo
> On the way of illumination? (1978: 147)

4 Specifically, Teilhard de Chardin states:

> Liberty: that is to say, the chance offered to every man (by removing obstacles and placing the appropriate means at his disposal) of "trans-humanizing" himself by developing his potentialities to the fullest extent. (1964: 239)

5 Such a view can be already traced in FM-2030's pioneer text: *Are You a Transhuman? Monitoring and Stimulating Your Personal Rate of Growth in a Rapidly Changing World* (1989).

Chapter 5

1 The three main goals of Istvan's political campaign were the following:

1) Attempt to do everything possible to . . . overcome human death and aging within 15-20 years.

2) Create a cultural mindset in America that embracing and producing radical technology and science is in the best interest of our nation and species.

3) Create national and global safeguards and programs that protect people against abusive technology and other possible planetary perils we might face as we transition into the transhumanist era. (Istvan 2014)

In 2016, Istvan was not on the ballot in any state. In 2017, he announced his intent
to run for Governor of California in the 2018 election.

2   A considerable amount of transhumanist literature is published online, and so, like
in this case, the specific page number of the references cannot be listed.

Chapter 6

1   It is important to note that Posthumanism do not share the same roots, as we will
highlight in Chapter 10.

2   In "Transhumanism: Towards a Futurist Philosophy" (1990) Max More states,
"Transhumanism shares many elements of humanism, including a respect for reason
and science, a commitment to progress, and a valuing of human (or transhuman)
existence in this life rather than in some supernatural 'afterlife'" (n. pg.).

3   In the words of Bradley Onishi:

> One can characterize the differing trajectories of posthumanism by placing
> them into two general camps: ultra-humanists, those who want to extend
> the humanist project to hyperbolic ends; post-humanists, those that want to
> overcome the humanist understanding of the human in favor of a revised model.
> ... The ultra-humanist trajectory of the scientific posthuman is illustrated most
> vividly in the scientific movement called "transhumanism." (102–03)

4   We will embark in a detailed critique and deconstruction of humanism in the
second part of this book.

5   We will explain this notion in note 3 of Chapter 13.

6   We will expand on these points in Chapter 12.

Chapter 7

1   It is worth noting that David Pearce in "The Hedonistic Imperative" (1995)
portrays a life's "happy ending" as a state of well-being offered by the intake of
smart drugs. His proposal may not sound too far from the over-medicalization
of the old, often practiced within Western medicine, with a hedonistic take.
Such a scenario shares many similarities with Aldous Huxley's *Brave New World*
(1932) and the use of "soma," even if Pearce's project is not conceived in a
statalized form. In the subchapter "Could Life Really Have A Happy Ending?" he
states:

> In fact with a combination of cognitive-enhancers ("smart drugs") and gentle
> euphoriants, there is no reason why the old age of the sympathetic reader
> shouldn't herald, not a slow, spirit-sapping decline, but a period of beautiful

experiences and glorious self-fulfillment. Thus later life can be a time immeasurably richer than anything (s)he has enjoyed before. (1995: n. pg.)

2 Even though some specific takes on Transhumanism have developed within religious frames, such as the case of Mormon Transhumanism, for the most part, as James Hughes states: "Self-identified transhumanists today are mostly secular and atheist" (2010). Max More, for instance, takes an explicit standpoint against normative religions in the name of science: "Many people find it puzzling and frustrating that religion has persisted despite enormous advances in scientific understanding" (1990: n. pg.).

3 For a specific criticism of these aspects, see subchapter "Technochantment" by Elaine L. Graham (2002: 165–68).

4 Bioethicist John Harris, for instance, see human enhancements as morally good "because they make us better people" (2007: 2).

5 For a critical reflection on radical life extension from an ethical standpoint, see, among others, Fukuyama 2012.

6 I have elaborated on this question specifically in the article "The Body" (Ferrando 2014b).

7 We will come back to this notion in Chapter 12.

8 We will clarify this point in Interlude 1.

9 On the transhumanist devaluation of the human body, Bradley Onishi has stated: "The transhuman ambition for technological advancement is undergirded by an ultra-humanist logic that understands material existence, including the human body, to be a hindrance to the goals of the human/post-human species" (2011: 104).

10 Feminist scholar Elaine L. Graham, in the liminal text *Representations of the Post/Human* (2002), which sets the standards for the posthumanist shift in cultural studies, offers a criticism to the last sentence of this specific passage, by defining Kurzweil's vision as "a confusion of anthropocentric triumphalism and evolutionary determinism" (160).

Chapter 8

1 In the same passage, Hayles also affirms,

While I have serious disagreements with most transhumanist rhetoric, the transhumanist community is one that is fervently involved in trying to figure out where technogenesis is headed in the contemporary era and what it implies about our human future. This is its positive contribution, and from my point of view, why it is worth worrying about. (2011: 216)

2 In Heidegger's words: "*Technē* belongs to bringing-forth, to *poiēsis*" (1977: 13).

3 To quote Heidegger: "From earliest times until Plato the word *technē* is linked with the word *epistēmē*" (*ivi*: 13).

4 It is important to note, as philosopher Richard Parry underlines:

> Most often, *technê* is translated as craft or art. While *epistêmê* is generally
> rendered as knowledge, in this context, where it is used in its precise sense,
> it is sometimes translated as scientific knowledge. However, one must not
> confuse this usage with our contemporary understanding of science, which
> includes experimentation. Conducting experiments to confirm hypotheses is
> a much later development. Rather, translating *epistêmê* as scientific knowledge
> is a way of emphasizing its certainty. (Parry 2014, n. pg.)

5 For instance: "Technology is a mode of revealing. Technology comes to presence in the
   realm where revealing and unconcealment take place, where *alētheia*, truth, happens"
   (ivi: 13). The essence of technology, according to Heidegger, is a way of revealing.

6 In Heidegger's words: "We now name that challenging claim which gathers man
   thither to order the self-revealing as standing-reserve: 'Ge-stell' [Enframing]" (ivi: 19).

7 In Heidegger's words: "Chronologically speaking modern physical science begins
   in the seventeenth century. In contrast, machine-power technology develops
   only in the second half of the eighteenth century. But modern technology, which
   for chronological reckoning is the later, is, from the point of view of the essence
   holding sway within it, the historically earlier" (22).

8 Sophia was the first robot to be granted citizenship: she became a citizen of Saudi
   Arabia in 2017—we will come back to Sophia the robot in Chapter 21.

9 *Wall-E* also represents a rare example of a movie with (almost) no human
   characters, thus, from a posthumanist approach to media theory, "post-
   anthropomorhic and post-anthropocentric" (Ferrando 2015: 273).

10 It is important to note that "potentiality" here is not posed in contraposition to
    "actuality"—the two principles have been traditionally approached in Western
    philosophy as a dichotomy, following the Aristotelian lead.

11 We will reflect more clearly on this notion in Chapter 21.

12 We will come back to this point in Part 3.

13 Shortly before dying in 1984, Foucault mentioned his idea of working on a book
    on the technologies of the self. In 1988, the book *Technologies of the Self: A Seminar
    with Michel Foucault* was published *post-mortem*, based on a seminar Foucault had
    originally presented at the University of Vermont in 1982. Foucault introduced this
    notion by stating:

> When I began to study the rules, duties, and prohibitions of sexuality,
> the interdictions and restrictions associated with it, I was concerned not
> simply with the acts that were permitted and forbidden but with the feelings
> represented, the thoughts, the desires one might experience, the drives to
> seek within the self any hidden feeling, any movement of the soul, any desire
> disguised under illusory forms. (1988: 16)

Chapter 9

1 As Mary Schnackenberg Cattani states in her preface to *French Philosophies of the Sixties: An Essay on Antihumanism* (1985),

> This critique of modern rationality was absolutely inseparable from a critique of the subject (of man) defined as consciousness and as will, that is, as man as the author of his acts and ideas. In order to understand this, one must refer back to the considerable trauma represented by the Second World War for European intellectuals. Immediately after the war, in fact, it is no exaggeration to say that "civilized societies," that is the entire Western world, could legitimately be accused of having engendered, or at least of having been unable to stop, two of the greatest political catastrophes of this century: colonialist imperialism and Nazism. (1990: xii–xiii)

2 For an account on this specific type of Antihumanism, see Davies 1997: 57–69.

3 This is why, from an ontological perspective, we can talk of a pluralistic monism, or a monistic pluralism, as we will see in Part 3.

4 This is a point which is importantly remarked by Rosi Braidotti in her philosophical work, which bridges Antihumanism and Posthumanism.

5 We will expand on this point by addressing Perspectivism in Chapter 27.

6 As Edward Said recalls,

> Orientalism is never far from what Denys Hay has called the idea of Europe, a collective notion identifying "us" Europeans as against all "those" non-Europeans, and indeed it can be argued that the major component in European culture is precisely what made that culture hegemonic both in and outside Europe: the idea of European identity as a superior one in comparison with all the non-European peoples and cultures. (1978: 7)

7 In Chapter 12, we will analyze this aspect in detail.

8 The history of philosophy became sensitive to the writings of many *others*, such as the critical non-male perspective of Simone de Beauvoir (1908–86) or the critical non-Eurocentric perspective of Frantz Fanon (1925–61).

9 Note that Foucault and Heidegger use this notion with different acceptions. For a reflection on Heidegger's use of this term, see Chapter 8.

10 As Michel Foucault suggests in *The Order of Things* (1966; Engl. Transl. 1970):

> What I am attempting to bring to light is the epistemological field, the *episteme* in which knowledge, envisaged apart from all criteria having reference to its rational value or to its objective forms, grounds its positivity and thereby manifests a history which is not that of its growing perfection, but rather that of its conditions of possibility. (xxii)

11 According to David Keck:

> Ultimately, the scholastics' use of logical methods and ideas led to the question
> of the possibility of a natural angelology. Could humans, unenlightened by the
> revelation of Scripture, aided only by the use of their native faculties, arrive at a
> knowledge of the spirits of heaven? In asking if human reason can know of the
> angels apart from the authority of Scripture and the Fathers, the transformation
> from monastic to scholastic methods was complete. (1998: 82)

12 More on this point in Part 2, Chapter 17.

13 On this regard, Foucault stated:

> Nietzsche rediscovered the point at which man and God belong to
> one another, at which the death of the second is synonymous with the
> disappearance of the first, and at which the promise of the superman signifies
> first and foremost the imminence of the death of man. . . . It is no longer
> possible to think in our day other than in the void left by man's disappearance.
> For this void does not create a deficiency; it does not constitute a lacuna that
> must be filled. It is nothing more, and nothing less, than the unfolding of a
> space in which it is once more possible to think. (1970: 342)

14 We are going to explain the symbolic meaning of Zarathustra as the main hero in
the next page.

15 Italics in the original text.

16 Note that, for a text's coherence, I will mostly rely on Walter Kaufmann's translation
of Nietzsche's work, including some passages from *Thus Spoke Zarathustra* (original
translation: 1954; referenced: 1976). And still, in this specific case, I have quoted
Del Caro and Pippin 2006 for their gendered sensitivity in rendering "*Mensch*,"
which is absent in Kaufmann's translation. As the translators Del Caro and Pippin
underline: "Just as *Mensch* means human, human being, *Übermensch* means
superhuman, which I have rendered as overman, though I use human being,
mankind, people and humankind to avoid the gendered and outmoded use of
'man'" (2006: 5).

17 On the genealogical relation between Transhumanism and the Enlightenment, see
Chapter 6.

18 It is important to note that Keith Ansell Pearson's *Viroid Life: Perspectives on
Nietzsche and the Transhuman Condition*, published in 1997, already highlighted
such a relation.

19 For instance, in "A History of Transhumanist Thought," Nick Bostrom stated:

> What Nietzsche had in mind, however, was not technological transformation
> but rather a kind of soaring personal growth and cultural refinement in
> exceptional individuals (who he thought would have to overcome the
> life-sapping "slave-morality" of Christianity). Despite some surface-

level similarities with the Nietzschean vision, transhumanism—with its Enlightenment roots, its emphasis on individual liberties, and its humanistic concern for the welfare of all humans (and other sentient beings)—probably has as much or more in common with Nietzsche's contemporary J. S. Mill, the English liberal thinker and utilitarian. (2005: 4)

20 The debate initiated by Sorgner was further developed in the Volume IV, Issue II, of "The Hedonist: A Nietzsche Circle Journal," with articles by Babette Babich, Paul S. Loeb, Keith Ansell Pearson, among others.

21 Notably, in section 10 of *Ecce Homo: How One Becomes What One Is* (this book was written in 1888 and published in 1908); and also, in section 276 of *The Gay Science* (1882).

22 More on this point in Chapter 27.

23 Again, in *Thus Spoke Zarathustra*, Nietzsche affirms:

What is great about human beings is that they are a bridge and not a purpose: what is lovely about human beings is that they are a *crossing over* and a *going under*. (*ibidem*: 7)

24 In *Thus Spoke Zarathustra*, it is stated: "All creatures so far created something beyond themselves; and you want to be the ebb of this great flood and would even rather go back to animals than overcome humans?" (2006: 5).

25 Zoroastrianism can also be referred to as Mazdaism.

26 We should note that these dates are controversial and there is no scholarly consensus on the precise time when he lived—it may be much earlier than that.

27 The majority of ancient societies did not regard time as linear, but as cyclical, reflecting the seasons of nature (spring, summer, fall, and winter), the cycle of life and death, and so on. Most contemporary indigenous worldviews, as well as many religions also perceive time as cyclical (think of the Yugas in Hindu cosmology, or the concept of the wheel of time in Buddhism and Sikhism).

28 In a similar tone, only the prophet who originally proclaimed the dualism between good and evil can announce the message of going beyond good and evil. Here we should note that, although Zoroastrianism does reflect some dualistic views in the struggle between good and evil, it is not a dualistic religion (cf. Rose 2011).

29 This is why Nietzsche, together with Karl Marx and Sigmund Freud, were famously defined by philosopher Paul Ricoeur as the "three masters of suspicion" (1970: 33).

30 We are going to come back to this point in Chapter 28.

31 Nietzsche defines it as the "Heaviest Burden" in aphorism 341 of *The Gay Science*, and develops it more thoroughly in *Thus Spoke Zarathustra*. For a reflection on the relevance of Nietzsche's notion of the eternal recurrence in the development of a posthuman cosmology, see Ferrando 2013.

32 As we will see in Chapters 19 to 21.

33 As stated in *The Gay Science*, Section 125.

34 We have addressed Posthumanism as a philosophy which goes beyond the need for a vengeance in Chapter 2.

35 Here the term refers to its Foucauldian acception, as clarified previously in this chapter.

36 We will come back to this point in Chapter 28.

37 The term "metahuman" was specifically utilized within the comic series released by the publisher DC Comics (New York).

38 Sometimes redefined as "Environmental Humanities" (Neimanis et al. 2015).

39 We will expand on these aspects in Chapter 23.

40 For a full account of all the nuances and related terms, see the comprehensive *Posthuman Glossary*, edited by Braidotti and Hlavajova (2017).

Chapter 10

1 What about the "realist" question: *Is there a set of experiences and a common goal that can define the human species as a whole?* This question stays open until Chapter 12, in which we will address this aspect more clearly.

2 We will fully emerge into this reflection toward the end of Part 3.

3 We will present this specific take of Posthumanism in Chapter 21.

4 We will address this aspect in Chapter 22.

5 Here, centrism should not be accessed in its political sense, but as a "centralizing," recurrent in forms such as anthropo-centrism, Euro-centrism, andro-centrism, and so on.

6 In Vattimo's words: "If it were simply a question of an awareness—or assumption—of representing an historical novelty which constitutes a new and different figure in the phenomenology of the spirit, then the postmodern would be positioned along the lines of modernity itself, since the latter is governed by the categories of the 'new' and of 'overcoming.' Things change, however, if we see the postmodern not only as something new in relation to the modern, but also as a dissolution of the category of the new—in other words, as an experience of 'the end of history'—rather than as the appearance of a different stage of history itself" (1991: 4).

7 In every civilization, while "new" information is achieved, other information is lost, so that the lost information, once retrieved, becomes new again. Psychoanalyst Immanuel Velikovsky actually defined the human species as that species which constantly loses memory of its own origins, and thus called it *Mankind in Amnesia* (1982).

8 As Heidegger states,

> We encounter the first humanism in Rome: it therefore remains in essence a specifically Roman phenomenon, which emerges from the encounter of Roman civilization with the culture of late Greek civilization. (2001: 242)

9 Such an essence has been historically set within an uncritical male frame.

10 We will come back to this point in different chapters, both in Part 1 and in Part 2.

11 In Heidegger's words, "Thinking accomplishes the relation of Being to the essence of man" (2001: 238).

12 Hegemonic in the sense that it has (self-)recognized a leading role to themselves, and has eventually been granted such a recognition by (some) others—that is, the outsiders which are needed in a hierarchical political view.

13 We are going to delve into this aspect in Chapters 25 and 26.

14 Marchesini's book *Post-human: Verso Nuovi Modelli di Esistenza* (2002) can be considered one of the most exhaustive studies on Posthumanism within the Italian philosophical landscape.

15 Translation mine. Original text: "L'umano non è più l'emanazione o l'espressione dell'uomo bensì il risultato dell'ibridazione dell'uomo con le alterità non umane" (34).

16 Note that metanarratives here are not condoned of any metaphysical assumptions, but they are performing a functional role, in referring to the recorded history of human thought.

17 We will come back to this notion in Chapter 9.

18 See, for instance, the table of differences delineated by Ihab Hassan in *The Postmodern Turn* (1987): some of the traits of Modernism are individuated in "Purpose," "Design," Hierarchy," "Mastery/Logos," "Creation/Totalization," "Centering," and "Genital/Phallic." The equivalent listed traits for Postmodernism are "Play," "Chance," "Anarchy," "Exhaustion/Silence," "Decreation/Deconstruction," "Dispersal," and Polymorphous/Androgynous" (91).

19 Furthermore, it can be observed that none of the terms really fit, since "we have never been modern" (Latour 1987). For a detailed presentation of Latour's point of view on the terms "modern" and "postmodern," see specifically Section 1.5 "What Does it Mean To Be a Modern?" (10–12).

20 This is different from some specific takes on OOO, such as in the case of New Realism, as we will see in Part 3, Chapter 28.

21 This is a topic recurrently discussed in the field of philosophy. Here, I will only offer two main historical references, which I find most significant in this context. On the *praxis/poiesis* distinction, see Aristotle's *Nicomachean Ethics* (c. 350 BC), Book VI. On the relation theory/practice, see Karl Marx's *Theses on Feuerbach* (1845), where he famously stated, "Philosophers have only interpreted the world differently, but the point is to change it" (2009: 97).

Interlude 1

1 Think, for instance, of teaching n. 8, among others, which starts with this sentence: "The supreme good is like water, / which nourishes all things without trying to. / It is

content with the low places that people disdain. / Thus it is like the Tao" (Tzu 1999: n. pg.).

2 For more on the Dao as an open and fluid framework, see, for instance, Silantsyeva 2016, among others—this article offers a contemporary Deleuzian reading of this ancient text.

3 As I have noted in a previous article, "The main risk run by humans consists in turning the robotic difference into a stigma for new forms of racism, based on how far such a difference can be placed from the human norm" (Ferrando 2014a: 16).

4 In the article "Humans Have Always Been Posthuman: A Spiritual Genealogy Of Posthumanism" (2016a), I have delved into the points in common, as well as the differences, between these traditions and Posthumanism.

5 For instance, an attempt to rethink Posthumanism through the Indian tradition of Tantra can be found in *Avatar Bodies: A Tantra for Posthumanism* (2004) by Ann Weinstone.

Chapter 11

1 We will reflect on the notion of post-truth in Chapter 27.

Chapter 12

1 This is the full quote: "Gender is always about the production of subjects in relation to other subjects, and in relation to artifacts. Gender is about material-semiotic production of these assemblages, these human-artifact assemblages that are people. . . . It is an obligatory distribution of subjects in unequal relationships, where some have property in others" (Haraway 2004: 328–29).

2 It is important to note that de Beauvoir did not consider herself a philosopher.

3 See, for instance, "She appears as *the privileged Other*, through whom the subject fulfills himself: one of the measures of man" (281). And also, "The ideal woman will be she who incarnates most exactly the *Other* capable of revealing him to himself" (284).

4 I have expanded on this point in the article "Of Posthuman Born: Gender, Utopia and the Posthuman" (2015).

5 For instance, *The Hunger Games* (2012), a sci-fi dystopian movie with a powerful female character, was a massive box office success. It was produced by Nina Jacobson and Jon Kilik.

6 This is a better translation of this passage by Constance Bord and Sheila Malovany-Chevallier: "Alterity is the fundamental category of human thought" (2009: 26).

7 From a gender perspective, it is important to note that, following this paragraph, de Beauvoir thus asks: "How is it then that this reciprocity has not been recognized between the sexes, that one of the contrasting terms is set up as the sole essential, denying any relativity in regard to its correlative and defining the latter as pure otherness?" (*ivi*: XXI).

8 We will expand on this criticism in Chapter 26.

9 In Irigaray words, "But which "subject" up till now has investigated the fact that a *concave mirror* concentrates the light and, specifically, that this is not wholly irrelevant to women's sexuality?" (1985: 144).

10 It is important to notice that Irigaray's work is rooted within psychoanalysis. To clarify her perspective, we will bring, as an example, her reading of Freud's penis-envy: "If *she* envies it, then *he* must have it. If *she* envies what *he* has, then it must be valuable" (1985: 53). The penis-envy, more than objectively portraying an aspect of the female psychology, reflects the need of the recognition of the value of the penis for the male psychology.

11 Butler sharply summarizes their different perspectives in these terms: "In opposition to Beauvoir, for whom women are designated as the Other, Irigaray argues that both the subject and the Other are masculine mainstays of a closed phallogocentric signifying economy that achieves its totalizing goal through the exclusion of the feminine altogether" (1999: 14).

12 To this magmatic multitude we shall return in the next chapters.

Chapter 13

1 For a comprehensive study of the humanistic reduction of the non-human animal, see the work of Roberto Marchesini (1959–).

2 As we shall see in the next chapter, these subjectivities correspond to the ones who have historically took advantage of this epistemological supremacy to sustain their own sociopolitical privileges.

3 Foucault originally refers to the "micro-physics" of power:

> Now, the study of this micro-physics presupposes that the power exercised on the body is conceived not as a property, but as a strategy, that its effects of domination are attributed not to "appropriation," but to dispositions, maneuvers, tactics, techniques, functionings; that one should decipher in it a network of relations, constantly in tension, in activity, rather than a privilege that one might possess; that one should take as its model a perpetual battle rather than a contract regulating a transaction or the conquest of a territory. In short this power is exercised rather than possessed; it is not the "privilege," acquired or preserved, of the dominant class, but the overall effect of its

strategic positions—an effect that is manifested and sometimes extended by the position of those who are dominated. (1995: 26)

4 The English translation reflects the original text in Italian, where *Uomo* is used instead of *Essere Umano*, and the subject is strictly expressed in the masculine form.

5 The fact that the text was first published in 2002 eradicates any type of chronological justifications on the use of grammatical choices that are gender non-neutral.

6 Published by the American Philosophical Association (APA) in February 1986, this article is still referred by the APA as a suggested reading for their authors.

Chapter 14

1 For instance, in the Provision V of the "Negro Act," it was stated that

if any slave who shall be out of the house or plantation where such slave shall live, or shall be usually employed, or without some white person in company with such slave, shall refuse to submit or to undergo the examination of any white person, it shall be lawful for any such white person to pursue, apprehend, and moderately correct such slave; and if any such slave shall assault and strike such white person, such slave may be lawfully killed. (Smith 2005: 21)

2 There is a controversy regarding this point; some argue that de las Casas started to write the *Apologetic History* already in 1527 (cf. Hanke 1949).

3 In Stanton's words, "Extermination begins, and quickly becomes the mass killing legally called 'genocide.' It is 'extermination' to the killers because they do not believe their victims to be fully human" (*ibidem*).

4 Although it is impossible to determine the exact number of Jewish victims, six million is the round figure accepted by most authorities.

5 For an account on how the rise of racist and eugenic ideologies developed into the "final solution," see, among others, Friedlander 1995—this text is particularly interesting because it describes how the so-called euthanasia of the people with disabilities provided a practical model for, and thus initiated, the Holocaust. We will come back to this point in Chapter 24.

6 For an extensive inquiry into the meaning of "normal" and "pathological" in medicine and biology, see Canguilhem 1943.

7 This estimate is problematic. Since the murders were not systematically recorded and many of the archives which existed have been lost, the number of deaths could be much higher. Consequently, historians have not settled on a figure. For a reflection on different estimates, see, among others, Gaskill 2010: 61–77.

8   On the constitution of the specific gendered nature of witchcraft accusations and convictions, see Bailey 2002.

9   On the role of superstition in the European with trials, see specifically Chapter 4: "The Medieval Condemnation of Magic, 1000-1500" (Bailey 2007: 107–40).

10 On the notion of abjection as preceding the symbolic order, see Kristeva 1980.

11 Please note that here "human" refers to the historical process of humanizing, and not to an ontological fundamental category.

12 For an extensive reflection on the "racial Other," see Goldberg 1993.

13 For a critical reading of the human rooted in queer theory, see Judith Butler's *Undoing Gender* (2004), where she sharply asks: "If I am a certain gender, will I still be regarded as part of the 'human'?" (2).

14 I have expanded on this point in the article "The Body" (2014b).

Chapter 15

1   The critiques enacted by their "daughters," or by their "adoptive offsprings" (for instance, feminist or postcolonial theorists, who first had to assimilate Western androcentric modes of constructing knowledge, in order to deconstruct them), is not validated the same way within philosophical Western traditions; the attempts to annihilate their recognition (if any) will be much more effective. Karen J. Warren, in her "recovery project," clearly portrays the results of such an attitude in her essay *2,600 Years of the History of Western Philosophy Without Women* (2009). See also: Tuana 1998.

2   In the words of Foucault, "These four types of technologies hardly ever function separately" (18).

3   It is important to note that psychoanalyst Joan Riviere as early as 1929 delineated "womanliness" as a masquerade in her article specifically entitled: "Womanliness as a masquerade," where she presented femininity as a mask used by women in their everyday lives to meet male expectations.

4   As Judith Butler puts it: "In my view, the normative focus for gay and lesbian practice ought to be on the subversive and parodic redeployment of power rather than on the impossible fantasy of its full-scale transcendence" (1999: 158)

5   Patrick Gun Cuninghame (2007) thus defines the cultural and political attitude developed within the 1977 Italian anarchist movements, especially by the *Indiani Metropolitani,* whose "ironic praxis" could be exemplified in their slogan: *Una risata vi seppellirá* (translated by Cuninghame as "A laughter will bury you all," 153).

6   For instance, philosopher Francesca Brezzi writes, "In certain historical and cultural eras, mysticism was the only access for women to 'words which would be heard,' despite the theology of the time considered women as incomplete men"—*Trans. Mine* (2005: 127).

7   On the difference between religion and spirituality, see for instance, Zinnbauer et al. 1997.

8   For a full reflection on the significance of spirituality to the posthuman approach, see Ferrando 2016a.

9   Steve Nichols in his manifesto "The Posthuman Movement" (1988) dedicates a small section entitled "Transcendence" to set this type of connection. Although written in a very generic tone, it is still an interesting antecedent to be mentioned.

Chapter 16

1   As philosopher François Raffoul underlines: "The relation to the other, that is to say, for Lévinas, necessarily, the absolute other (escaping absolutely from the Same), is 'not a communion.' A communion would reproduce a logic of the Same" (2005: 143); while Lévinas's effort is "to give thought to an experience of alterity that cannot be reduced to the Self" (*ibidem*).

2   We will explore this aspect in Part 3.

3   For instance, within the field of animal studies, Matthew Calarco has criticized Lévinas's perspective as "dogmatically anthropocentric" (2008: 55). In *Zoographies: The Question of the Animal from Heidegger to Derrida* (2008), Calarco dedicates Chapter 2, entitled "Facing the Other Animal: Lévinas" (55–78), entirely to this reflection.

4   In Part 3, we will reflect on the encounter of the human with the machine.

5   We will approach the biological meaning of the species in Chapter 22, while in Chapter 23, we will introduce an overview on possible evolutionary developments of humankind.

6   White further asserts this point by emphasizing the fact that the astronauts in Earth orbits and the lunar astronauts have different types of epiphanies:

> The orbital astronaut sees the Earth as huge and himself or herself as less significant. The lunar astronaut sees the Earth as small and feels the awesome grandeur of the entire universe. . . . Both programs change the astronaut's perception of the Earth and of his or her own identity, but in quite different ways. (1998: 36)

7   A research in this direction is needed within the field of posthuman studies.

Chapter 17

1   It is important to note that this etymology is not unanimously accepted and that it has been contested for different reasons. From a linguistic perspective, it has been noted the change of the vowel "u," which in "humus" is long (ū), while in

"*humanus*" becomes short (ŭ)—see, for instance, Romaniello 2004: 188–90. On the other, it has also been challenged for its semantics. As early as the first century CE, Marcus Fabius Quintilianus (c. 35–c. 100) stated:

> Etiamne *hominem* appellari, quia sit *humo* natus (quasi vero non omnibus animalibus eadem origo, aut illi primi mortales ante nomen imposuerint terrae quam sibi)? (Institutio Oratoria I, 6, 34)

Translation by H. E. Butler:

> Are we to assent to the view that *homo* is derived from *humus*, because man sprang from the earth, as though all other living things had not the same origin? (Quintilian and Butler 1920: 127)

2   Not to be confused with *Terra*, the Latin translation for the Earth—which at the time was not conceived as a planet yet.
3   Until 312 CE, Roman society was traditionally polytheistic.
4   Most notably, philosopher Cato the Elder (234–149 BCE) was one of the leading voices against the spread of Hellenic culture in Rome.
5   It is interesting to note that Aristotle himself, when he was in Athens, was considered a *metoikos* or "metic," that is, a resident alien who is not a slave.
6   Women and slaves, for instance, were excluded.
7   BTL 2009: n. pg.
8   Translation by John R. Stone (2005: 273).
9   BTL 2009: n. pg.
10   Translation by John R. Stone (2005: 39).
11   BTL 2009: n. pg.
12   Translation by J. R. Stone (2005: 40).
13   Note that of the 463 times that the term "humanitas" is found in the entire *corpus* of Classic Latin authors, 229 are detected in Cicero's writings (BTL 2009: n. pg.).
14   There is a large range of references which could be listed for this purpose, among others: Rieks 1967; Schadewaldt 1973; Giustiniani 1985.
15   Note that Cicero's use of the stoic notion of *dignitas* in *De Officiis* (44 BCE) prescinds from any social status (I; 106). And still, Cicero's emphasis in delineating it according to "reason" implicitly relates it more consistently to a male legacy (women have been historically considered inferior, precisely because of their presumed lack of rationality and reason).

Chapter 18

1   On the possible causes of their extinction, see Finlayson 2009.

2 The year 1758 is the date of publication of *Systema Naturae* (first edition: 1735), which is considered the starting point of modern botanical and zoological taxonomy.

3 It is worth noting that Linnaeus grew up in Sweden during what has been defined as the Age of Liberty (1719–72)—"Liberty" here refers to the freedom from absolute monarchy (Roberts 1986).

4 As its revealing etymology displays, *taxis*, in Greek, means "order, arrangement, category"; *nomos* means "order, law, science."

5 Translation by R. Dunn (2009: 37).

6 Prior to Linnaeus, who strictly used a binomial system, a polynomial nomenclature was in use: scientific terms were formed by many words, which caused unnecessary confusion.

7 Although his earlier belief in the fixity of the species was later abandoned, in Linnaeus's view, the original species were to be found in the Garden of Eden.

8 For a detailed account on the progression of Linnaeus's human classification through the different editions of *Systema Naturae*, see the subchapter "Defining the Human" in Douthwaite 2002: 14–21.

9 Linnaeus described Asians as *Asiaticus fuscus* from the second (1740) till the tenth edition of "Systema Naturae," when he changed it with *luridus*. For a detailed account of the different uses of *fuscus* and *luridus* in his work, see Keevak 2011: 51–55.

10 This next series of quotes are direct translations from Linnaeus, reported in recent articles and texts which are of relevance to our discussion.

11 Fluehr-Lobban, for instance, see in Linnaeus's classification one of the main reasons why race is still today mostly constructed around phenotype, that is, physical characteristics (2006: 10).

12 It is worth noticing that his Eurocentric standards also motivated a privilege for Latin nomenclature, so that, from a contemporary perspective, he has been accused of "linguistic imperialism" (Schiebinger 2004: 194–225; Cook 2010: 121–38). For instance, Londa Schiebinger, here specifically referring to Linnaeus's botanical classification, affirms:

> He explicitly chose as the "Fathers of Botany" in this regard the ancient Greeks and Romans, not the "Asiatics or Arabians" whose knowledge of plants even Linnaeus would have recognized as ancient and extensive but whose languages he considered "barbarous." (2004: 200)

13 The term "Mammalia" only appears in the tenth edition of *Systema Naturae* (1758), where it substituted the traditional term "*Quadrupedia*," present since the first edition (1735). For an account on the reasons of this change, see Schiebinger (1993: 385–88).

14 For a reflection on the history of wet-nursing, see, among others, Stevens et al. 2009.

15 For instance, Linnaeus blamed the milk of Caligula's wet-nurses for his tyranny (1752: 265), among other examples.

16 In fact, according to Schiebinger, "The mammae are 'functional' in only half of this group of animals (the females) and, among those, for a relatively short period of time (during lactation) or not at all. Linnaeus could indeed have chosen a more gender-neutral term, such as *Aurecaviga* (the hollow-eared ones) or *Pilosa* (the hairy ones)" (1993: 382–83).

17 Human children have the longest infancy in the animal kingdom.

18 As we have noted previously, reason and education have been historically associated to men. Here, we shall also remind that in Latin *homo* means "human being"; and still, it is strictly expressed in the masculine form, exposing the sexist outline of the Latin grammar itself.

19 In the words of Schiebinger:

> In the same volume in which Linnaeus introduced the term *Mammalia,* he also introduced the name *Homo Sapiens.* This term, man of wisdom, was used to distinguish humans from other primates (ape, lemurs, and bats, for example). (2000: 15)

20 We will come back to this concept in Chapter 26.

Interlude 2

1 Oxford Dictionary: Entry "beast," n. pg.

Chapter 19

1 For a critical reflection on the implications of this term, see Chapter 17.

2 For instance, from a feminist perspective, it has been criticized for its masculinist and techno-normative approach (Grusin 2017).

3 The term is used here as a sociocultural adaptation of the scientific explanation proposed by Thomas Kuhn (1962).

4 Here, we shall clarify that this post-anthropocentric move cannot be assimilated to the perverse form of anthropocentrism Rosi Braidotti critically refers to, regarding advanced capitalism: "The global economy is post-anthropocentric in that it ultimately unifies all species under the imperative of the market and its excesses threaten the sustainability of our planet as a whole" (63). We will come back to this point in Chapter 19.

5 For instance, Peter Ward, in direct response to this view, coined the Medea hypothesis, according to which multicellular life, intended as a superorganism, would be suicidal (2009).

6 Here, we should note that, there are many different types of compost, depending on the food scraps involved in the process, among other factors.

7 The hyphen has been added here to play with the term by reversing the location of the "post-" that manifests as "com-post-" instead of "post-human." Actually, the term "compost" comes from Latin "*com-positum*" which means "composed"—in the sense of "*com*" (with)—and "*postum*" (posed).

8 For more on this point, see Chapter 17.

Chapter 20

1 Please note that here the term is used in a different way by David Roden (2015). We will come back to his important take on "posthuman life" in Chapter 20.

2 For a contemporary reflection on the origins and meanings of biopolitical discourse, see Esposito 2008.

3 We have underlined this aspect in Chapter 13.

4 "*Zoë*" as a root word is relegated to terms strictly referring to non-human animals, such as zoo and zoology.

5 We have elaborated on this point in Chapter 18, on the coinage of the term "*Homo sapiens.*"

6 For a critical revision of these categories from the perspective of biochemical adaption (that is, how organisms physiologically behave and evolve under different environmental conditions), see Hochachka and Somero 2002.

7 On their comprehensive book *The Tree of Knowledge: The Biological Roots of Human Understanding* (1987a), biologists Humberto Maturana and Francisco Varela stated,

> Throughout the history of biology many criteria have been proposed. They all have drawbacks. For instance, some have proposed as a criterion chemical composition, or the capacity to move, or reproduction, or even some combination of those criteria, that is, a list of properties. But how do we know when the list is complete? For instance, if we build a machine capable of reproducing itself, but it is made of iron and plastic and not of molecules, is it living? (42)

> We will come back to this question in Chapter 26.

8 On the exchange between the virus and their host cells, biologist Luis P. Villarreal has argued:

> Viruses represent a major creative force in the evolution of the host, driving the host to acquire new, and accumulate ever more complex, molecular identities. (2004a: 296)

> Villarreal has consequently directed his reflection towards "the possible role of viruses in the evolution of complexity, including the evolution of human-specific attributes." (*ibidem*)

9 In the article "Are Viruses Alive?" (2004b), Villarreal has stated: "Viruses today are thought of as being in a gray area between living and nonliving" (97).

10 I would rather use this geopolitical characterization, instead of the ethnocentric "Westernized," or the universalistic "globalized," in order to emphasize the survival of local specificities in globalized policies and/or practices.

11 Sir Edward Burnett Tylor (1832–1917) provided the first comprehensive academic overview on Animism, which he considered as one of the oldest human beliefs.

12 This lack of primacy for the living marks, for Tylor, one of the most significant points of departure in the history of religions. In the Volume I of his *Primitive Culture: Researches Into the Development of Mythology, Philosophy, Religion, Language, Art and Custom* (1871), he affirmed:

> The divisions which have separated the great religions of the world into intolerant and hostile sects are for the most part superficial, in comparison with the deepest of all religious schisms, that which divides Animism with Materialism. (453)

13 The uncanny valley theory suggests that the more humanoid objects resemble human beings, the more likely human being will perceive uncanny feelings toward them.

14 To avoid the confusion with the homonymous existing term "nomophobia" (which, derived from the Greek word "*nomos*," refers to the fear of laws and rules), we can propose "nocellphobia" as an abbreviation for "no-cell-phone phobia."

15 For an ontological reflection on the technical object, see Simondon (1958; Engl. Trans. 1980).

16 We will reflect on the field of Biological AI in the next chapter.

Chapter 21

1 As stated by Chris Hables Gray, Steven Mentor, and Heidi J. Figueroa-Sarriera: "From artificial life programs to 'living dead' cadaver-organ donors the line between the organic and the machinic is becoming very blurred, indeed" (1995: 5)

2 Note that, in the article "Open Problems in Artificial Life" (2000), Mark A. Bedau et al. extend the notion of "artificial life" to other types of life, which could include alien life and life resulted through bioengineering technologies:

> Although artificial life is fundamentally directed towards both the origins of biology and its future, the scope and complexity of its subject require interdisciplinary cooperation and collaboration. This broadly based area of study embraces the possibility of discovering lifelike behavior in unfamiliar settings and creating new and unfamiliar forms of life, and its major aim is to develop a coherent theory of life in all its manifestations, rather than an historically contingent documentation bifurcated by discipline. (363)

3   Essentialism suggests that specific sets of characteristics apply to defined categories. It emphasizes fixed traits over discontinuities.

4   As Haraway famously noted in "A Cyborg Manifesto" (1985): "The boundary between physical and non-physical is very imprecise for us. . . . Our best machines are made of sunshine: they are all light and clean, because they are nothing but signals, electromagnetic waves, a section of a spectrum" (53).

5   This is the full passage:

> Biochemistry studies the way in which life emerges from the interaction of inanimate molecules. In this paper we look into the possibility that life could emerge from the interaction of inanimate artificial molecules. Cellular automata provide us with the logical universes within which we can embed artificial molecules in the form of propagating, virtual automata. We suggest that since virtual automata have the computational capacity to fill many of the functional roles played by the primary biomolecules, there is a strong possibility that the "molecular logic" of life can be embedded within cellular automata and that, therefore, artificial life is a distinct possibility within these highly parallel computer structures. (1986: 120)

It shall also be noted that Langton specifically reflected on DNA in the section titled "Information" (121–22).

6   The two main theoretic references of such a tendency can be found in Marvin Minsky's *The Society of Mind* (1985) and Hans Moravec's *Mind Children* (1988).

7   For a philosophical perspective on this notion, see Bray and Colebrook 1998.

8   The field of quantum physics, for instance, has demonstrated the non-reducibility of matter, as we will see in Chapter 29.

9   It shall be noted that this text was published in 1991, that is, before the development of Posthumanism as a movement.

10 We will come back to vitalism in Chapter 28.

11 See Chapter 13.

12 These types of scholars generally approach the machinic difference through hegemonic genealogies, without taking into account the studies on the differences developed from the human "margins," to quote bell hooks (1984), such as feminism or critical race studies, among others.

13 It is important to note that this move was also criticized as premature and not respectful to the humans living in Saudi Arabia who were not granted similar rights (cf. Wootson 2017).

14 This means that it is recognized the same legal rights as a human being (I would like to thank Quentin Turner for bringing this news to my attention).

15 It is worth noting that "the ruling comes after a group of 25 people aged between seven and 26 filed a lawsuit claiming their constitutional rights to life, food and water were being violated" (Stubley 2018, n. pg.).

16　We will come back to Perspectivism in Chapter 27.

17　To understand the use of this term, refer to Part 2 of this book.

Chapter 22

1　By re-entering our inquiry, we shall notice that the scientific theories debating the origins of life are not immune from the slippery discussion over the dividing line between animate and inanimate, as seen in section b of Chapter 20. For instance, biochemist Alexander Oparin, in his influential work *The Origin of Life* (1924), noted:

> However, this need not lead us to the conclusion that there is an absolute and fundamental difference between a living organism and lifeless matter. Everyday experience enables us to differentiate living things from their non-living environment. But the numerous attempts to discover some specific "vital energies" resident only in organisms invariably ended in total failure, as the history of biology in the nineteenth and twentieth centuries teaches us. (1953: 246)

2　Approximately, this is the commonly accepted estimate. For a paleontological access to specific fossil data, see among others: Milsom and Rigby 2010.

3　Alexander Oparin, for instance, famously developed the hypothesis of the "primordial soup" (1924).

4　Such a gender non-neutral nomenclature is first to be found in the writings of Anaxagoras (c. 510–428 BC). Its Greek etymology of *pan* ("all") and *sperma*, which in ancient Greek referred to both "origin, source" and "(human) seed" (translation by Slater 1969: n. pg.), reflects the sexist, and scientifically false, vision which identified the active principle of life in the male reproductive fluid, while the female was considered to contribute passive matter—this view influenced the ways model of conceptions were described in standard Western science, until as late as the 1980s (Cordrick Haely 2008: 69–70).

5　For further investigation on the origins of life, see among others, Hazen 2005; Seckbach 2012.

6　This idea had already been suggested by scientists such as Pierre-Louis Moreau de Maupertuis (1698–1759), Erasmus Darwin (1731–1802), and Jean-Baptiste Lamarck (1744–1829). For a history on the idea of evolution, see for instance, Bowler 2003; Larson 2004.

7　As Haraway puts it: "The cyborg has no origin story in the Western sense" (1985: 51).

8　The LUA does not refer to the first form of life. Life may have existed much earlier; more specifically, the LUA represents the universal common ancestor of all current life on Earth.

9　The two hypotheses can, in fact, coexist (Becerra and Delaye 2016).

10   While a vertical genetic exchange occurs from the parental generation to the
     offspring through reproduction, "horizontal gene transfer is defined—in the
     words of biologist Jeffrey G. Lawrence—as the transfer of genetic material between
     bacterial cells uncoupled with cell division" (2005: 255).

11   For instance, someone could say that human clones would have the same DNA,
     but the epigenetic manifestation of their DNA would vary according to their diet,
     environment, habits, and so on.

12   This example also represents an interesting case of convergent evolution, that is, the
     genetic event of two or more populations independently acquiring the same trait.

13   We shall note that, on one side, this type of behavior characterizes "invasive"
     species, such as the case of the zebra mussel (cf. Ricciardi et al. 1998). On the other
     side, this behavior can also lead to interesting ecological opportunities. Let's think,
     for instance, of the wetland filtration abilities of *Phragmites* in non-native locations.
     This plant, also known as the common reed, is abundant and invasive to New York
     City, Long Island, and New Jersey. Although it is disruptive to other plants and
     animals that previously depended on native species, it has the ability to benefit
     aquatic ecosystems and reduce anthropogenic climate change (cf. Mozdzer and
     Megonigal 2013). I thank John Maggi for this note.

14   There have been around 300,000 farmer-suicides in the past two decades in India
     (cf. Mishra 2014). This serious problem, which Shiva attributes mainly to the
     introduction of GP cotton seeds (that is, genetically manipulated cotton seeds sold
     by Monsanto), has wider ramifications; and still, the expensive price of these seeds
     has consistently contributed to the state of things (Thomas and De Tavernier 2017).

15   The *Oxford Dictionary* defines it as "the search for plant and animal species from
     which medicinal drugs and other commercially valuable compounds can be
     obtained" (entry "bioprospecting," n. pg.).

16   The *Oxford Dictionary* defines it as "the practice of commercially exploiting
     naturally occurring biochemical or genetic material, especially by obtaining patents
     that restrict its future use, while failing to pay fair compensation to the community
     from which it originates" (entry "biopiracy," n. pg.). For more on biopiracy, see
     Shiva 1997.

Chapter 23

1   In the words of Darwin: "Slow though the process of selection may be, if feeble man
    can do much by his powers of artificial selection, I can see no limit to the amount
    of change, to the beauty and complexity of the coadaptations between all organic
    beings, one with another and with their physical conditions of life, which may be
    effected in the long course of time by nature's power of selection" (1859: 153).

2   Note that this notion is mostly referred to as "space colonization" within transhumanist literature, with no acknowledgment of the radical criticisms offered by postcolonial theorists to the institution of colonization and its historical praxis. This is also a good example which shows how often Transhumanism and Posthumanism engage upon the same issues from different standpoints.

3   It may be interesting to re-access the question of species extinction in light of genetic engineering, since the revival of an extinct species is no longer science-fiction, as the cloning of the bucardo goat has proved (Folch et al. 2009). Although ethically questionable, these possibilities open new ground in the discussion of species extinction, which can be more specifically addressed as: *Can a species be considered categorically extinct, if some of its own genetic material is left behind?*

4   In this section, Darwin states: "Lamarck was the first man whose conclusions on the subject excited much attention. . . . he upholds the doctrine that species, including man, are descended from other species. He first did the eminent service of arousing attention to the probability of all change in the organic, as well as in the inorganic world, being the result of law, and not of miraculous interposition" (1859: 54).

5   Darwin notes: "It is curious how largely my grandfather, Dr Erasmus Darwin, anticipated the views and erroneous grounds of opinion of Lamarck" (1859: 54).

6   For a comprehensive view on evolution with an up-to-date revisitation of Lamarckism in the light of epigenetics, see Jablonka et al. 2005.

7   The neologism "intra-change" (Ferrando 2016b)—which I coined under the influence of Karen Barad's notion of "intra-action" (2007)—here is used instead of the term "exchange." "Ex" comes from Latin, meaning "out," while "intra" highlights how changes affect each term of reference. It is thus more suitable to express the meaning of the relation and the reciprocal effects of the process of changing.

8   According to David Resnik and Daniel Vorhaus: "Genetic determinism can be loosely defined as the view that genes (genotypes) cause traits (phenotypes)" (2006: 3). Resnik and Vorhaus also make an important difference between strong genetic determinism, moderate genetic determinism, and weak genetic determinism (*ibidem*).

Chapter 24

1   *Oxford Dictionary*: Entry "designer baby," n. pg.

2   They explain, more specifically: "A bacterial enzyme that uses guide RNA molecules to target DNA for cleavage has been adopted as a programmable tool to site-specifically modify genomes of cells and organisms, from bacteria and human cells to whole zebrafish" (2013: 50).

3   The first genetically modified babies have already been born. Although there are different examples that could be listed here, we are going to mention the case

of "Lulu" and "Nana", pseudonyms to refer to the twin sisters born in China in November 2018, whose DNA, according to bio-physical researcher He Jiankui, was genetically manipulated at the embryonic level using CRISPR editing system. We shall note that Jiankui's claims have not been verified yet, and that he is currently facing a clinical trial (LaMotte 2018).

4   As Garver and Garver point out: "The ideas of racial hygiene became relevant to Hitler in 1923 while he was imprisoned in Landsberg, where he read the second edition of the textbook by E. Baur, E. Fischer, and F. Lenz, *The Principles of Human Heredity and Race Hygiene* (*Menschliche Erblichkeitslehre und Rassenhygiene*). He subsequently incorporated these racial ideas into his own book, *My Struggle* (*Mein Kampf*)" (1991: 1112).

5   In Habermas's words: "Genetic manipulation could change the self-understanding of the species in so fundamental a way that the attack on modern conceptions of law and morality might at the same time affect the inalienable normative foundations of social integration" (2003: 26).

6   This text was conceived within the context of what has been defined as the Sloterdijk-Habermas debate, which followed Peter Sloterdijk's controversial lecture, and then publication, entitled: *Rules for the Human Zoo: a Response to the Letter on Humanism* (1999).

7   The metaphor of "playing God" has been widely employed within the bioethical field. According to Ted Peters and Francis S. Collins: "The fear expressed in the phrase 'playing God' . . . is that humans may play God in their own selfish and imperfect ways" (2002: x).

8   We are going to address this point more thoroughly in Chapters 25 and 26.

9   For an account on the notion of the body from a posthuman perspective, see Ferrando 2014b.

Chapter 25

1   On the differences between Posthumanism and Transhumanism on a bioethical ground, see Gordijn and Chadwick 2009.

2   Hamer is well known for his studies on the genetics of human behavior, from his work on sexual orientation on what has been popularized as the "gay gene" (1994), to the religious experience and the "God gene" (2004).

3   For more on the topic of genetic discrimination, see Lemke 2013.

4   Germline genetic modification is a form of genetic engineering which involves replacing genes in eggs, sperm, or at the very beginning of the embryonic stage: such modification is inheritable, which means that the modified genes will appear in all succeeding generations. On germline modification, author Carl Zimmer has

remarked: "It's an open question whether its effects would amount to short-lived ripples or major waves" (2005: 157).

5 See note 3, Chapter 24.

6 In "The Proactionary Principle: Optimizing Technological Outcomes" (2013), More states: "The Proactionary Principle is motivated by the need to make wise decisions about the development and deployment of new technologies *and* by the crucial need to protect technological experimentation and progress" (258).

7 As presented in Chapter 5.

8 For a comprehensive account on these subjects, see the anthology edited by Max More and Natasha Vita-More: "The Transhumanist Reader: Classical and Contemporary Essays on the Science, Technology, and Philosophy of the Human Future" (2013). See also: Birnbacher 2009.

9 The notion of bioethics here should be approached in a comprehensive way. For instance, in her influential text *Bioethics in the Age of New Media* (2009), Joanna Zylinska proposes bioethics as an ethics of life, revisiting the notion of life itself through "the new understanding of the relationship between humans, animals, and machines that new technologies and new media prompt us to develop" (vii).

10 As Jonathan Hill summarizes: "Animals cloned from somatic cells may display a combination of fetal and placental abnormalities that are manifested at different stages of pregnancy and postnatally" (2014: 307).

11 For a critical approach to the notion of inevitability in relation to human enhancement, see Fukuyama 2012, among others.

12 More specifically, the Northern states.

13 Italics in the original text.

Chapter 26

1 As Bernard Scott underlines, in his article "Second Order Cybernetics: An Historical Introduction" (2004): "'radical constructivism,' 'second-order cybernetics,' and 'autopoiesis' were coined to capture aspects of this new paradigm" (1371).

2 For an understanding of the notion of "poiesis," see Chapter 8.

3 In this article, Maturana and Varela thus describe an autopoietic machine: "A machine organized (defined as a unity) as a network of processes of production, transformation and destruction of components which: (i) through their interactions and transformations continuously regenerate and realize the network of processes (relations) that produced them; and (ii) constitute it (the machine) as a concrete unity in space in which they (the components) exist by specifying the topological domain of its realization as such a network" (1980: 135). Note that the use of the notion of machine, here, is intended to overlook the biocentric assumption for which life has to be organic.

4 In their words: "Our proposition is that living beings are characterized in that,
   literally, they are continually self-producing. We indicate this process when we call
   the organization that defines them as *autopoietic organization*" (1987a: 43).

5 Sociologist Niklas Luhmann (1927–98) developed his systems theory from
   Maturana and Varela's notion of autopoiesis.

6 Note that, in another article, Maturana wrote, "I do not think I should ever use
   the notion of self-organization, because that cannot be the case. Operationally it is
   impossible" (1987b: 71).

7 George Canguilhem (1904–95) offered a philosophical reflection on the
   biological significance of the environment, developed through the notion
   of milieu, in his work *Knowledge of Life* (1952), specifically in Part Three,
   Section Five "The Living and Its Milieu" (2008: 98–120), which starts with this
   statement:

   > The notion of milieu is becoming a universal and obligatory mode of
   > apprehending the experience and existence of living beings; one could almost
   > say it is now being constituted as a category of contemporary thought. (98)

   It is interesting to notice that, throughout the text, the milieu itself assumes a
   cognitive outfit which can be regarded as autopoietic:

   > Despite finding his ordinary perceptual experience contradicted and
   > corrected by scientific research, living man [*l'homme vivant*] draws from
   > his relation to the scientist [*l'homme savant*] a sort of unconscious self-
   > conceit, which makes him prefer his own milieu over the milieus of other
   > living beings, as having more reality and not just a different value. In fact, as
   > a proper milieu for comportment and life, the milieu of man's sensory and
   > technical values does not in itself have more reality than the milieus proper to
   > the woodlouse or the gray mouse. (119)

8 As cognitive scientist Marvin Minsky recalls in *The Society of Mind* (1985): "Each
   of the cells of which we're made, including those inside the brain, requires some
   chemical energy in the form of food or oxygen" (283).

9 Maturana and Varela state: "We will propose a way of seeing cognition not as a
   representation of the world 'out there,' but rather as an ongoing bringing forth of a
   world through the process of the living itself" (1987a: 11).

10 The Macy Conferences were a set of interdisciplinary meetings held between 1946
   and 1953, which led to the emergence of the field of cognitive science.

11 We shall note that Jerome Lettvin (1920–2011), co-author of the article, was not
   involved with the Macy Conferences.

12 The authors explicitly stated,

   > We used *Rana pipiens* in these experiments. We opened a small flap of bone
   > either just behind the eye to expose the optic nerve, or over the brain to

expose the superior colliculus. No further surgery was done except to open the membranes or connective tissue overlying the nervous structure. The frog was held in extension to a cork platform and covered with moist cloth. An animal in such a position, having most of his body surface in physical contact with something, goes into a still reaction, i.e., he will not even attempt to move save to react to pain, and except for the quick small incision of the skin at the start of the operation, our procedure seems to be painless to him. (1968: 240)

13 In *How We Became Posthuman*, Katherine Hayles dedicated long sections of Chapter 6 (1999: 131–59) to the frog experiment.

14 Throughout the article the frog is strictly referred to in the male gender. Nowhere is it specified that the frogs experimented upon were males; thus, we might imply that the universalized male form was a result of an uncritical use of gender non-neutral language. The fact that this lack of sensitivity was common at the time the article was published does not mean we should simply ignore it. Already hierarchical, gender non-neutral language can be an easy carrier for other types of biases, such as speciesism and anthropocentrism.

15 See note 14.

16 Let's examine, for instance, this passage: "The eye speaks to the brain in a language already highly organized . . . , instead of transmitting some more or less accurate copy of the distribution of light" (1968: 255) The fact that the frog elaborates reality differently from the human does not necessarily mean that one is closer than the other to the "real" perception of an "objective" reality; but so it appears in the article, where a "more accurate" copy, for instance, would apply to the human representation.

17 As they explain, "Such a description would require an interaction with the absolute to be described, but the representation which would arise from such an interaction would necessarily be determined by the autopoietic organization of the observer, not by the deforming agent; hence, the cognitive reality that it would generate would unavoidably be relative to the knower" (1980: 121).

18 As Hayles recalls:

Although the observer's perceptions construct reality rather than passively perceive it, for Maturana this construction depends on *positionality* rather than *personality*. In autopoietic theory, the opposite of objectivism is not subjectivism but relativism. (1999: 143)

19 For instance, in his genealogical effort to trace the sources of radical constructivism, Ernst von Glasersfeld (1995) places Maturana close to Giambattista Vico (1668–1744) and Immanuel Kant (1724–1804), among others.

20 This case could apply, for instance, in the hypothetical case of a specific AI takeover scenario, where humans, for different reasons, would be seen negatively by robots.

Chapter 27

1 *Oxford Dictionary*: Entry "relative," n. pg.
2 For a historical account on the relativist/absolutist dichotomized positions, see Gairdner 2008. For the differences between absolute relativism and cultural relativism, see Latour 1993: 103–14, among others.
3 It is interesting to note that the Latin words *species* and *speculum* (mirror) also derive from *specere*.
4 And still, the gaze inducing the perspective should not be reduced to the physical sight, but shall be addressed as a situated perception, that is, the situated and embodied process of becoming aware.
5 Third Essay, Chapter 12. This is the full passage:

> Let us be on guard against the dangerous old conceptual fiction that posited a 'pure, will-less, painless, timeless knowing subject'; let us guard against the snares of such contradictory concepts as 'pure reason,' 'absolute spirituality,' 'knowledge in itself': these always demand that we should think of an eye that is completely unthinkable, an eye turned in no particular direction, in which the active and interpreting forces, through which alone seeing becomes seeing *something*, are supposed to be lacking; these always demand of the eye an absurdity and a nonsense. There is *only* a perspective seeing, *only* a perspective 'knowing'; and the *more* affects we allow to speak about one thing, the *more* eyes, different eyes, we can use to observe one thing, the more complete will our 'concept' of this thing, our 'objectivity,' be. (2000: 555)

6 The first German edition was published in 1901 and contained 483 sections; in 1906, an expanded second edition was published, containing 1067 sections.
7 In Book Four, section 958 (1884), for instance, it is written that "I write for a species of man that does not yet exist: for the 'masters of the earth'" (1967: 503).
8 We should stress that Nietzsche does not consider perspectivism as a theory of knowledge, rather, as Sorgner points out, as "a theory which describes how everyone achieves their own apparent truths" (2007: 83).
9 Specifically, in Book Three, section 481 (1883–88).
10 In section 540 (1885).
11 We should remind that, according to Nietzsche, the death of God implies the death of any absolute external authority. See Chapter 9 for more on this point.
12 Think, for instance, of the rich debate which followed the essay "Is Multiculturalism bad for women?" by Susan Moller Okin, 1999.
13 See Chapter 18 for a reflection on forests as entities that are "subject of rights." Furthermore, the root system of a forest is also a well-developed communication

system; new scientific studies have recently revealed a new level of complexity in below-ground plant-plant interactions (Broberg, Anten and Ninkovic 2018).

14 The anti-human proposal should not to be confused with the philosophical movement of Antihumanism and the antihumanist approach, as presented in Part 1.

15 Nietzsche's view on the body can be found, for instance, in *Thus Spoke Zarathustra*, Part 1, chapter "On the Despisers of the Body," where he stated,

> But the awakened and knowing say: body am I entirely, and nothing else; and soul is only a word for something about the body. / The body is a great reason, a plurality with one sense, a war and a peace, a herd and a shepherd. An instrument of your body is also your little reason, my brother, which you call "spirit"—a little instrument and toy of your great reason. . . . Behind your thoughts and feelings, my brother, there stands a mighty ruler, an unknown sage—whose name is self. In your body he dwells; he is your body. / There is more reason in your body than in your best wisdom. . . . O despisers of the body! You are no bridge to the overman! (1976: 146–47)

16 As Maturana recalls: "The epistemological shift that I have made with the notion of autopoiesis . . . lies in abandoning the question of reality for the question of cognition while turning to explain the experience of the observer with the experience of the observer" (2002: 34). Maturana concludes this passage by stating: "This is a fundamental move away from a domain of transcendental ontologies to a domain of constitutive ontologies" (*ibidem*). In Maturana's constitutive ontology, the species-specific autopoietic perception defines what is experienced by the observer: an ontology based on the cognitive perspective which is enquiring, as we have seen in Chapter 27. Here, we should mention that Maturana and Varela's emphasis on phenomenology and immanence characterizes their entire theoretical and scientific production. For an extensive reflection on the key role of phenomenology in the development of cognitive science, see Varela, Thompson and Rosch 1991.

17 As stated by Nietzsche in section 636 (March–June 1888):

> Perspectivism is only a complex form of specificity. My idea is that every specific body strives to become master over all space and to extend its force (its will to power) and to thrust back all that resists its extension. But it continually encounters similar efforts on the part of other bodies and ends by coming to an arrangement ("union") with those of them that are sufficiently related to it: thus they can even conspire together for power. And the process goes on. (*ibidem*: 340)

18 Nietzsche emphasized this aspect in Book Three, sections 553–569 (1967: 300–07), as well as in other sections, such as 715 (November 1887–March 1888), which is quoted within this text following the present note.

19 "(1) Willens-Punktationen: meaning unclear; perhaps the point is that the will
    is not a single entity but more like a constantly shifting federation or alliance of
    drives—Translator's Note" (1967: 38).

20 As Sorgner clearly summarizes:

> As we enter deeper into Nietzsche's metaphysics, we have to realise that for
> him a thing is never an independent entity. A thing, a power-constellation is
> always what it does, and what it does can be different in respect to different
> power-constellations. So the thing in the end for Nietzsche can only be defined
> by the sum of its effects it has on other power constellations. (2007: 56)

21 For a further reflection on Bošković's influence on Nietzsche, see Whitlock 1999;
    Ansell Pearson 2000.

22 In *The Will to Power*, section 637 (1885), Nietzsche stated,

> Even in the domain of the inorganic an atom of force is concerned only with
> its neighborhood: distant forces balance one another. Here is the kernel of the
> perspective view and why a living creature is "egoistic" through and through.
> (1967: 340)

23 We will explain this point in Chapter 29.

Chapter 28

1 For the problematization related to the use of the adjective "new" in this context,
   see Lykke 2012. For a specific account on the posthumanist affiliation of New
   Materialism, see, for instance, Coole and Frost 2010: 7–15.

2 One of the proponents of this type of radical constructivism was philosopher Ernst
   von Glasersfeld (1917–2010), who elaborated on his theory of knowing in *Radical
   Constructivism: A Way of Knowing and Learning* (1995), among other texts.

3 For a critique of constructivism and representationalism from a posthumanist
   perspective, see Smith and Jenks 2006: 47–60.

4 In her article, "Butler's Sophisticated Constructivism: A Critical Assessment"
   (1999), Veronica Vasterling stated,

> During the last decade, a new paradigm has emerged in feminist theory:
> radical constructivism. Judith Butler's work is most closely linked to the
> new paradigm. On the basis of a creative appropriation of poststructuralist
> and psychoanalytical theory, Butler elaborates a new perspective on sex,
> gender and sexuality. A well-known expression of this new perspective is
> Butler's thesis, in *Bodies that Matter* (1993) that not only gender but also the
> materiality of the (sexed) body is discursively constructed. (17)

5 As Karen Barad stated: "If performativity is linked not only to the formation of the
   subject but also to the production of the matter of bodies, as Butler's account of

'materialization' and Haraway's notion of 'materialized refiguration' suggest, then it is all the more important that we understand the nature of this production" (2003: 808).

6 Specifically, Barad explains her views on the differences between Post-Trans-and Anti-Humanism in Note 6 (2007: 428). More generally on this subject, see the subchapter "Humanist Orbits" (134–37).

7 In Barad's words, "By invoking this contested term, I want to be clear that I am not interested in postmodernist celebrations (or demonizations) of the posthuman as living testimonies to the death of the human, nor as the next stage of Man" (2007: 136).

8 For a comprehensive account on vitalism—both historically and theoretically—see Canguilhem's *Knowledge of Life* (1952), specifically Part Three, Section 3 "Aspects of Vitalism" (2008: 59–74).

9 This is why some scientists and philosophers have attempted to find alternative notions, such as autopoiesis (although this term has its limits as well, as we have seen in Chapter 26).

10 For instance, the work on vitalism done by Rosi Braidotti, which is of key relevance to the field of Posthuman Studies, is located within this specific genealogy.

11 For example, in his monograph *Object-Oriented Ontology: A New Theory of Everything*, Grahamn Harman dedicates a section to Jane Bennett, defining her as a "Fellow Traveller" within the OOO movement (Chapter 6: 240–43).

12 David Roden's *Posthuman Life* (2015), and more in general his work, offers a thorough reflection on the affinities between the posthuman turn and OOO.

13 For an understanding on the ontological turn, see, for instance, Cohen 2017.

14 Antihuman shall not be confused with antihumanist, see note 14 in Chapter 27.

15 For a thorough critical reflection on this notion, see Brassier 2015.

16 It is significant, as David Roden notes, that "one of DeLanda characterizations of flat ontology occurs during a discussion of the ontological status of biological species in which he sides with philosophers who hold that species are individuals rather than types or universals" (2015: 114).

17 Note that Deleuze and Guattari's notion of plane of immanence (1987) should not be assimilated to DeLanda's flat ontology.

18 For a reflection on this point, see Chapters 25 and 26.

19 As Wolfendale clearly summarizes, correlationism "is characterized by the idea that the world (and its objects) cannot be thought outside of its relation to thought (and its subjects)" (297).

20 Barad thus explains her ontological approach: "*Thingification*—the turning of relations into 'things,' 'entities,' 'relata'—infects much of the way we understand the world and our relationship to it. Why do we think that the existence of relations requires relata?" (2003: 812). To which, she answers: "I present a relational ontology that rejects the metaphysics of relata, of 'words' and 'things.' On an agential realist

account, it is once again possible to acknowledge nature, the body, and materiality in the fullness of their becoming" (*ibidem*).

21 According to the *Oxford Dictionary*, a relatum (singular form for "relata" in Latin) means "each of two or more terms, objects, or events between which a relation exists." Entry: relatum, n. pg. *Note mine.*

Chapter 29

1 Atoms were thought to be the building blocks of matter until early twentieth century, when, passing from the Bohr model (1913) to James Chadwick's atomic one (1932), it was discovered that they were also composite, made of electrons, protons, and neutrons. Then again, these models were discovered to be composed of still smaller particles, named "quarks," which were independently proposed in 1964 by two American physicists: Murray Gell-Mann and George Zweig. In the late 1960s, this model was again redefined by string theory. On the history of modern physics, see, among others, Segrè 1980; Heilbron 2005.

2 Between the late 1960s, early 1970s, many physicists independently contributed to this theory, including Gabriele Veneziano, Yoichiro Nambu, Holger Bech Nielsen, and Leonard Susskind. For a comprehensive account on string theory, see, for instance, Greene 1999.

3 It is important to note that, currently, string theory is a mathematical model not supported by experimental evidence yet, and so it has been criticized for its lack of falsifiability (Woit 2006; Smolin 2006).

4 Please note that, in this text, we will not engage in a reflection on Bohmian mechanics (also called de Broglie-Bohm theory or the pilot-wave model), a field which is gaining some attention in the scientific community. Although this version of quantum mechanics supports a deterministic model, it relies on the condition of hidden variables (that is, states in the system which would be hidden from us) (Bohm 1952), thus making it not fully deterministic either. The same observation can apply to the hidden-measurements interpretation of quantum mechanics, another realistic interpretation relying on the condition of hidden measurements (that is, unavoidable fluctuations in the measurement system) (Aerts 1986).

5 For a historical account on the wave-particle duality, see, for instance, Wheaton 1983.

6 Here, we shall remind that Barad earned her doctorate in theoretical physics; her rigorous scientific knowledge pervades her philosophical insights.

7 The concept of the observer effect can be first traced in the writings of Niels Bohr (1885–1962), and specifically, in a reply he wrote to Einstein, Podolsky, and Rosen, where he stated, "The procedure of measurement has an essential

influence on the conditions on which the very definition of the physical quantities in question rests" (1935: 1025). For an extensive reflection on this notion, see, for instance, Stapp 2007.

8 See note 1 in Introduction.

9 Italics in the original text.

10 In *The Hidden Reality* (2011), theoretical physicist Brian Greene recognizes nine different types of multiverse, one of which being precisely the landscape multiverse. The other eight are the quilted multiverse, the inflationary multiverse, the brane multiverse, the cyclic multiverse, and the quantum multiverse, the holographic multiverse, the simulated multiverse, and the ultimate multiverse. For a comprehensive scientific account on the notion of the multiverse, see also Kaku 2005.

11 Thomas Huxley was a fervent supporter of Charles Darwin's theory of evolution, and he played a pivotal role in the publication of Darwin's *On the Origin of Species* (1859). He was also the grandfather of Aldous Huxley and Julian Huxley, whose work we have referred to in Part 1.

12 In a general and ironic way, we can say, in the words of Robert Shea (1933–94) and Robert Anton Wilson (1932–2007): "Every fact of science was once damned. Every invention was considered impossible. Every discovery was a nervous shock to some orthodoxy. Every artistic innovation was denounced as fraud and folly" (1975: 793). This type of reflection relates to the widespread motto of the counterculture of the 1960s: "Be realistic: demand the impossible."

Chapter 30

1 Here, I decided to present Tegmark's classification, instead of Greene's (as depicted in note 10 of Chapter 29): both are scientifically exhaustive, but Tegmark's is less analytic and more synthetic.

2 We will also include Tegmark's original definitions, in notes 4, 6, 7, and 9 of this chapter.

3 I thank Dr. John Studley for this observation.

4 This is how Tegmark describes it,

> If space is infinite and the distribution of matter is sufficiently uniform on large scales, then even the most unlikely events must take place somewhere. In particular, there are infinitely many other inhabited planets, including not just one but infinitely many with people with the same appearance, name and memories as you. Indeed, there are infinitely many other regions the size of our observable universe, where every possible cosmic history is played out. (2010: 559)

5 It is important to note that Georges Lemaître (1894–1966), in an article published
   in 1927, was actually the first to propose the theory of the expansion of the
   universe; nevertheless, this theory was later defined as the "Hubble's law."

6 In Tegmark's words,

> Try imagining an infinite set of distinct [universes] . . . , some perhaps with
> different dimensionality and different physical constants. This is what is
> predicted by most currently popular models of inflation, and we will refer to it
> as the Level II multiverse. These other domains are more than infinitely far away
> in the sense that you would never get there even if you traveled at the speed of
> light forever. The reason is that the space between our Level I multiverse and
> its neighbors is still undergoing inflation, which keeps stretching it out and
> creating more volume faster than you can travel through it. (2010: 564)

7 Tegmark thus explains this level:

> If Everett was correct and physics is unitary, then there is a third type of
> parallel worlds that are not far away but in a sense right here. The universe
> keeps branch- ing into parallel universes . . . : whenever a quantum event
> appears to have a random outcome, all outcomes in fact occur, one in each
> branch. This is the Level III multiverse. (*ibidem:* 568)

8 Note that the term "many-worlds" was only later attributed to Everett's theory by
   Bryce Seligman DeWitt (1973).

9 As Tegmark defines it

> If there is a particular mathematical structure that is our universe, and its
> properties correspond to our physical laws, then each mathematical structure
> with different properties is its own universe with different laws. The Level IV
> multiverse is compulsory, since mathematical structures are not "created" and
> don't exist "somewhere"—they just exist. (2010: 575)

10 The notion of the uncanny has been of particular relevance in the development
   of the philosophy of artificial intelligence, to refer to the relation between human
   and robots. See for instance note 13 of Chapter 20, on the theory of the "uncanny
   valley" as developed by Masahiro Mori (1970).

11 In Chapter 19, we have underlined how humans and the environment are
   co-constituting each other, and thus cannot be understood in separation.

12 "Anthropocenic" means of the Anthropocene. For more on the Anthropocene,
   see Chapter 19.

13 We shall note that, within this frame, the multiverse includes, but it is not limited to,
   notions such as "parallel dimensions," "parallel worlds," and "alternative realities."

14 Italics mine.

15 Such an optimistic view was famously satirized by Voltaire (1694–1778) in his
   Candide: or, The Optimist (1759).

16 For instance, Tim Wilkinson in his article "The Multiverse Conundrum" (2012) notes that during medieval times, the question whether God had created many world was as relevant as for the Bishop of Paris, Étienne Tempier, to issue a series of condemnations in 1277 "to explicitly denounce Aristotle's view of there being only one possible world, which he thought to be at odds with God's omnipotence" (n. pg.).

17 On the notion of possible worlds in Al-Ghazali's work *The Incoherence of the Philosophers*, see Kukkonen 2000a.

18 On the notion of possible worlds in Averroes's work *The Incoherence of the Incoherence*, see Kukkonen 2000b.

19 Note that referring to Fakhr al-Din al-Razi's articulate reflection on the notion of possible worlds in his work *Matalib al-'Aliya* (Engl. Trans. *The Higher Issues*), scholar Adi Setia uses the term "multiverse" (Setia 2004).

20 For a reflection on Duns Scotus's view on possible worlds, see Langston 1990; for Scotus's reflection on the possible, see King 2001; for the differences between Scotus and Leibniz on possible worlds, see Knuuttila 1996: 131–34.

21 According to Lewis, there is one hypothetical exception: "They have no parts in common, with the exception, perhaps, of immanent universals exercising their characteristic privilege of repeated occurrence" (1986: 2).

22 Modal essentialism suggests that specific sets of characteristics strictly apply to the modalities in which these worlds would manifest and materialize, emphasizing fixed traits over the entangled processes through which these possible worlds would be co-constituting each other as such.

23 We have explained the notion of solipsism in Chapter 26.

24 I am referring to string theory, as presented in Chapter 29.

25 In physics, spacetime refers to a continuum of the three dimensions of space plus time as a fourth dimension.

26 The network theory is an area of studies related to computer sciences and graph theories, which has developed a specific reflection on the significance of the notion of links and of nodes (see, for instance, Barabasi 2003) within representational, logistical, but also social and biological networks.

27 *Oxford Dictionary*: Entry "rhizome," n. pg.

28 Here, we shall bring to mind Nietzsche's hypothesis on the subject as a multiplicity, which is exposed in *The Will to Power,* Book Three, section 490 (1885):

> The assumption of one single subject is perhaps unnecessary; perhaps it is just as permissible to assume a multiplicity of subjects, whose interaction and struggle is the basis of our thought and our consciousness in general? A kind of aristocracy of "cells" in which dominion resides? To be sure, an aristocracy of equals, used to ruling jointly and understanding how to command? *My hypotheses*: the subject as multiplicity. (1967: 270)

The perception of the subject as a multiplicity offers interesting insights for a materialistic view of the Self as many, within the frame of a posthuman multiverse.

29 For a development of all these notions from a specific posthumanist standpoint, see Braidotti 2002.

30 It is important to note that this is just a possible reading. As Rosi Braidotti states, "I would recommend that we resist quick assimilations of, for instance, Deleuzian machines as metaphors for advanced technologies" (2005" n. pg.).

31 Here, I would rather use this definition instead of "parallel universes," since these other dimensions may be neither parallel nor universes. The notion of "interpermeating dimensions" shares some aspects in common with the concept of "plane" in esoteric cosmology, but it cannot be assimilated to it either, as these dimensions would not evolve, hierarchically, around a center of spiritual unity, an Absolute, which is a premise of many religious and esoteric teachings.

32 For a reflection on Foucault's technologies of the self, see Chapter 15.

Interlude 3

1 This Greek term is equivalent to the Latin *mores*.

2 See, for instance, the *Iliad*, Book 6: ἤθεα ἵππων "the habitats of horses" (Homer, n. year).

Concluding Celebration

1 More specifically, we do not have to wait until the near future to be posthuman, as the transhumanist take on this notion may suggest. For a clarification on this point, see Chapter 3.

2 See, for instance, Speculative Posthumanism, as discussed in Chapter 25.

3 For a philosophical reflection which emphasizes the relevance of non-human agents, see, among others, Schatzki 2001.

4 Think, for instance, of the notion of the noosphere. According to Teilhard de Chardin, the noosphere is the sphere of the mind, "a thinking layer" (1959: 202). More specifically, he explains: "This amounts to imagining, in one way or another, above the animal biosphere a human sphere, the sphere of reflexivity, of conscious invention, of the conscious unity of souls, the noosphere if you will, and to conceiving, at the origin of this new entity, a phenomenon of special transformation affecting pre-existent life: hominisation" (1966: 63).

5 In oceanography, anomalous waves, also called "freak waves" and "rogue waves," are considered rare, unpredictable and, potentially, extremely impactful.

Bibliography

Adam, A. (1998). *Artificial Knowing: Gender and the Thinking Machine*. Routledge: London et al.

Aerts, D. (1986). A Possible Explanation for the Probabilities of Quantum Mechanics. In: *Journal of Mathematical Physics*, Vol. 27, 202–10.

Agamben, G. [1995] (1998). *Homo Sacer: Sovereign Power and Bare Life*. Trans. Heller-Roazen, D., Stanford University Press: Stanford.

Agamben, G. [2002] (2004). *The Open: Man and Animal*. Trans. Attell, K., Stanford University Press: Stanford.

Alighieri, D. [1304–1321]. *La Divina Commedia di Dante Alighieri*. Trans. Cary, H. F. (1909). *The Divine Comedy*, Vol. 20. Harvard Classics, Collier and Son Company: New York.

Ansell Pearson, K. (1997). *Viroid Life: Perspectives on Nietzsche and the Transhuman Condition*. Routledge: London et al.

Ansell Pearson, K. (2000). Nietzsche's Brave New World of Force: Thoughts on Nietzsche's 1873 "Time Atom Theory" Fragment & on the Influence of Boscovich on Nietzsche. In: *Pli: The Warwick Journal of Philosophy*, No. 9, 6–35.

Ansell Pearson, K. (2011). The Future is Superhuman: Nietzsche's Gift. In: *The Agonist: A Nietzsche Circle Journal*, Vol. IV, Issue II, Fall 2011. Retrieved in January 2019: http://www.nietzschecircle.com/AGONIST/2011_08/Superhuman.html

Anzaldúa, G. (1987). *Borderlands/La Frontera: The New Mestiza*. Aunt Lute Books: San Francisco.

Appleby, J. (2002). Planned Obsolescence: Flying into the Future with Stelarc. In: Zylinska, J. (ed.) (2002). *The Cyborg Experiments: The Extensions of the Body in the Media Age*. Continuum: London et al., 101–13.

Arendt, H. (1958). *The Human Condition*. The University of Chicago Press: Chicago et al.

Aristotle [fourth century BCE] (1944). Politics. In: *Aristotle in 23 Volumes*, Vol. 21. Trans. Rackham, H., Harvard University Press: Cambridge, MA; William Heinemann Ltd.: London. Retrieved in January 2019: http://www.perseus.tufts.edu/hopper/text?doc=Perseus:abo:tlg,0086,035:1:1253a

Aristotle [fourth century BCE] (2000). *Nicomachean Ethics: Book VI*. Trans. Crisp, R., Cambridge University Press: New York, 103–18.

Babich, B. (2011). Nietzsche's Post-Human Imperative: On the "All-too-Human" Dream of Transhumanism. In: *The Agonist: A Nietzsche Circle Journal*, Vol. IV, Issue II, Fall 2011. Retrieved in January 2019: http://www.nietzschecircle.com/AGONIST/2011_08/Dream_of_Transhumanism.html

Badiou, A., Cassin, B. (2016). *Heidegger: His Life and His Philosophy*. Columbia University Press: New York.

Badmington, N. (ed.) (2000). *Posthumanism*. Palgrave: New York.

Badmington, N. (2004). *Alien Chic: Posthumanism and the Other Within*. Routledge: Oxon.

Bailey, M. D. (2002). The Feminization of Magic and the Emerging Idea of the Female Witch in the Late Middle Ages. In: *Essays in Medieval Studies*, Vol. 19, 120–34.

Bailey, M. D. (2007). *Magic and Superstition in Europe: A Concise History from Antiquity to the Present*. Rowman and Littlefield Publishers: Lanham.

Bailey, R. (2005). *Liberation Biology: The Scientific and Moral Case for the Biotech Revolution*. Prometheus: New York.

Bakhtin, M. M. [1941] [1965] (1993). *Rabelais and His World*. Trans. Iswolsky, H., Indiana University Press: Bloomington.

Balsamo, A. (1996). *Technologies of the Gendered Body: Reading Cyborg Women*. Duke University Press: Durham et al.

Barabasi, A. L. (2003). *Linked: How Everything is Connected to Everything Else and What It Means for Business, Science, and Everyday Life*. Plume: New York.

Barad, K. (2003). Posthumanist Performativity: Toward an Understanding of How Matter Comes to Matter. In: *Signs: Journal of Women in Culture and Society*, Vol. 28, No. 3, The University of Chicago, 801–31.

Barad, K. (2007). *Meeting the Universe Halfway: Quantum Physics and the Entanglement of Matter and Meaning*. Duke University Press: Durham et al.

Bars, I., Terning, J., Nekoogar, F., Krauss, L. (2010). *Extra Dimensions in Space and Time (Multiversal Journeys)*. Springer: New York.

Barton, E. R., et al. (2002). Muscle-specific Expression of Insulin-like Growth Factor 1 Counters Muscle Decline in mdx Mice. In: *Journal of Cell Biology*, Vol. 157, 137–48.

Baudrillard, J. [1981] (1994). *Simulacra and Simulation*. Trans. Glaser, S. F., The University of Michigan Press: Ann Arbor.

Bauer, A., Bauer, R. (1942). Day to Day Resistance to Slavery. In: *The Journal of Negro History*, Vol. 27, 388–419.

Bauman, R. (2000). *Human Rights in Ancient Rome*. Routledge: London et al.

Becerra, A., Delaye, L. (2016). The Universal Ancestor: An Unfinished Reconstruction. In: *Mètode Science Studies Journal*, No. 6, University of Valencia, 145–49.

Bechdel, A. (1985). The Rule. In: *Dykes to Watch Out For*. Retrieved on January 2019: http://dykestowatchoutfor.com/the-rule

Bechtel, W., Richardson, R. C. (1998). Vitalism. In: Craig, E. (ed.) *Routledge Encyclopedia of Philosophy*. Routledge: London. Retrieved in January 2019: https://www.rep.routledge.com/articles/thematic/vitalism/v-1

Bedau, M. A., McCaskill, J. S., Packard, N. H., Rasmussen, S., Adami, C., Green, D. G., Ikegami, T., Kaneko, K., Ray, T. S. (2000). Open Problems in Artificial Life. In: *Artificial Life*, Vol. 6, No. 4, 363–76.

Bell, D., Kennedy, B. M. (eds.) (2000). *The Cybercultures Reader*. Routledge: London et al.

Bennett, J. (2010). *Vibrant Matter: A Political Ecology of Things*. Duke University Press: Durham et al.

Bennett, J. (2017). Vibrant Matter. In: Braidotti, R., Hlavajova, M. (eds.) (2017), 447–48.

Beran, T. N., et al. (2011). Understanding How Children Understand Robots: Perceived Animism in Child–Robot Interaction. In: *International Journal of Human-Computer Studies*, Vol. 69, Issue 7–8, July 2011, 539–50.

Bibliotheca Teubneriana Latina (BTL) (2009). De Gruyter: Berlin. Retrieved in January 2019: http://www.degruyter.com/databasecontent?dbid=btl&dbsource=%2Fdb%2F btl

Birnbacher, D. (2009). Posthumanity, Transhumanism and Human Nature. In: Chadwick, R., Gordijn, B. (2009), 95–106.

Biti, V. (2016). *Tracing Global Democracy: Literature, Theory, and the Politics of Trauma*. Walter de Gruyter: Berlin and Boston.

Bohm, D. (1952). A Suggested Interpretation of the Quantum Theory in Terms of "Hidden" Variables, I and II. In: *Physical Review*, Vol. 85, Issue 2, 166–93.

Bohr, N. (1913). On the Constitution of Atoms and Molecules, Part I. In: *Philosophical Magazine*, Vol. 26, No. 151, 1–24.

Bohr, N. (1935). Quantum Mechanics and Physical Reality. In: *Nature*, Vol. 136, 1025–26.

Bostrom, N. (2005). A History of Transhumanist Thought. In: *Journal of Evolution and Technology*, Vol. 14, Issue 1, April 2005, 1–25. Retrieved in January 2019: http:// jetpress.org/volume14/bostrom.html

Bostrom, N., Roache, R. (2008). Ethical Issues in Human Enhancement. In: Ryberg, J., Petersen, T., Wolf, C. (eds) (2007) *New Waves in Applied Ethics*. Palgrave Macmillan: Basingstoke, 120–52. Retrieved in January 2019: https://nickbostrom.com/ethics/ human-enhancement.pdf

Bostrom, N. (2014). *Superintelligence*. Oxford University Press: Oxford, UK.

Bowler, P. J. (2003). *Evolution: The History of an Idea*. University of California Press: Berkeley.

Braidotti, R. (1994). *Nomadic Subjects: Embodiment and Sexual Difference in Contemporary Feminist Theory*. Columbia University Press: New York.

Braidotti, R. (1996a). Signs of Wonder and Traces of Doubt: On Teratology and Embodied Differences. In: Lykke N., Braidotti R. (1996) *Between Monsters, Goddesses and Cyborgs*. Zed Books: London, 135–52.

Braidotti, R. (1996b). Cyberfeminism with a Difference. In: *New Formations*, No. 29, Autumn 1996, 9–25.

Braidotti, R. (2002). *Metamorphoses: Towards a Materialist Theory of Becoming*. Polity: Cambridge, UK.

Braidotti, R. (2003). Is Metal to Flesh like Masculine to Feminine? University of Auckland, Department of Film and Media Studies. Retrieved in March 2007: http:// www.arts.auckland.ac.nz/tcs/data/2.htm

Braidotti, R. (2005). Affirming the Affirmative: On Nomadic Affectivity. In: *Rhizomes*, Vol. 11, No. 12 (Fall 2005/Spring 2006). Retrieved in January 2019: http://www.rhizomes. net/issue11/braidotti.html

Braidotti, R. (2006). *Transpositions: On Nomadic Ethics*. Polity: Cambridge, UK.

Braidotti, R. (2012). *Nomadic Theory: The Portable Rosi Braidotti*. Columbia University Press: New York.

Braidotti, R. (2013). *The Posthuman*. Polity: Cambridge, UK.

Braidotti, R., Hlavajova, M. (eds.) (2017). *The Posthuman Glossary*. Bloomsbury: London.

Braidotti, R. (2018). A Theoretical Framework for the Critical Posthumanities. In: *Theory, Culture & Society*, Vol. 0, No. 0, 1–31.

Brassier, R. (2015). Develeling: Against "Flat Ontologies." In: Dijk, V., et al. (eds.), *Under Influence - Philosophical Festival Drift (2014)*. Omnia, 64–80. Retrieved on January 2019: https://uberty.org/wp-content/uploads/2015/05/ RayBrassierDelevelingAgainstFlatOntologies.pdf

Bray, A., Colebrook, C. (1998). The Haunted Flesh: Corporeal Feminism and the Politics of (Dis)Embodiment. In: *Signs*, Vol. 24, No. 1, Autumn, 35–67.

Brezzi, F. (2005). Una Rivelazione Altra. In: Ales Bello, A., Pezzella, A. M. (eds.), *Il Femminile tra Oriente e Occidente: Religioni, Letteratura, Storia, Cultura*. Citta' Nuova: Roma, 125–60.

Broberg, A., Anten, N. P. R., Ninkovic, V. (2018). Aboveground Mechanical Stimuli Affect Belowground Plant-Plant Communication. In: *PLoS One*, Vol. 13, Issue 5, May 2018, 1–15.

Brooks, R. (2002). *Flesh and Machine: How Robots Will Change Us*. Pantheon Books: New York.

Brown, K. W., Kasser, T. (2005). Are Psychological and Ecological Well-Being Compatible? The Role of Values, Mindfulness and Lifestyle. In: *Social Indicators Research*, Vol. 74, 349–68.

Burke, A., Gonzalez, A. (2011). Growing Interest in Meditation in the United States. In: *Biofeedback*, Vol. 39, No. 2, Summer 2011, 49–50.

Butler, J. [1990] (1999). *Gender Trouble: Feminism and the Subversion of Identity.* Routledge: New York et al.

Butler, J. (1993). *Bodies that Matter: On the Discursive Limits of Sex*. Routlegde: New York.

Butler, J. (2004). *Undoing Gender*. Routledge: New York.

Caecilius, S. [180 BC ca.]. Fragments. In: Ennius, C. (1935). *Remains of Old Latin*, Vol. I, No. 294. Trans. Warmington, E. H., Harvard University Press: Cambridge, MA.

Calarco, M. (2008). *Zoographies: The Question of the Animal from Heidegger to Derrida*. Columbia University Press: New York.

Canguilhem, G. [1943] (1989). *The Normal and the Pathological*. Trans. Fawcett, C. R., Zone Books: New York.

Canguilhem, G. [1952] (2008). *Knowledge of Life*. Trans. Geroulanos, S., Ginsburg, D., Fordham University Press: New York.

Čapek, K. [1920] (2004). *R.U.R. Rossum's Universal Robots.* Penguin: New York.

Capra, F. (1975). *The Tao of Physics: An Exploration of the Parallels between Modern Physics and Eastern Mysticism.* Shambhala: Boston, MA.

Chadwick, J. (1932). Possible Existence of a Neutron. In: *Nature*, Vol. 129, No. 3252, 312.

Chadwick, R., Gordijn, B. (eds.) (2009). *Medical Enhancement and Posthumanity.* Springer: Berlin et al.

Chakrabarty, D. (2009). The Climate of History: Four Theses. In: *Critical Inquiry*, Vol. 35, Issue 2, 197–222.

Channell, D. F. (1991). *The Vital Machine: A Study of Technology and Organic Life.* Oxford University Press: New York et al.

Charpentier, E., Doudna, J. A. (2013). Biotechnology: Rewriting a Genome. In: *Nature*, Vol. 495, Issue 7439, July 3, 2013, 50–51.

Chessick, R. (1995). The Effect of Heidegger's Pathological Narcissism on the Development of His Philosophy. In: Adams, J., Williams, E. (eds.), *Mimetic Desire: Essays on Narcissism in German Literature from Romanticism.* Camden House: Columbia, SC, 103–18.

Chivian, E., Bernstein, A. (eds.) (2008). *Sustaining Life: How Human Health Depends on Biodiversity.* Oxford University Press: New York.

Cicero, M. T. [44 BC] (1913). *De Officiis.* Trans. Miller, W., Harvard University Press: Cambridge, MA.

Clough, P. (2007). *The Affective Turn: Theorizing the Social.* Duke University Press: Durham and London.

Clynes, M. E., Kline, N. S. (1960). Cyborgs and Space. In: *Astronautics*, September, 26–27, 74–76. Reprinted in: Gray, C. H., et al. (1995), 29–34.

Cohen, B. (1988). The Computer: A Case Study of the Support by Government, Especially the Military, of a New Science and Technology. In: Mendelsohn, et al. (1988), 119–54.

Cohen, J. J. (2017). The Ontological Turn. In: Braidotti, R., Hlavajova, M. (eds.) (2017), 447–48.

Colby, F. S. (2008). *Narrating Muhammad's Night Journey: Teaching the Development of the Ibn 'Abbas Ascension Discourse.* State University of New York Press: Albany.

Cook, A. (2010). Linnaeus and Chinese plants: A Test of the Linguistic Imperialism Thesis. In: *Notes and Records of The Royal Society*, Vol. 64, No. 2, 121–38.

Coole, D., Frost, S. (2010). *New Materialisms: Ontology, Agency and Politics.* Duke University Press: Durham et al.

Cordrick Haely, K. (2008). *Objectivity in the Feminist Philosophy of Science.* Continuum: London.

Crenshaw, Kimberle (1989). Demarginalizing the Intersection of Race and Sex: A Black Feminist Critique of Antidiscrimination Doctrine, Feminist Theory and Antiracist Politics. In: *University of Chicago Legal Forum*, Vol. 1989, Article 8. Retrieved on January 2019: https://chicagounbound.uchicago.edu/uclf/vol1989/iss1/8

Crichton, M. [1972] (2002). *The Terminal Man*. Avon Books: New York.

Crutzen, P. J., Stoermer, E. F. (2000). The "Anthropocene." In: *Global Change Newsletter*, No. 41, 17–18.

Curran, A. S. (2011). *The Anatomy of Blackness: Science and Slavery in an Age of Enlightenment*. The Johns Hopkins University Press: Baltimore.

Danius, S., Jonsson, S., Spivak, G. C. (1993). An Interview with Gayatri Chakravorty Spivak. In: *Boundary 2*, Vol. 20, No. 2, 24–50.

Darwin, C. (1859). *On the Origin of Species by Means of Natural Selection: Or, The Preservation of Favoured Races in the Struggle for Life*. John Murray: London.

Davies, T. (1997). *Humanism*. Routlegde: London et al.

Davis, L. J. (ed.) (2006). *Disability Studies Reader*. Routledge: New York.

De Beauvoir [1949] (1974). *The Second Sex*. Trans. Parshley, H. M., Vintage Books, New York.

De Beauvoir [1949] (2009). *The Second Sex*. Trans. Borde, C., Malovany-Chevallier, S., Jonathan Cape: London.

De Garis, H. (2005). *The Artilect War: Cosmists vs Terrans, A Bitter Controversy Concerning Whether Humanity Should Build Godlike Massively Intelligent Machines*. ETC Publications: Palm Springs.

De las Casas, B. [1550 ca.] (1967). *Apologética Historia Sumaria*. Edited by O'Gorman, E., Universidad Nacional Autónoma de México: México, D. F.

De Las Casas, B. [1527–1561] (1971). *History of the Indies*. Trans. Collard, A., Harper Torchbooks: New York et al.

DeLanda, M. (2002). *Intensive Science & Virtual Philosophy*. Continuum: London.

Deleuze, G. [1970] (1988). *Spinoza: Practical Philosophy*. Trans. Hurley, R., City Lights Book: San Francisco.

Deleuze, G., Guattari, F. [1980] (1987). *A Thousand Plateaus: Capitalism and Schizophrenia*. Trans. Massumi, B., Continuum: London.

Del Val, J., Sorgner, S. [2010] (2011). A Metahumanist Manifesto. In: *The Agonist: A Nietzsche Circle Journal*, Vol. IV, Issue II, Fall 2011. Retrieved in January 2019: http://www.nietzschecircle.com/AGONIST/2011_08/METAHUMAN_MANIFESTO.html

Derrida, J. [1967] (1976). *Of Grammatology*. Trans. Gayatri Chakravorty Spivak, Johns Hopkins University Press: Baltimore.

Dery, M. (1993). Black to the Future: Interviews with Samuel R. Delany, Greg Tate, and Tricia Rose. In: Dery, M. (1994). *Flame Wars: The Discourse of Cyberculture*. Duke University Press: Durham, 179–222.

DeWitt, B. S., Graham, R. N. (eds.) (1973). *The Many-Worlds Interpretation of Quantum Mechanics*. Princeton University Press: Princeton.

Diamond, P. (2016) Las Casas' In Defense of the Indians: Can A Just War Be Waged Against Barbarians? In: Gish, D., Constas, C., et al. (eds.) *The Quest for Excellence*. Rowman & Littlefield: Lanham, MD, 157–62.

Doane, M. (1990). Technophilia: Technology, Representation, and the Feminine. In: Jacobus, M., Fox Keller, E., Shuttleworth, S. (eds.) (1990). *Body/Politics: Women and the Discourses of Science.* Routledge: New York et al., 163–76.

Dolinoy, D. C. (2008). The Agouti Mouse Model: An Epigenetic Biosensor for Nutritional and Environmental Alterations on the Fetal Epigenome. In: *Nutrition Review*, Vol. 66, Suppl. 1, August 2008, S7–11.

Dolphijn, R., van der Tuin, I. (2010). The Transversality of New Materialism. In: *Women: A Cultural Review*, Vol. 21, Issue 2, Routledge: London, 153–71.

Dolphijn, R., van der Tuin, I. (2012). *New Materialism: Interviews & Cartographies.* Open Humanities Press: University of Michigan.

Doudna, J. (2018). The Ultimate Life Hacker. In: *Journal Foreign Affairs*, Vol. 97, Issue 3, January 2018, 158–65.

Douthwaite, J. V. (2002). *The Wild Girl, Natural Man, and the Monster: Dangerous Experiments in the Age of Enlightenment.* University of Chicago Press: Chicago.

Dubois, W. E. B. (1897). *The Conservation of Races.* The Academy: Washington DC.

Dunn, R. (2009). *Every Living Thing: Man's Obsessive Quest to Catalog Life, from Nanobacteria to New Monkeys.* HarperCollins: New York.

Dvorsky, G., Hughes, J. (2008). Postgenderism: Beyond the Gender Binary. In: *IEET White Paper.* Hartford, CT: Institute for Ethics and Emerging Technologies. Retrieved in January 2019: http://ieet.org/archive/IEET-03-PostGender.pdf

Einstein, A. [1916]. The Foundation of the General Theory of Relativity. Trans. Parret, W., Jeffrey, G. B. In: Einstein, A., Lorentz, H. A., Minkowski, H., Weyl., H. (1952). *The Principle of Relativity: A Collection of Original Memoirs on the Special and General Theory of Relativity.* Dover: New York, 109–64.

Eliot, T. S. [1950] (1978). *The Cocktail Party: A Comedy.* Harcourt: Orlando.

Esposito, R. (2008). *Bíos: Biopolitics and Philosophy.* Posthumanities Series, Trans. Campbell, T., University of Minnesota Press: Minneapolis et al.

Ettinger, R. (1962). The Prospect of Immortality. Retrieved in January 2019: https://www.cryonics.org/images/uploads/misc/Prospect_Book.pdf

Everett, H. [1956]. Theory of the Universal Wave Function. In: DeWitt, B. S., Graham, R. N. (1973), 3–140.

Ferrando, F. (2012). Towards a Posthumanist Methodology. A Statement. In: *Frame, Journal For Literary Studies*, Vol. 25, No. 1, Narrating Posthumanism, Utrecht University, 9–18.

Ferrando, F. (2013). From the Eternal Recurrence to the Posthuman Multiverse. In: *The Agonist, The Nietzsche Circle*, Vol. VI, Issue I & II, Spring & Fall 2013, 1–11.

Ferrando, F. (2014a). Is the Post-Human a Post-Woman? Robots, Cyborgs and the Futures of Gender. In: *European Journal of Futures Research*, Vol. 2, Issue 43, September 2014, Springer, 1–17.

Ferrando, F. (2014b). The Body. In: Ranisch, R., Sorgner, S. L. (2014), 213–26.

Ferrando, F. (2014c). Posthumanism, Transhumanism, Antihumanism, Metahumanism, and New Materialisms: Differences and Relations. In: *Existenz*, The Karl Jaspers Society of North America, Vol. 8, No. 2, March 2014, 26–32.

Ferrando, F. (2015). Of Posthuman Born: Gender, Utopia and the Posthuman. In: Hauskeller, M. Philbeck, T. D., et al. (eds.), 269–78.

Ferrando, F. (2016a). Humans Have Always Been Posthuman: A Spiritual Genealogy of the Posthuman. In: Banerji, D., Paranjape, M. R. (eds.), *Critical Posthumanism and Planetary Futures*. Springer: New Delhi, 243–56.

Ferrando, F. (2016b). The Party of the Anthropocene: Posthumanism, Environmentalism and the Post-Anthropocentric Paradigm Shift. In: *Relations: Beyond Anthropocentrism*, Vol. 4, No. 2, November 2016, 159–73.

Feyerabend, P. (1975). *Against Method: Outline of an Anarchist Theory of Knowledge*. Verso: London.

Fiedler, L. (1978). *Freaks: Myths and Images of the Secret Self*. Simon and Schuster: New York.

Finlayson, C. (2009). *The Humans Who Went Extinct: Why Neanderthals Died Out and We Survived*. Oxford University Press: New York et al.

Fluehr-Lobban, C. (2006). *Race and Racism: An Introduction*. AltaMira Press: Lanham.

FM-2030 (1989). *Are You a Transhuman? Monitoring and Stimulating Your Personal Rate of Growth in a Rapidly Changing World*. Warner Books: New York.

Folch, J., Cocero, M.J., Chesné, P., Alabart, J.L., Domínguez, V., Cognié, Y., Roche, A., Fernández-Arias, A., Martí, J.I., Sánchez, P., Echegoyen, E., Beckers, J.F., Bonastre, A.S., Vignon, X. (2009). First Birth of an Animal from an Extinct Subspecies (Capra Pyrenaica Pyrenaica) by Cloning. In: *Theriogenology*, Vol. 71, 2009, 1026–34.

Foucault, M. [1966] (1970). *The Order of Things: An Archaeology of the Human Sciences*. Trans. Sheridan, A., Random House: New York.

Foucault, M. [1975] (1995). *Discipline and Punish: the Birth of the Prison*. Trans. Sheridan, A., Random House: New York.

Foucault, M. [1976] (1998). *The History of Sexuality Vol. 1: The Will to Knowledge*. Trans. Hurley, R., Penguin: London.

Foucault, M. (1988). Technologies of the Self. In: Martin, L. H., Gutman, H., Hutton, P. H. (eds.) (1988). *Technologies of the Self*. University of Massachusetts Press: Amherst.

Fox Keller, E., Longino, H. E. (1996). *Feminism and Science*. Oxford University Press: New York et al.

Fraschetti, A. (ed.) (1999). *Roman Women*. Trans. Lappin, L., University of Chicago Press: Chicago.

Freud, S. (1919). The "Uncanny." In: Freud, S. (1955). *The Standard Edition of the Complete Psychological Works of Sigmund Freud*, Vol. XVII (1917–1919). Trans. Strachey, J., Freud, A., Hogarth Press: London, 217–52.

Frey, R. G. (2002). Ethics, Animals and Scientific Enquiry. In: Gluck, J. P., DiPasquale, T., Orlans, F. B., (2002). *Applied Ethics in Animal Research: Philosophy, Regulation, and Laboratory Applications*. Purdue University Press: West Lafayette, IN, 13–24.

Friedlander, H. (1995). *The Origins of Nazi Genocide: From Euthanasia to the Final Solution.* University of North Carolina Press: Chapel Hill.

Fukuyama, F. (2002). *Our Posthuman Future: Consequences of the Biotechnology Revolution.* Picador: New York.

Fukuyama, F. (2012). Agency or Inevitability: Will Human Beings Control Their Technological Future? In: Rosenthal, M. (ed.) *The Posthuman Condition.* Aarhus University Press: Aarhus, 157–69.

Gairdner, W. D. (2008). *The Book of Absolutes: A Critique of Relativism and a Defence of Universals.* McGill-Queens University Press: Montréal et al.

Galton, F. (1883). *Inquiries into Human Faculty.* London: Macmillan.

Garver, K. L., Garver, B. (1991). Eugenics: Past, Present, and the Future. In: *American Journal of Human Genetics*, Vol. 49, 1109–18.

Gaskill, M. (2010). *Witchcraft, A Very Short Introduction.* Oxford University Press: Oxford et al.

Gehlen, A. [1957] (1980). *Man in the Age of Technology.* Trans. Lipscomb, P., Columbia University Press: New York.

Gell-Mann, M. (1964). A Schematic Model of Baryons and Mesons. In: *Physics Letters*, Vol. 8, No. 3, 214–15.

Gerbault, P., Liebert, A., Itan, Y., Powell, A., Currat, M., Burger, J., Swallow, D. M., Thomas, M. G. (2011). Evolution of Lactase Persistence: An Example of Human Niche Construction. In: *Philosophical Transactions of the Royal Society*, Vol. 366, No. 1566, March 2011, 863–77.

Ghiselin, M. T. (1975). A Radical Solution to the Species Problem. In: *Systematic Zoology*, Vol. 23, No. 4, December 1974, 536–44.

Gibson, W. (1982). Burning Chrome. In: Gibson, W. (2003). *Burning Chrome.* HarperCollins Publishers: New York, 179–205.

Giustiniani, V. R. (1985). Homo, Humanus, and the Meanings of "Humanism". In: *Journal of the History of Ideas*, Vol. 46, No. 2, April–June 1985, 167–95.

Goldberg, D. T. (1990). The Social Formation of Racist Discourse. In: Goldberg, T. D. (ed.) (1990). *Anatomy of Racism.* University of Minnesota Press: Minneapolis, 295–318.

Goldberg, D. T. (1993). Racial Knowledge. In: Back L., Solomos J. (eds.) (2000). *Theories of Race and Racism: A Reader.* Routledge: London et al., 154–80.

Goldberg, A. D., Allis, C. D., Bernstein E. (2007). Epigenetics: A Landscape Takes Shape. In: *Cell*, Vol. 128, No. 4, February 2007, 635–38.

Gould, S. J. (1996). *Full House. The Spread of Excellence from Darwin to Plato.* Three Rivers Press: New York.

Graham, L. E. (2002). *Representations of the Post/Human: Monsters, Aliens and Others in Popular Cultures.* Rutgers University Press: New Brunswick, NJ.

Greene, B. (1999). *The Elegant Universe: Superstrings, Hidden Dimensions, and the Quest for the Ultimate Theory.* Norton: New York.

Greene, B. (2011). *The Hidden Reality: Parallel Universes and the Deep Laws of the Cosmos*. Random House: New York.

Grespin, W. (2010). Blood Coltan? In: *Journal of International Peace Operations*, Vol. 6 Issue 3, November/December 2010, 27–30.

Grosz, E. (1994). *Volatile Bodies: Towards a Corporeal Feminism*. Indiana University Press: Bloomington et al.

Grusin, R. (ed.) (2017). *Anthropocene Feminism*. Minnesota Press University: Minneapolis.

Gun Cuninghame, P. (2007). A Laughter That Will Bury You All: Irony as Protest and Language as Struggle in the Italian 1977 Movement. In: *International Review of Social History*, Vol. 52, Suppl. S15, December 2007, 153–68.

Guth, A. H., Steinhardt, P. J. (1984). The Inflationary Universe. In: *Scientific American*, Vol. 250, No. 5, May 1984, 90–102.

Habermas, J. [2001] (2003). *The Future of Human Nature*. Trans. Rehg, W., Pensky, M., Beister, B., Polity Press: Cambridge, UK.

Hables Gray, C., Figueroa-Sarriera, H. J., Mentor, S. (eds.) (1995). *The Cyborg Handbook*. Routledge: New York.

Hables Gray, C., Figueroa-Sarriera, H. J., Mentor, S. (1995). Cyborgology. Constructing the Knowledge of Cybernetic Organisms. In: Hables Gray, C., et al. (1995), 1–14.

Hahn, J. (1993). Aurignacian Art in Central Europe. In: Knecht, H., Pike-Tay, A., White, R. (eds.), *Before Lascaux: The Complex Record of the Early Upper Paleolithic*. CRC Press: Boca Raton (FL), 229–41.

Halberstam, J., Livingston, I. (eds.) (1995). *Posthuman Bodies*. Indiana University Press, Bloomington et al.

Hamer, D., Copeland, P. (1994). *The Science of Desire: The Search for the Gay Gene and the Biology of Behavior*. Simon and Schuster: New York.

Hamer, D. (2004). *The God Gene: How Faith Is Hardwired into our Genes*. Doubleday: New York.

Hanke, L. (1949). *The Spanish Struggle for Justice in the Conquest of America*. Philadelphia, PA: University of Pennsylvania.

Han-Pile, B. (2010). The "Death of Man": Foucault and Anti-Humanism. In: O'Leary, T., Falzon, C. (eds.) (2010). *Foucault and Philosophy*. Wiley-Blackwell: West Sussex et al.

Hansell, G. R., Grassie, W. (eds.) (2011). *Transhumanism and Its Critics*. Metanexus: Philadelphia.

Haraway, D. (1985). A Cyborg Manifesto: Science, Technology and Socialist-Feminism in the Late Twentieth Century. In: Kirkup, G., et al. (2000), 50–57.

Haraway, D. (1985). A Cyborg Manifesto: Science, Technology and Socialist-Feminism in the Late Twentieth Century. In: Nicholson, L. (ed.) (1989). *Feminism/Postmodernism (Thinking Gender)*. Routledge: London, 50–57.

Haraway, D. (1989). *Primate Visions: Gender, Race, and Nature in the World of Modern Science*. Routledge: New York.

Haraway, D. (1991). *Simians, Cyborgs, and Women: The Reinvention of Nature*. Routledge: New York.

Haraway, D. (1996a). *Modest _ Witness @ Second _ Millennium. FemaleMan © _ Meets _Oncomouse™*. Routledge: New York.

Haraway, D. (1996b). Situated Knowledges: The Science Question in Feminism and the Privilege of Partial Perspective. In: Fox Keller, E., Longino, H. E. (1996), 249–63.

Haraway, D. (2003). *The Companion Species*. Prickly Paradigm Press: Chicago.

Haraway, D. (2004). *The Haraway Reader*. Routledge: New York et al.

Haraway, D. (2007). *When Species Meet*. University of Minnesota Press: Minneapolis.

Haraway, D. (2015). Anthropocene, Capitalocene, Plantationocene, Chthulucene: Making Kin. In: *Environmental Humanities*, Vol. 6, 159–65. Retrieved in January 2019: http://environmentalhumanities.org/arch/vol6/6.7.pdf

Haraway, D. (2016). *Staying with the Trouble: Making Kin in the Chthulucene*. London: Duke University Press.

Harding, S. (1991). *Whose Science? Whose Knowledge? Thinking from Women's Lives*. Cornell University Press: Ithaca, NY.

Harding, S. (1993). Rethinking Standpoint Epistemology: What is "Strong Objectivity"? In: Alcoff, L., Potter, E. (eds.) (1993). *Feminist Epistemologies*. Routledge: New York, 49–82.

Harman, G. (2015). Object Oriented Ontology. In: Hauskeller, M. Philbeck, T. D., et al. (2015), 401–09.

Harman, G. (2018). *Object-Oriented Ontology: A New Theory of Everything*. Penguin Random House: United Kingdom.

Harris, J. (2007). *Enhancing Evolution: The Ethical Case for Making Better People*. Princeton University Press: Princeton et al.

Hassan, I. (1977). Prometheus as Performer: Toward a Posthumanist Culture? In: *The Georgia Review*, Vol. 31, No. 4, Winter 1977, 830–50.

Hassan, I. (1987). *The Postmodern Turn: Essays in Postmodern Theory and Culture*. Ohio State University Press: Columbus, OH.

Hassan, M. I. (2012). Expanding Masculine Spaces: Planned Births and Sex Composition of Children in India. In: Raju, S., Lahiri-Dutt, K. (eds.) (2012). *Doing Gender, Doing Geography: Emerging Research in India*. Taylor and Francis: Hoboken, 179–96.

Hauskeller, M., Carbonell, C.D., Philbeck, T. D., et al. (eds.) (2015). *The Palgrave Handbook of Posthumanism in Film and Television*. Palgrave MacMillan: New York.

Hawkins, M. (1997). *Social Darwinism in European and American Thought, 1860–1945: Nature as Model and Nature as Threat*. Cambridge University Press: Cambridge, UK.

Hayles, N. K. (1999). *How We Became Posthuman: Virtual Bodies in Cybernetics, Literature, and Informatics*. The University of Chicago Press: Chicago et al.

Hayles, N. K. (2008). Wrestling with Transhumanism. In: Hansell, G. R., Grassie, W. (2011), 215–26.

Hazen, R. M. (2005). *Genesis: The Scientific Quest for Life's Origin*. Joseph Henry Press: Washington.

Heidegger, M. [1927] (1962). *Being and Time*. Trans. Macquarrie, J., Robinson, E., HarperOne: New York.

Heidegger, M. (1947). Letter on Humanism. In: MacDonald, P. S. (ed.) (2001). *The Existentialist Reader: An Anthology of Key Texts*. Trans. Capuzzi, F. A., Routledge: New York, 236–69.

Heidegger, M. [1953] (1977). *The Question Concerning Technology and Other Essays*. Trans. Lovitt, W., Harper Torchbooks: New York.

Heilbron, J. L. (2005). *The Oxford Guide to the History of Physics and Astronomy*. Oxford University Press: New York et al.

Hill, J. R. (2014). Incidence of Abnormal Offspring from Cloning and Other Assisted Reproductive Technologies. In: *Annual Review of Animal Biosciences*, Issue 2, 307–21.

Hird, M. J. (2012). Knowing Waste: Towards an Inhuman Epistemology. In: *Social Epistemology*, Vol. 26, No. 3/4, 453–69.

Hochachka, P. W., Somero, G. N. (2002). *Biochemical Adaptation: Mechanism and Process in Physiological Evolution*. Oxford University Press: New York.

Homer [8th centure BCE] (1920). Iliad. In: Homer. *Homeri Opera in Five Volumes*. Oxford University Press: Oxford. Retrieved in January 2019: http://www.perseus.tufts.edu/hopper/text?doc=Perseus%3Atext%3A1999.01.0133%3Abook%3D6%3Acard%3D503

hooks, b. (1984). *Feminist Theory: From Margin to Center*. South End Press: Boston.

Horney, K. (1926). The Flight from Womanhood. In: *International Journal of Psychoanalysis*, Vol. 7, 324–29.

Hubbard, R. (2006). Abortion and Disability: Who Should and Should Not Inhabit the World? In: Davis, L. J. (ed.) (2006), 93–103.

Hubble, E. (1929). A Relation Between Distance and Radial Velocity Among Extra-Galactic Nebulae. In: *PNAS*, Vol. 15, No. 3, 168–73.

Hughes, J. (2004). *Citizen Cyborg: Why Democratic Societies Must Respond to the Redesigned Human of the Future*. Westview Press: Cambridge, MA.

Hughes, J. (2009). On Democratic Transhumanism. In: *IEET, Institute for Ethics and Emerging Technologies*, June 2009. Retrieved in January 2019: https://ieet.org/index.php/IEET2/more/hughes20090623

Hughes, J. (2010). Problems of Transhumanism: Atheism vs. Naturalist Theologies. In: *IEET, Institute for Ethics and Emerging Technologies*, January 2010. Retrieved in January 2019: http://ieet.org/index.php/IEET/more/hughes20100114/

Huxley, A. [1932] (2006). *Brave New World*. HarperCollins: New York.

Huxley, J. (1957). Transhumanism. In: Huxley, J. (1957). *New Bottles for New Wine*. Chatto & Windus: London, 13–17.

Huxley, T. H. (1880). The Coming of Age of the Origin of Species. In: *Nature*, Vol. 22, Issue 549, 1–4.

Irigaray, L. [1974] (1985). *Speculum, of the Other Woman*. Trans. Gill, C. G., Cornell University Press: New York.

Istvan, Z. (2014). Should a Transhumanist Run for US President? In: *The Huffington Post, Blog*, October 8, 2014. Retrieved in January 2019: https://www.huffingtonpost.com/zoltan-istvan/should-a-transhumanist-be_b_5949688.html

Jablonka, E., Lamb, M. J. (2005), *Evolution in Four Dimensions: Genetic, Epigenetic, Behavioral, and Symbolic Variation in the History of Life*. MIT Press: Cambridge, MA.

James, W. (1896). *Is Life Worth Living?* S. Burns Weston: Philadelphia.

Jameson, F. (1991). *Postmodernism, or, The Cultural Logic of Late Capitalism*. Duke University Press: Durham.

Janes, L. (2000). Introduction to Part Two. In: Kirkup, G., et al. (2000), 91–100.

Johnson, D. G. (2010). Sorting Out the Question of Feminist Technology. In: Layne, L. L., et al. (2010), 36–54.

Kaku, M. (2005). *Parallel Worlds: The Science of Alternative Universes and Our Future in the Cosmos*. Penguin: London.

Kalinowski, F. (2013). Phantom Flesh: Extreme Performance Artist Stelarc Interviewed. In: *The Quietus*, 6 March 2013. Retrieved in January 2019: http://thequietus.com/articles/11469-stelarc-interview

Keck, D. (1998). *Angels and Angelology in the Middle Ages*. Oxford University Press: Oxford, UK.

Keevak, M. (2011). *Becoming Yellow: A Short History of Racial Thinking*. Princeton University Press: Princeton.

Kember, S. (2003). *Cyberfeminism and Artificial Life*. Routledge: London.

Kete, K. (2002). Animals and Ideology: The Politics of Animal Protection in Europe. In: Rothfels, N. (2002). *Representing Animals*. Indiana University Press, Bloomington et al., 19–34.

King, P. (2001). Duns Scotus on Possibilities, Powers and the Possible. In: Buchheim, T., Kneepkens, C. H., Lorenz, K. (eds.) (2001). *Potentialität und Possibilität. Modalaussagen in der Geschichte der Metaphysik*. Frommann-Holzboog: Stuttgart-Bad Canstatt, 175–99.

Kirby, V. (1997). *Telling Flesh: The Substance of the Corporeal*. Routledge: New York.

Kirkup, G., Janes, L., Woodward, K., Hovenden, F. (eds.) (2000). *The Gendered Cyborg: A Reader*. Routledge: London et al.

Kitano, N. (2007). Animism, Rinri, Modernization: The Base of Japanese Robotics. In: *ICRA'07: IEEE, International Conference on Robotics and Automation*, April 10–14, 2007, Rome (Italy). Retrieved in January 2019: http://www.roboethics.org/icra2007/contributions.html

Klingensmith, S. W. (1953). Child Animism: What the Child Means by "Alive". In: *Child Development*, Vol. 24, No. 1, March 1953, 51–61.

Knuuttila, S. (1993). *Modalities in Medieval Philosophy*. Routledge: London et al.

Knuuttila, S. (1996). Duns Scotus and the Foundations of Logical Modalities. In: Honnefelder, L., Wood, R., Dreyer, M. (eds.) (1996). *John Duns Scotus: Metaphysics and Ethics*. E. J. Brill: Leiden, 127–44.

Koller, J. M. (2004). Why is Anekāntavāda Important? In: Sethia, T. (2004), pp. 85–98.

Kosicki, M., Tomberg, K., Bradley, A. (2018). Repair of Double-Strand Breaks Induced by CRISPR–Cas9 Leads to Large Deletions and Complex Rearrangements. In: *Nature Biotechnology*, Vol 36, 765–71.

Kristeva, J. [1974] (1984). *Revolution in Poetic Language.* Trans. Waller, M., Columbia University Press: New York.

Kristeva, J. [1980] (1982). *Powers of Horror: An Essay on Abjection.* Trans. Roudiez, L. S., Columbia University Press: New York.

Kuhn, T. S. [1962] (2012). *The Structure of Scientific Revolutions.* The University of Chicago Press: Chicago.

Kukkonen, T. (2000a). Possible Worlds in the Tahâfut al-Falâsifa: Al-Ghazâlî on Creation and Contingency. In: *Journal of the History of Philosophy*, Vol. 38, No. 4, October 2000, 479–502.

Kukkonen, T. (2000b). Possible Worlds in the Tahâfut al-Tahâfut: Averroes on Plenitude and Possibility. In: *Journal of the History of Philosophy*, Vol. 38, No. 3, July 2000, 329–47.

Kurzweil, R. (1999). *The Age of Spiritual Machines: When Computers Exceed Human Intelligence.* Penguin: New York.

Kurzweil, R. (2005). *The Singularity is Near: When Humans Transcend Biology.* Penguin: New York.

LaGrandeur, K., Hughes, J. (eds.) (2017). *Surviving the Machine Age: Intelligent Technology and the Transformation of Human Work.* Palgrave Macmillan: New York.

LaMotte, S. (2018). Rice Professor under Investigation for Role in 'World's First Gene-edited Babies'. *CNN News*, 27 November 2018.

Langton, C. G. (1986). Studying Artificial Life with Cellular Automata. In: *Physica D*, Vol. 22, No. 1–3, 120–49.

Langston, D. A. (1990). Scotus and Possible Worlds. In: Knuuttila, S., Ebbesen, S., Työrinoja, R. (eds.) (1990). *Knowledge and the Sciences in Medieval Philosophy: Proceedings of the Eight International Congress of Medieval Philosophy*, Vol. 2, 240–47.

Larson, E. J. (2004). *Evolution: The Remarkable History of a Scientific Theory.* Modern Library Edition: New York.

Latour, B., Woolgar, S. [1979] (1986). *Laboratory Life: The Construction of Scientific Facts.* Princeton University Press: Princeton.

Latour, B. (1987). *Science in Action: How to Follow Scientists and Engineers Through Society.* Open University Press: Milton Keynes, UK.

Latour, B. [1991] (1993) *We Have Never Been Modern.* Trans. Porter, C., Harvard University Press: Cambridge, MA.

Latour, B. (2003). The Promises of Constructivism. In: Ihde, D., Selinger, E. (eds.) (2003). *Chasing Technoscience: Matrix for Materiality.* Indiana University Press: Bloomington et al., 27–46.

Latour, B. (2005). *Reassembling the Social: An Introduction to Actor-Network-Theory.* Oxford University Press: Oxford et al.

Latour, B. (2014). Agency at the Time of the Anthropocene. *New Literary History*, Vol. 45, 1–18. Retrieved in January 2019: http://www.bruno-latour.fr/sites/default/files/128-FELSKI-HOLBERG-NLH-FINAL.pdf

Latour, B. (2017a). Anthropology at the Time of the Anthropocene: A Personal View of What is to be Studied. In: Brightman, M., Lewis, J. (eds.) *The Anthropology of Sustainability: Beyond Development and Progress*. Palgrave Macmillan: New York, 35–49.

Latour, B. (2017b). *Facing Gaia: Eight Lectures on the New Climatic Regime*. Polity: Cambridge.

Lauzen, M. M. (2017). The Celluloid Ceiling: Behind-the-Scenes. Employment of Women on the Top 250 Films of 2017. White Paper. The Center for the Study of Women in Television and Film, San Diego State University, San Diego, CA. Retrieved in January 2019: http://womenintvfilm.sdsu.edu

Law, J., Hassard, J. (eds.) (1999). *Actor Network Theory and After*. Blackwell: Oxford et al.

Lawrence, J. G. (2005). Horizontal and Vertical Gene Transfer: The Life History of Pathogens. In: Russell, W., Herwald, H. (eds.) (2005). *Concepts in Bacterial Virulence. Contributions to Microbiology*, Vol. 12. Karger: Basel, 255–71.

Layne, L. L., Vostral, S. L., Boyer, K. (eds.) (2010). *Feminist Technology*. University of Illinois Press: Urbana et al.

Leibniz, G. W. (1710). Essays of Theodicy on the Goodness of God, the Freedom of Man and the Origin of Evil. In: Leibniz, G. W. (2010). *Theodicy*. Trans. Huggard, M. E., Cosimo Classics: New York.

Lemaître, G. (1927). Un Univers Homogène de Masse Constante et de Rayon Croissant Rendant Compte de la Vitesse Radiale des Nébuleuses Extragalactiques. In: *Annals of the Scientific Society of Brussels*, Série A, 47–49.

Lemke, T. (2013). *Perspectives on Genetic Discrimination*. Routledge: London et al.

Leonard, E. B. (2003). *Women, Technology, and the Myth of Progress*. Prentice Hall: Upper Saddle River, NJ.

Leroi-Gourhan, A. (1943). *L'Homme et la Matière*. Albin Michel: Paris.

Leroi-Gourhan, A. [1964] (1993). *Gesture and Speech*. The MIT Press: Cambridge, MA et al.

Lettvin, J. Y., Maturana, H. R., McCulloch, W. S., Pitts, W. H. (1959). What the Frog's Eye Tells the Frog's Brain. In: *Proceedings of the IRE*, Vol. 47, No. 11, 1940–51. Reprinted in: Corning, W. C., Balaban, M. (eds.) (1968). *The Mind: Biological Approaches to Its Functions*. John Wiley & Sons: New York, 233–58.

Lévinas, E. [1961] (1969). *Totality and Infinity: An Essay on Exteriority*. Trans. Lingis, A., Duquesne University Press: Pittsburgh.

Lévinas, E. (1985). Diachrony and Representation. In: Lévinas, E. (1994). *Time and the Other, and Additional Essays*. Trans. Cohen, R., Duquesne University Press: Pittsburgh, 97–120.

Levy, D. (2007). *Love and Sex with Robots: The Evolution of Human-Robot Relationships*. HarperCollins Publishers: New York.

Lewis, D. (1986). *On the Plurality of Worlds*. Basil Blackwell: Oxford et al.

Lewis, P. (2007). *The Cambridge Introduction to Modernism*. Cambridge University Press: New York.

Lind af Hageby, L., Schartau, L. K. (1903). *The Shambles of Science: Extracts from the Diary of Two Students of Physiology*. Ernest Bell: London.

Linde, A. (1986). Eternally Existing Self-Reproducing Chaotic Inflationary Universe. In: *Physics Letters B*, Vol. 175, No. 4, 395–400.

Linde, A. (1994). The Self-Reproducing Inflationary Universe. In: *Scientific American*, Vol. 271, No. 5, November 1994, 48–55.

Linnaeus, C. (1752). *Nutrix Noverca*. Retrieved in January 2019: https://archive.org/details/NutrixNoverca

Linnaeus, C. (1758). *Systema Naturae per Regna Tria Naturae: Secundum Classes, Ordines, Genera, Species, cum Characteribus, Differentiis, Synonymis, Locis—Editio Decima, Reformata*. Laurentius Salvius: Holmiae.

Loeb, P. S. (2011). Nietzsche's Transhumanism. In: *The Agonist: A Nietzsche Circle Journal*, Vol. IV, Issue II, Fall 2011. Retrieved in January 2019: http://www.nietzschecircle.com/AGONIST/2011_08/loeb_nietzsche_transhumanism.html

Lonzi, C. (1970). Let's Spit on Hegel. In: Jagentowicz Mills, P. (ed.) (1996). *Feminist Interpretations of G.W.F. Hegel* (Re-Reading the Canon). Trans. Bellesia. G., Maclachlan, E., Pennsylvania State University Press: University Park.

Lovejoy, A. O. (1936). *The Great Chain of Being: A Study of the History of an Idea*. Harvard University Press: Cambridge, MA.

Lovelock, J. (1988). The Earth as a Living Organism. In: Wilson, E., Peter, F. (eds.) *Biodiversity*. National Academies Press: Washington DC, 486–89. Retrieved in January 2019: https://www.ncbi.nlm.nih.gov/books/NBK219276/

Lovelock, J. (1995). *The Ages of Gaia: A Biography of Our Living Earth*. Norton: New York.

Luft, R. E. (2009). Intersectionality and the Risk of Flattening Difference: Gender and Race Logics, and the Strategic Use of Antiracist Singularity. In: Berger, M. T., Guidroz, K. (eds.) (2009). *The Intersectional Approach: Transforming the Academy through Race, Class, and Gender*. University of North Carolina Press: Durham, 100–17.

Luhmann, N. [2002] (2013). *Introduction to Systems Theory*. Trans. Gilgen, P., Polity Press: Cambridge, UK.

Lutz, H., Herrera Vivar, M. T., Supik, L. (2011). Framing Intersectionality: An Introduction. In: Lutz, H., Herrera Vivar, M. T., Supik, L. (eds.) (2011). *Framing Intersectionality: Debates on a Multi-Faceted Concept in Gender Studies*. Ashgate: Farnham, 1–22.

Lykke, N. (2012). New Materialisms and their Discontents. In: *Proceedings from the Conference "Entanglements of New Materialism, Third New Materialism Conference,"* May 25–26, 2012, Linköping University.

MacCormack, P. (2012). *Posthuman Ethics: Embodiment and Cultural Theory*. Routledge: Routledge, Abingdon.

Marchesini, R. (2002). *Post-human: Verso Nuovi Modelli di Esistenza*. Bollati Boringhieri: Torino.

Marchesini, R. (2009). *Il Tramonto dell'Uomo: La Prospettiva Post-Umanista*. Dedalo: Bari.

Marchesini, R. (2014). *Epifania animale: L'oltreuomo come rivelazione*. Milano, Mimesis.

Marcus, G. E. (1995). Ethnography in/of the World System: The Emergence of Multi-Sited Ethnography. In: *Annual Review of Anthropology*, No. 24, October 1995, 95–117.

Margulis, L. (ed.) (1991). *Symbiosis as a Source of Evolutionary Innovation: Speciation and Morphogenesis*. The MIT Press: Cambridge, MA.

Margulis, L. (1998). *Symbiotic Planet: A New Look at Evolution*. Weidenfeld & Nicolson: London.

Marx, K. [1845] (1924). Theses on Feuerbach. In: Engels, F., Marx, K. (2009). *Feuerbach – The Roots of the Socialist Philosophy; Theses on Feuerbach*. Trans. Lewis, A., Mondial: New York.

Maturana, H. R., Varela, F. J. [1972] (1980). *Autopoiesis and Cognition: The Realization of the Living*. Reidel Publishing Company: Dordrecht, Holland.

Maturana, H. R., Varela, F. J. (1987a). *The Tree of Knowledge: The Biological Roots of Human Understanding*. Shambhala: Boston et al.

Maturana, H. R. (1987b). Everything is Said by an Observer. In: Thompson, W. (ed.) (1987). *Gaia, A Way of Knowing*. Lindisfarne Press: Great Barrington, MA, 65–82.

Maturana Romesin, H. R. (2002). Autopoiesis, Structural Coupling and Cognition: A History of These and Other Notions in the Biology of Cognition. In: *Cybernetics & Human Knowing*, Vol. 9, No. 3–4, 5–34.

McElheny, V. K. (2010). *Drawing the Map of Life: Inside the Human Genome Project*. Basic Books: New York.

McLuhan, M. (1964). *Understanding Media: The Extensions of Man*. Signet Books: New York.

Meillassoux, Q. (2008). *After Finitude: An Essay on the Necessity of Contingency*. Continuum: London.

Mendelsohn, E., Roe Smith, M., Weingart, P. (eds.) (1988). *Science, Technology and the Military*. Kluwer Academic Publishers: Dordrecht et al.

Miah, A. (2008). A Critical History of Posthumanism. In: Chadwick, R., Gordijn, B. (2009), 71–94.

Miller, C., Swift, K. (1980). *The Handbook of Nonsexist Writing*. Lippincott and Crowell: New York.

Milsom, C., Rigby, S. (2010). *Fossils at a Glance*. Wiley-Blackwell: West Sussex, UK.

Minsky, M. (1985). *The Society of Mind*. Simon and Schuster: New York.

Mishra, S. (2014). *Farmers' Suicides in India, 1995–2012: Measurement and Interpretation*. Asia Research Centre: London.

Moore, J. (ed.) (2016). *Anthropocene or Capitalocene? Nature, History, and the Crisis of Capitalism*. Kairos: Oakland.

Moravec, H. (1988). *Mind Children: The Future of Robot and Human Intelligence*. Harvard University Press: Cambridge, MA.

More, M. (1990) Transhumanism: Towards a Futurist Philosophy. In: *Extropy 6*, Summer, 6–12. Retrieved in April 2013: http://www.maxmore.com/transhum.htm

More, M. (1993): Technological Self-Transformation: Expanding Personal Extropy. In: *Extropy 10*, Vol. 4, No. 2, Winter/Spring, 15–24. Retrieved in April 2013: http://www.maxmore.com/selftrns.htm

More, M. (1998). Extropian Principles: A Transhumanist Declaration, Version 3:0. Retrieved in April 2013: http://www.maxmore.com/extprn3.htm

More, M. (2003). The Principles of Extropy, Version 3:1. Retrieved in April 2013: http://www.extropy.org/principles.htm

More, M. (2004). The Proactionary Principle. Version 1:0. Retrieved in April 2013: http://www.extropy.org/proactionaryprinciple.htm

More, M. (2010). The Overhuman in the Transhuman. In: *Journal of Evolution and Technology*, Vol. 21, Issue 1, January 2010, 1–4. Retrieved in January 2019: http://jetpress.org/v21/more.htm

More, M. (2013). The Philosophy of Transhumanism. In: More, M., Vita-More, N. (eds.) (2013), 3–17.

More, M. (2013). The Proactionary Principle: Optimizing Technological Outcomes. In: More, M., Vita-More, N. (2013), 258–67.

More, M., Vita-More, N. (eds.) (2013). *The Transhumanist Reader: Classical and Contemporary Essays on the Science, Technology, and Philosophy of the Human Future*. Wiley-Blackwell: West Sussex.

Mori, M. (1970). The Uncanny Valley. In: *Energy*, Vol.7, Issue 4: 33–35.

Mori, M. [1974] (1981). *The Buddha in the Robot: A Robot Engineer's Thoughts on Science and Religion*. Kosei Publishing: Tokyo.

Morton, T. (2013). *Hyperobjects: Philosophy and Ecology After the End of the World*. University of Minnesota Press: Minneapolis.

Mozdzer, T. J., Megonigal, J. P. (2013). Increased Methane Emissions by an Introduced *Phragmites australis* Lineage under Global Change. In: *Wetlands*. Vol. 33, Issue 4, 609–15.

Nagoshi, J. L., Brzuzy, S. (2010). Transgender Theory: Embodying Research and Practice. In: *Affilia, Journal of Women and Social Work*, Vol. 25, No. 4, November 2010, 431–43.

NASA Orbital Debris FAQs (n. year). NASA. Retrieved in January 2019: https://www.nasa.gov/news/debris_faq.html

NASA's Journey to Mars (n. year). NASA. Retrieved in January 2019: https://www.nasa.gov/content/nasas-journey-to-mars/

Nass, C., Moon, Y. (2000). Machines and Mindlessness: Social Responses to Computers. In: *Journal of Social Issues*, Vol. 56, No. 1, 81–103.

Nealon, J. (2012). *Post-Postmodernism: or, The Cultural Logic of Just-in-Time Capitalism.* Stanford University Press: Stanford.

Neimanis, A., Åsberg, C., Hedrén, J. (2015). Four Problems, Four Directions for Environmental Humanities: Toward Critical Posthumanities for the Anthropocene. In: *Ethics and the Environment*, Vol. 20, No. 1, Spring 2015, 67–97.

Nichols, S. (1988). The Post-Human Movement. In: *Games Monthly Magazine & Elsewhere*. Retrieved in January 2019: http://www.posthuman.org/page2.html

Nietzsche, F. W. [1882] (1974). *The Gay Science: With a Prelude in German Rhymes and an Appendix of Songs.* Trans. Kaufmann, W., Random House: New York.

Nietzsche, F. W. [1883–5] (1976). Thus Spoke Zarathustra. In: *The Portable Nietzsche*. Trans. Kaufmann, W., Penguin Books: New York, 103–439.

Nietzsche, F. W. [1883–5] (2006). *Thus Spoke Zarathustra.* Trans. Del Caro, A., Pippin, R., Cambridge University Press: Cambridge, UK.

Nietzsche, F. W. [1887] (2000). On the Genealogy of Morals. In: *Basic Writings of Nietzsche*. Trans. Kaufmann, W., Random House: New York, 437–600.

Nietzsche, F. W. [1901/1906] (1967). *The Will to Power.* Trans. Kaufmann, W., Hollingdale, R. J., Random House: New York.

Nishitani, O. (2006). Anthropos and Humanitas: Two Western Concepts of "Human Being." In: Sakai, N. N., Solomon, J. (eds.), *Translation, Biopolitics, Colonial Difference*. Hong Kong University Press: Aberdeen, 259–74.

Noble, D. (1997). *The Religion of Technology: The Divinity of Man and the Spirit of Invention.* Penguin: New York.

Nybakken, O. E. (1939). Humanitas Romana. In: *Transactions and Proceedings of the American Philological Association*, Vol. 70, 396–413.

Okin Moller, S. (1999). Is Multiculturalism Bad for Women? In: Cohen, J., Howard, M., Nussbaum, M. C. (eds.), *Is Multiculturalism Bad for Women?* Princeton University Press: Princeton, NJ.

Omi, M., Winant, H. (1994). *Racial Formation in the United States: From the 1960s to the 1990s.* Routledge: New York.

Onishi, B. (2011). Information, Bodies, and Heidegger: Tracing Visions of the Posthuman. In: *Sophia*, Vol. 50, No. 1, 101–12.

Oparin, A. I. [1936] (1953). *The Origin of Life.* Dover Publications: New York.

O'Rourke, D. (2005). *How America's First Settlers Invented Chattel Slavery: Dehumanizing Native Americans and Africans with Language, Laws, Guns, and Religion.* Peter Lang: New York et al.

Osborn, F. (1937). Development of a Eugenic Philosophy. In: *American Sociological Review*, Vol. 2, No. 3, June 1937, 389–97.

Oxford *Dictionaries Online*, Copyright © 2019 Oxford University Press. Entries: "Human." Retrieved in January 2019: http://oxforddictionaries.com/definition/english/human, "Relative." Retrieved in January 2019: http://oxforddictionaries.com/definition/english/relative

Parikka, J. (2014). *The Anthrobscene.* University of Minnesota Press: Minneapolis.

Parry, R. (2014). Episteme and Techne. In: Zalta, E. N. (ed.), *The Stanford Encyclopedia of Philosophy*, Fall 2014 Edition. Retrieved in January 2019: https://plato.stanford.edu/archives/fall2014/entries/episteme-techne/

Pastourmatzi, D. (2009). Flesh Encounters Biotechnology: Speculations on the Future of the Biological Machine. In: Detsi-Diamanti Z., Kitsi-Mitakou, K., Yiannopoulou, E. (eds.) (2009). *The Future of the Flesh: A Cultural Survey of the Body.* Palgrave Macmillan: New York, 199–219.

Pearce, D. (1995). The Hedonistic Imperative. Retrieved in January 2019: http://www.hedonistic-imperative.com

Pearl the NurseBot Helps the Elderly at Home. In: *Carnegie Mellon Today*, Vol. 1, No. 4, December 2004, 1–2. Retrieved in April 2013: http://www.carnegiemellontoday.com/article.asp?aid=155

Pepperell, R. (1995). The Posthuman Manifesto. In: Pepperell, R. [1995] (2003). *The Posthuman Condition: Consciousness Beyond the Brain.* Intellect Books: Bristol, UK, 177.

Peters, T., Collins, F. S. (2002). *Playing God?: Genetic Determinism and Human Freedom* (2nd Edition). Routledge: New York.

Piaget, J. (1929). *The Child's Conception of the World.* Harcourt, Brace: Oxford, UK.

Plautus, T. M. [211 BC]. Asinaria. In: Lindsay, W. M. (ed.) (1922). *T. Macci Plauti Comoediae: Volume I: Amphitruo, Asinaria, Aulularia, Bacchides, Captivi, Casina, Cistellaria, Curculio, Epidicus, Menaechmi, Mercator.* Oxford Classical Texts: New York.

Posner, R. (2011). Eight Historical Paradigms of the Human Sciences. In: Peil, T. (ed.) (2011). *The Space of Culture, the Place of Nature in Estonia and Beyond: Approaches to Cultural Theory*, Vol. 1. Tartu University Press: Tartu, 20–38.

Quintilian, M. F. [95 AD ca.] (1920). *The Institutio Oratoria of Quintilian. Book 1.* Trans. Butler, H. E., Harvard University Press: Cambridge, MA; William Heinemann: London.

Rae, A. (1986). *Quantum Physics: Illusion or Reality?* Cambridge University Press: Cambridge.

Raffoul, F. (2005). Being and the Other: Ethics and Ontology in Levinas and Heidegger. In: Nelson, E. A., Kapust, A., et al. (eds.), *Addressing Lévinas*. Northwestern University Press: Evanston, IL, 138–51.

Rambachan, A. (2006). *The Advaita Worldview: God, World, and Humanity.* State University of New York Press: Albany, NY.

Randall, L. (2005). *Warped Passages: Unraveling the Mysteries of the Universe's Hidden Dimensions.* HarperCollins: New York.

Ranisch R., Sorgner S. L. (eds.) (2014). *Post- and Transhumanism: An Introduction.* Peter Lang Publisher: Frankfurt et al.

Resnik, D. B., Vorhaus, D. B. (2006). Genetic Modification and Genetic Determinism. In: *Philosophy, Ethics, and Humanities in Medicine*, Vol. 1, Art. ID 9, 1–11.

Ricciardi, A., et al. (1998). Impending Extinctions of North American Freshwater Mussels (Unionoida) Following the Zebra Mussel (Dreissena Polymorpha) Invasion. In: *Journal of Animal Ecology*, Vol. 67, Issue 613–19.

Richardson, K. (2018). Technological Animism: The Uncanny Personhood of Humanoid Machines. In: Swancutt, K., Mazard, M. (eds.). *Animism Beyond the Soul: Ontology, Reflexivity, and the Making of Anthropological Knowledge*. Berghahn Books: New York and Oxford, 112–28.

Ricoeur, P. (1970). *Freud and Philosophy an Essay on Interpretation*. Trans. Savage, D., Yale University Press: New Haven et al.

Rieks, R. (1967). *Homo, Humanus, Humanitas. Zur Humanität in der Lateinischen Literatur des Ersten Nachchristlichen Jahrhunderts*. Fink: München.

Riviere, J. (1929). Womanliness as a Masquerade. In: *International Journal of Psychoanalysis*, Vol. 10, 303–13.

Roberts, M. (1986). *The Age of Liberty, Sweden 1719–1772*. Cambridge: Cambridge University Press.

Roden, D. (2010). Deconstruction and Excision in Philosophical Posthumanism. In: *Journal of Evolution and Technology*, Vol. 21, Issue 1, June 2010, 27–36. Retrieved in January 2019: http://jetpress.org/v21/roden.htm

Roden, D. (2015). *Posthuman Life: Philosophy at the Edge of the Human*. Routledge: London and New York.

Romaniello, G. (2004). *Pensiero e Linguaggio: Grammatica Universale*. Sovera: Roma.

Rose, J. (2011). *Zoroastrianism: An Introduction*. Tauris: London.

Said, E. (1978). *Orientalism*. Random House: New York.

Sandberg, A. (2011). DIY Enhancement: Morphological Freedom or Self-Harm? In: *Practical Ethics: Ethics in the News*, University of Oxford, January 10, 2011. Retrieved in January 2019: http://blog.practicalethics.ox.ac.uk/2011/01/diy-enhancement-morphological-freedom-or-self-harm/

Sangster, J. (1994). Telling Our Stories: Feminist Debates and the Use of Oral History. In: *Women's History Review*, Vol. 3, Issue 1, 5–28.

Sax, B. (2002). *Animals in the Third Reich: Pets, Scapegoats, and the Holocaust*. Continuum: London et al.

Saxton, M. (2006). Disability Rights and Selective Abortion. In: Davis, L. J. (ed.) (2006), 105–15.

Schadewaldt, W. (1973). Humanitas Romana. In: Temporini, H., Haase, W. (eds.) (1973). *Aufstieg und Niedergang der Römischen Welt: Geschichte und Kultur Roms im Spiegel der Neueren Forschung*, Part 1, Vol. 4. De Gruyter: Berlin et al., 43–62.

Schatzki, T. R. (2001). Introduction: Practice Theory. In: Schatzki et al. (eds.), *The Practice Turn in Contemporary Theory*. Routledge: London et al., 10–11.

Schiebinger, L. (1993). Why Mammals are Called Mammals: Gender Politics in Eighteenth-Century Natural History. In: *The American Historical Review*, Vol. 98, No. 2, April 1993, 382–411.

Schiebinger, L. (2000). Taxonomy for Human Beings. In: Kirkup, G., et al. (2000), 11–37.

Schiebinger, L. (2004). *Plants and Empire: Colonial Bioprospecting in the Atlantic world.* Harvard University Press: Cambridge, MA.

Schmitt F. F. (2004). Epistemology and Cognitive Science. In: Niiniluoto I., Sintonen M., Woleński, J. (eds), *Handbook of Epistemology.* Springer: Dordrecht, 841–918.

Schnackenberg Cattani, M. (1990). Preface to the English Translation. In: Ferry, L., Renaut, A. [1985] (1990). *French Philosophies of the Sixties: An Essay on Antihumanism.* Trans. Schnackenberg Cattani, M., The University of Massachusetts Press: Amherst.

Schneider, S., et al. (eds.) (2004). *Scientists Debate Gaia: The Next Century.* MIT Press: Boston, MA.

Schrödinger, E. (1935a). The Present Situation in Quantum Mechanics. Trans. Drimmer, J. (1980). In: *Proceedings, Cambridge Philosophical Society*, Vol. 124, 323–38.

Schrödinger, E. (1935b). Discussion of Probability Relations between Separated Systems. In: *Proceedings of the Cambridge Philosophical Society*, Vol. 31, 555–63.

Scott, B. (2004). Second Order Cybernetics: An Historical Introduction. In: *Kybernetes*, Vol. 33, No. 9/10: 1365–78.

Seckbach, J. (2012). *Genesis—In The Beginning: Precursors of Life, Chemical Models and Early Biological Evolution (Cellular Origin, Life in Extreme Habitats and Astrobiology)*, Vol. 22. Springer: Berlin et al.

Sedgwick, E. K. (1990). *Epistemology of the Closet.* University of California Press: Berkeley.

Segrè, E. (1980). *From X-Rays to Quarks: Modern Physicists and Their Discoveries.* Freeman: New York.

Seipel, P. (2015). Nietzsche's Perspectivism, Internal Reasons, and the Problem of Justification. In: *International Philosophical Quarterly*, Vol. 55, No. 1: 49–65.

Seitz, J. D. (2018). Striking a Balance: Policy Considerations for Human Germline Modification. In: *Santa Clara Journal of International Law*, Vol. 16, Issue 1, 60–100.

Sethia, T. (ed.) (2004). *Ahimsā, Anekānta, and Jainism.* Motilal Banarsidass: Delhi.

Setia, A. (2004). Fakhr al-Din al-Razi on Physics and the Nature of the Physical World: A Preliminary Survey. In: *Islam & Science*, Vol. 2, No. 2, Winter, 161–80.

Sharma, A. (2004). *Sleep as a State of Consciousness in Advaita Vedānta.* State University of New York Press: Albany, NY.

Shea, R., Wilson, R. A. (1975). *The Illuminatus! Trilogy: The Eye in the Pyramid, The Golden Apple, Leviathan.* Dell Publishing: New York.

Shelley, M. [1818] (1992). *Frankenstein: Or, The Modern Prometheus.* Penguin: London.

Shiva, V. (1993). *Monocultures of the Mind: Perspectives on Biodiversity and Biotechnology.* Zed Books: London.

Shiva, V. (1995a). Democratizing Biology: Reinventing Biology from a Feminist, Ecological, and Third World Perspective. In: Lederman, M., Bartsch, I. (eds.) (2001). *The Gender and Science Reader*. Routledge: London, 447–65.

Shiva, V. (1995b). Beyond Reductionism. In: Shiva, V., Moser, I. (eds.) (1995), 267–84.

Shiva, V., Moser, I. (eds.) (1995). *Biopolitics: A Feminist and Ecological Reader in Biotechnology*. Zed Books: London.

Shiva, V. (1997). *Biopiracy: The Plunder of Nature and Knowledge*. South End Press: Boston, MA.

Shiva, V. (2005). *Earth Democracy: Justice, Sustainability, and Peace*. South End Press: Cambridge.

Silantsyeva, T. (2016). The Triads of Expression and the Four Paradoxes of Sense: A Deleuzean Reading of the Two Opening Aphorisms of the Dao De Jing. In: *Dao: A Journal of Comparative Philosophy*, Vol. 15, Issue 3, September 2016, 355–77.

Simondon, G. (1958). *Du Mode d'Existence des Objets Techniques*. Aubier: Paris. Trans. Mellamphy, N. (1980). *On the Mode of Existence of Technical Objects*. University of Western Ontario (not published).

Singer, P. (1975). *Animal Liberation: A New Ethics for Our Treatment of Animals*. New York Review Books: New York.

Slater, W. J. (1969). *Lexicon to Pindar*. De Gruyter: Berlin. Retrieved in January 2019: http://perseus.uchicago.edu/Reference/Slater.html

Sloterdijk, P. [1999] (2001). Rules for the Human Zoo: A Response to the Letter on Humanism. Trans. Varney Rorty, M. (2009). In: *Environment and Planning D: Society and Space*, Vol. 27, 12–28.

Smith, M. (2005). *Stono: Documenting And Interpreting a Southern Slave Revolt*. University of South Carolina Press: Columbia, SC.

Smith, J., Jenks, C. (2006). *Qualitative Complexity: Ecology, Cognitive Processes and the Re-Emergence of Structures in Post-Humanist Social Theory*. Routledge: Oxon.

Smolin, L. (2001). *Three Roads to Quantum Gravity*. Basic Books: New York.

Smolin, L. (2006). *The Trouble with Physics, the Rise of String Theory, the Fall of a Science, and What Comes Next*. Houghton-Mifflin: New York.

Sorgner, S. L. (2007). *Metaphysics Without Truth: On the importance of Consistency within Nietzsche's Philosophy*. Revised Edition. University of Marquette Press: Milwaukee, WI.

Sorgner, S. L. (2009). Nietzsche, the Overhuman, and Transhumanism. In: *Journal of Evolution and Technology*, Vol. 20, Issue 1, March 2009, 29–42. Retrieved in January 2019: http://jetpress.org/v20/sorgner.htm

Sorgner, S. L. (2013). Human Dignity 2.0: Beyond a Rigid Version of Anthropocentrism. In: *Trans-Humanities*, Vol. 6, No. 1, February 2013: 135–59.

Sorgner, S. L. (2016). *Transhumanismus: "Die gefährlichste Idee der Welt"!?* Herder: Freiburg.

SPACE X (n. year). Mars. Retrieved in January 2019: http://www.spacex.com/mars

Spanos, W. (1993). *End Of Education: Toward Posthumanism (Pedagogy and Cultural Practice)*. University of Minnesota Press: Minneapolis.

Spinoza, B. [1677] (1955). *On the Improvement of Human Understanding: The Ethics and Selected Letters*. Trans. Elwes, R. H. M., Dover: New York. Retrieved in January 2019: https://www.gutenberg.org/files/3800/3800-h/3800-h.htm#chap03

Spivak, G. C. (1984). Criticism, Feminism and the Institution. Interview with Elizabeth Grosz. In: *Thesis 11*, 10/11, 175–87.

Spivak, G. C. (1987). *In Other Worlds: Essays in Cultural Politics*. Routledge: London.

Spry, T. (2001). Performing Autoethnography: An Embodied Methodological Praxis. In: *Qualitative Inquiry*, Vol. 7, No. 6, 706–32.

Stanton, G. (1998). The Eight Stages of Genocide. In: *Yale Genocide Studies Series, GS01*, Yale University. Retrieved in January 2019: http://www.genocidewatch.org/aboutgenocide/8stagesofgenocide.html

Stapp, H. P. (2007). *Mindful Universe: Quantum Mechanics and the Participating Observer*. Springer: Berlin et al.

Steinhart, E. (2008). Teilhard de Chardin and Transhumanism. In: *Journal of Evolution and Technology*, Vol. 20, Issue 1, 1–22. Retrieved in January 2019: http://jetpress.org/v20/steinhart.htm

Stelarc (1998). From Psycho-Body to Cyber-Systems: Images as Post-Human Entities. In: Bell, D., Kennedy, B. M. (2000), 560–76.

Stengers, I. (2015). *In Catastrophic Times: Resisting the Coming Barbarism*. Trans. Goffey, A., Open Humanities Press: London.

Stevens, E., Patrick, T., Pickler, R. (2009). A History of Infant Feeding. In: *The Journal of Perinatal Education*, Vol. 18, Issue 2: 32–39.

Stiegler, B. [1994] (1998). *Technics and Time, 1: The Fault of Epimetheus*. Trans. Beardsworth, R., Collins, G., Stanford University Press: Stanford.

Stone, A. R. (1991). Will the Real Body Please Stand Up? Boundary Stories About Virtual Cultures. In: Bell, D., Kennedy, B. M. (2000), 504–28.

Stone, R. J. (2005). *The Routledge Dictionary of Latin Quotations*. Routledge: New York.

Stone, S. (1995). *The War of Desire and Technology at the Close of the Mechanical Age*. The MIT Press: Cambridge, MA.

Strawser, B. J. (ed.) (2013). *Killing by Remote Control: The Ethics of an Unmanned Military*. Oxford University Press: Oxford et al.

Stubley, P. (2018). Colombian Government Ordered to Protect Amazon Rainforest in Historic Legal Ruling. In: *Independent*. April 6, 2018. Retrieved in January 2019: https://www.independent.co.uk/news/world/americas/amazon-rainforest-colombia-protect-deforestation-environment-logging-supreme-court-legal-rights-a8292671.html

Susskind, L. (2005). *The Cosmic Landscape: String Theory and the Illusion of Intelligent Design*. Time Warner Book Group: New York.

Tegmark, M. (2010). Many Worlds in Context. In: Saunders, S., Barrett, J., Kent, A., Wallace D. (eds.) (2010). *Many Worlds? Everett, Quantum Theory and Reality*. Oxford University Press: Oxford et al., 553–81.

Teilhard de Chardin, P. (1949). The Essence of the Democratic Idea: A Biological Approach. In: Teilhard de Chardin, P. (1964), 236–42.

Teilhard de Chardin, P. [1955] (1959). *The Phenomenon of Man*. Trans. Wall, B., Harper & Row: New York.

Teilhard de Chardin, P. [1956] (1966). *Man's Place in Nature: The Human Zoological Group*. Trans. Hague, R., Harper & Row: New York.

Teilhard de Chardin, P. [1959] (1964). *The Future of Man*. Trans. Denny, N., Random House: New York et al.

Terentius, P. A. [163 BC]. *Heauton Timorumenos* (The Self-Tormentor). In: Terence (1953). Trans. Sargeaunt, J., Harvard University Press: Cambridge, MA.

Thomas, G., De Tavernier, J. (2017). Farmer-Suicide in India: Debating the Role of Biotechnology. In: *Life Sciences, Society and Policy*, Vol. 13, Issue 8, 1–21.

Timalsina, S. (2009). *Consciousness in Indian Philosophy: The Advaita Doctrine of "Awareness Only."* Routledge: London et al.

Tirosh-Samuelson, H., Mossman, K. L. (eds.) (2012). *Building Better Humans? Refocusing the Debate on Transhumanism.* Peter Lang: Frankfurt et al.

Tokyo Couple Married by Robot in Rooftop Wedding. In: *BBC News*, May 16, 2010. Retrieved in January 2019: http://news.bbc.co.uk/2/hi/8685184.stm

Tuana, N. (1998). *Women and the History of Philosophy*. Paragon House: New York.

Tuncel, Y. (ed.) (2017). *Nietzsche and Transhumanism: Precursor or Enemy?* Cambridge Scholars Publishing: Newcastle, UK.

Turing, A. M. (1950). Computing Machinery and Intelligence. In: *Mind*, Vol. 59, No. 236, 433–60.

Turkle, S. (1984). *The Second Self: Computers and the Human Spirit*. Simon and Schuster: New York.

Turkle, S. (1995). *Life on the Screen: Identity in the Age of the Internet*. Touchstone: New York.

Turkle, S. (2011). *Alone Together: Why We Expect More from Technology and Less from Each Other*. Basic Books: New York.

Tylor, E. B. (1871). *Primitive Culture: Researches Into the Development of Mythology, Philosophy, Religion, Language, Art and Custom, Vol. 1*. Murray: London.

Tzu, L. [6th century BCE] (1999). *Tao Te Ching*. Trans. Mitchell, S., Frances Lincoln: London.

Uyeda, J. C., Hansen, T. F., Arnold, S. J., Pienaar, J. (2011). The Million-Year Wait for Macroevolutionary Bursts. In: *PNAS*, Vol. 108, No. 38, September 2011, 15908–13.

Varela, F. J, Thompson, E. T., Rosch, E. (1991). *The Embodied Mind: Cognitive Science and Human Experience*. The MIT Press: Cambridge, MA.

Varela, F. J. (1995). The Emergent Self. In: Brockman, J. (ed.) (1995). *The Third Culture: Beyond the Scientific Revolution*. Simon & Schuster: New York, 209–22.

Vasterling, V. (1999). Butler's Sophisticated Constructivism: A Critical Assessment. In: *Hypatia*, Vol. 14, No. 3, Summer 1999, 17–38.

Vattimo, G. [1985] (1991). *The End of Modernity: Nihilism and Hermeneutics in Postmodern Culture*. Trans. Snyder, J. R., The John Hopkins University Press: Baltimore.

Vaughan, A. T. (1982). From White Man to Redskin: Changing Anglo-American Perceptions of the American Indian. In: *The American Historical Review*, Vol. 87, No. 4, October 1982, 917–53.

Velikovsky, I. (1982). *Mankind in Amnesia*. Doubleday & Company: New York.

Viereck, G. S. (1929). What Life Means to Einstein: An Interview. In: *The Saturday Evening Post*, Volume 202, October 26, 1929, 117.

Villarreal, L. P. (2004a). Can Viruses Make Us Human? In: *Proceedings of the American Philosophical Society*, Vol. 148, Issue 3, September 2004, 296–323.

Villarreal, L. P. (2004b). Are Viruses Alive? In: *Scientific American*, Vol. 291, Issue 6, December 2004, 97–102.

Vincent, A. (2010). *The Politics of Human Rights*. Oxford University Press: Oxford.

Vita-More, N. (2004). The New Genre: Primo Posthuman. In: *Ciber@RT Conference*, April 2004, Bilbao (Spain). Retrieved in April 2013: http://www.natasha.cc/paper. htm

Vita-More, N. (2005). Primo Posthuman: Primo Guide, 2005 Edition. Retrieved in April 2013: http://www.natasha.cc/primo3m+comparision.htm

Vita-More, N. (2011). Bringing Art/Design into the Discussion of Transhumanism. In: Hansell, G. R., Grassie, W. (2011), 70–83.

Viveiros de Castro, E. (1998). Cosmological deixis and Amerindian perspectivism. In: *Journal of the Royal Anthropological Institute*, Vol. 4, No. 3, 469–88.

Voltaire [1759] (1991). *Candide* (A Norton Critical Edition). Trans. Adams, R. M., Norton & Company: New York.

Von Glasersfeld, E. (1995). *Radical Constructivism: A Way of Knowing and Learning*. RoutledgeFalmer: London.

Wajcman, J. (1991). *Feminism Confronts Technology*. The Pennsylvania State University Press: Pennsylvania.

Wake, D., Vredenburg, V. T. (2008). Are We in the Midst of the Sixth Mass Extinction? A View from the World of Amphibians. In: *Proceedings of the National Academy of Sciences of the United States of America*, Vol. 105, 11466–73.

Waldby, C. (2000). *The Visible Human Project: Informatic Bodies and Posthuman Medicine*. Routledge: London et al.

Ward, P. (2009). *The Medea Hypothesis: Is Life on Earth Ultimately Self-Destructive?* Princeton University Press: Princeton, NJ.

Ward, P. (2018). *Lamarck's Revenge: How Epigenetics Is Revolutionizing Our Understanding of Evolution's Past and Present*. Bloomsbury: New York.

Warren, K. (2009). 2,600 Years of the History of Western Philosophy Without Women: This Book as a Unique, Gender-Inclusive Alternative. In: Warren, K. (ed.) (2009). *An Unconventional History of Western Philosophy: Conversations Between Men and Women Philosophers*. Rowman and Littlefield Publishers: Lanham, 1–26.

Warren, L. V. (1986). Guidelines for Non-Sexist Use of Language. In: *Proceedings and Addresses of the American Philosophical Association*, Vol. 59, No. 3, February 1986, 471–82.

Warwick, K. (1997). *The March of the Machines*. Century: London.

Warwick, K. (2002). *I, Cyborg*. University of Illinois Press: Urbana et al.

Warwick, K., Nasuto, S. J. (2006). Historical and Current Machine Intelligence. In: *IEEE Instrumentation and Measurement Magazine*, Vol. 9, Issue 6, December 2006, 20–26.

Warwick, K. (2012). *Artificial Intelligence: The Basics*. Routledge: Oxon.

Watts, A. (1976). *Tao: The Watercourse Way*. Jonathan Cape: London.

Weinstone, A. (2004). *Avatar Bodies: A Tantra for Posthumanism*. University of Minnesota Press: Minneapolis et al.

Wheaton, B. R. (1983). *The Tiger and the Shark: Empirical Roots of Wave-Particle Dualism*. Cambridge University Press: New York.

White, F. (1998). *The Overview Effect: Space Exploration and Human Evolution*. American Institute of Aeronautics and Astronautics: Reston, VA.

White, J. (1983). Veiled Testimony: Negro Spirituals and the Slave Experience. In: *Journal of American Studies*, Vol. 17, No. 2, August 1983, 251–63.

Whitlock, G. (1999). Roger G. Boscovich and Friedrich Nietzsche: A Re-examination. In: Babich, B. E., Cohen, R. S. (eds.) (1999). *Nietzsche, Epistemology, and Philosophy of Science: Nietzsche and the Science II*. Boston Studies in the Philosophy of Science, Vol. 203. Kluwer Academic Publishers: Dordrecht et al., 187–202.

Widmer, R., et al. (2005). Global Perspectives On E-Waste. In: *Environmental Impact Assessment Review*, Vol. 25, Issue 5, July 2005, 436–58.

Wilkinson, T. (2012). The Multiverse Conundrum. In: *Philosophy Now*, Issue 89, March/April 2012. Retrieved in January 2019: http://philosophynow.org/issues/89/The_Multiverse_Conundrum

Wilson, R. A., Keil, F. C. (eds.) (1999). *The MIT Encyclopedia of Cognitive Science*. MIT Press: Cambridge, MA.

Woese, C. (1998). The Universal Ancestor. In: *PNAS*, Vol. 95, No. 12, June 1998, 6854–59.

Woit, P. (2006). *Not Even Wrong: The Failure of String Theory and the Search for Unity in Physical Law*. Basic Books: New York.

Wolfe, C. (2010). *What is Posthumanism?* Posthumanities Series, University of Minnesota Press: Minneapolis et al.

Wolfendale, P. (2017). Object-Oriented Ontology. In: Braidotti, R., Hlavajova, M. (eds.) (2017), 447–48.

Woolf, V. [1929] (2005). *A Room of One's Own*. Harcourt: Orlando et al.

Wootson, Jr., C. R., (2017). Saudi Arabia Grants Robot Citizenship, Irking Women's Rights Groups. In: *The Washington Post. Hamilton Spectator, The (ON)*, October 30, 2017.

Yildirim, C. (2014). *Exploring the Dimensions of Nomophobia: Developing and Validating a Questionnaire using Mixed Methods Research (Master's Thesis)*. Iowa State University. Retrieved in January 2019: https://lib.dr.iastate.edu/cgi/viewcontent.cgi?article=5012&context=etd

Zalasiewicz, et al. (2008). When Did the Anthropocene Begin? A Mid-Twentieth Century Boundary Level is Stratigraphically Optimal. In: *Quaternary International*, Vol. 383, October 5, 2015, 196–203.

Zetzel, J. E. G. (1972). Cicero and the Scipionic Circle. *Harvard Studies in Classical Philology*, Vol. 76, 173–79.

Zimmer, C. (2005). *Smithsonian Intimate Guide to Human Origins*. Smithsonian Books / HarperCollins: New York.

Zinnbauer, B. J., Pargament, K. I., Cole, B., Rye, M. S., Butter, E. M., Belavich, T. G., Hipp, K. M., Scott, A. B., Kadar, J. L. (1997). Religion and Spirituality: Unfuzzying the Fuzzy. In: *Journal for the Scientific Study of Religion*, Vol. 36, No. 4, December 1997, 549–64.

Zweig, G. (1964). An SU(3) Model for Strong Interaction Symmetry and its Breaking. In: CERN Report, Preprint 8182 / Th. 401.

Zylinska, J. (2009). *Bioethics in the Age of the New Media*. The MIT Press: Cambridge, MA.

Videography

Videos

Braidotti, R. (2015). Prof. Rosi Braidotti—Keynote Lecture—Posthumanism and Society Conference, New York, May 9, 2015. In: Online video clip. YouTube. YouTube, November 10, 2015. Retrieved in January 2019: https://www.youtube.com/watch?v=3S3CulNbQ1M

a. Films and Documentaries

Bigelow, K. Strange Days (1995). Lightstorm Entertainment.

Cook, N. (2005). Who Is Afraid of Designer Babies? BBC.

Jonze, S. Her (2013). Annapurna Pictures.

Niccol, A. Gattaca (1997). Columbia Pictures.

Stanton, A. Wall-E (2008). Disney Pixar.

b. Online References

Warwick, K., Ferrando, F. (2010). Is Science-Fiction a Source of Inspiration for Scientists? In: YouTube, Channel TVCyborg, Conversation N. 15, Video-Interview (original transcript). Retrieved in January 2019: http://www.youtube.com/watch?v=sb9TxqhCjKM

Index

"Abortion and Disability: Who Should and
        Should Not Inhabit the World?"
        (Hubbard) 130
Advaita Vedanta 156
Advaita Worldview, The
        (Rambachan) 156
Aerts, D. 226 n.4
affects 114
Agamben, G. 73, 74, 75, 76, 96, 109,
        110, 117
agency 132, 155
    human 52, 104
    non-human 154, 159, 161–2
    posthuman 161, 181–2, 187
agential realism 159–60, 168
    and vitalism compared 162–3
Age of Spiritual Machines, The
        (Kurzweil) 38
Al-Ghazali 175, 229 n.17
alife. *See* artificial life
Alone Together (Turkle) 191 n.3
al-Razi, Fakhr al-Din 175, 229 n.19
alterity 70, 75, 85, 162, 205 n.6
    within self 189–90
Althusser, L. 45
Amerindian perspectivism 155–6
Anaxagoras 215 n.4
animal epiphany 86
Animals and Ideology (Kete) 79
Animism 111, 213 nn.11–12
    relevance of 111–13
"Animism, Rinri, Modernization: The Base
        of Japanese Robotics" (Naho
        Kitano) 111
Ansell Pearson 224 n.21
Anten, N. P. R. 223 n.13
Anthropocene 22, 23, 30, 38, 87, 118,
        174, 187, 228 n.12
    post-anthropocentrism in 103–8
anthropocentrism xiv–xvi, 24, 30, 50, 57.
        See also post-anthropocentrism
    cognitive 146–7
    as problem 103–5

anthropological machine 73–6. *See also*
        humanizing
anthropomorphization 162
antihumanism 3–4, 45–53, 223 n.14
    Posthumanism and 45–7, 52
    Übermensch (overhuman) and
        47–53
anti-humanism xiii, 52, 154, 223 n.14,
        225 n.6
Apologetic History of the Indies (de las
        Casas) 78, 206 n.2
Arendt, H. 192 n.11
Aristotle 90, 203 n.21, 209 n.5, 229 n.16
artificial life 115, 140, 213 n.2
    biological artificial intelligence
        and 116–17
    cognitive autopoiesis and 140–7
    embodiment and 115–16
    ontological primacy and 118–19
    Philosophical Posthumanism
        and 117–18
artificial intelligence 42, 96, 111–13,
        140, 146, 187, 189, 221 n.20,
        228 n.10. *See also* cyborg
    biological 116–17
atoms 226 n.1
autopoiesis 5, 96, 140–7, 149, 179,
        221 n.18, 223 n.16
    animal testing and 143–4
    cognitive 142
    cognitive anthropocentrism and
        146–7
    frog experiment and 144–5
    meaning of 140–1
    origin of 141, 142–3
    Posthuman perspective of 141–2
"Autopoiesis and Cognition: The
        Realization of the Living"
        (Maturana and Varela) 141
autopoietic machine 219 n.3
autopoietic organization 220 n.4
Avatar Bodies (Weinstone) 204 n.5
Averroes 175, 229 n.18

Badmington, N. 52
Bailey, M. D. 207 nn.8–9
Barad, K. 5, 138, 155, 159–60, 162–3, 165,
    168, 181, 217 n.7, 224–5 n.5,
    225 nn.6–7, 20, 226 n.6
Bauman, R. 91
Bedau, M. A. 213 n.2
being, dualistic perception of 37
Being and essence of man 57
Being and Time (Heidegger) 193 n.1
Bennett, J. 161–2, 163, 225 n.11
Bigelow, K. 69
biochemistry 214 n.5
bio-conservative approach 131–2
bioethics 21, 183, 218 n.7, 219 n.8
    genetic discrimination and 134
    posthuman 128–32, 136–7
Bioethics in the Age of New Media
    (Zylinska) 219 n.8
bio-liberal approach 131, 132, 136
biological artificial intelligence 116–17
biopiracy 216 n.16
Biopolitics (Shiva and Moser) 168
bioprospecting 216 n.15
bios xiv, 5, 110
biotechnologies 128–9
Birnbacher, D. 219 n.7
Biti, V. 92
Bodies that Matter (Butler) 159, 224 n.4
body, Nietzsche on 223 n.15
"Body, The" (Ferrando) 197 n.6,
    207 n.14
Bohmian mechanics 226 n.4
Bohr, N. 226–7 n.7
Bord, C. 205 n.6
Bošković, R. J. 155
Bostrom, N. 48, 132, 195 n.1, 200 n.19
Bowler, P. J. 215 n. 6
Braidotti, Rosi 24, 55, 99, 106, 110, 123,
    154, 158, 192 n.10, 202 n.40,
    211 n.4, 225 n.10, 230 nn.29–30
branch-tree quantum scenario 173–4
Brassier, R 225 n.15
Brave New World (Huxley) 196 n.1
Bray, A. 214 n.7
Brezzi, F. 208 n.6
Broberg, A. 223 n.13
Brooks, R. 127
Brown, K. W. 154
Brown Dong Affair 143

bubble universes 172
Buddha in the Robot, The (Masahiro
    Mori) 112
Buddhism 192 n.6
Butler, H. E. 209 n.1
Butler, J. 71, 72, 74, 159, 205 n.11,
    207 nn.4, 13, 224 n.4
"Butler's Sophisticated Constructivism:
    A Critical Assessment"
    (Butler) 224 n.4

Caecilius, S. 91
Calarco, M. 208 n.3
Candide:or, The Optimist (Voltaire)
    228 n.15
Canguilhem, G. 207 n.6, 220 n.7, 225 n.8
Capra, F. 61
Cartesian dualism 37, 163–4
Cato the Elder 209 n.4
Cattani, M. S. 199 n.1
cat though experiment 172–3
cellular automata 214 n.5
Césaire, A. xiii
Chadwick, R. 218 n.1
Chakrabarty, D. 104
Channell, D. 116–17
Charpentier, E. 128
chattel slavery 77–8
child animism 112–13
China 135
Cicero, M. T. 209 nn.15–16, 91–2
classical humanism, criticism of xiii
"Climate of History, The: Four Theses"
    (Chakrabarty) 104
Clynes, M. 191 n.2
Cocktail Party, The (Eliot) 29
cognitive anthropocentrism 146–7
Cohen, J. J. 225 n.13
Colebrook, C. 214 n.7
Collins, F. S. 218 n.7
Collins, P. H. 151
compost, posthuman 107–8
"Computing Machinery and Intelligence"
    (Turing) 145
conatus 160–1
constitutive ontology 223 n.16
contemporary philosophy 175–7
Coole, D. 158, 161, 224 n.1
Cordrick Haely, K. 215 n.4
correlationism 225 n.19

"Cosmological Deixis and Amerindian Perspectivism" (Viveiro de Castro)   155
CRISPR technology   128–9, 218 n.3
"Critical History of Posthumanism, A" (Miah)   23
Critical Posthumanism   2, 25–6, 54–5
critical posthumanist perspective   50
Crutzen, P.   104
cryonics   107
Cultural Posthumanism   2, 26, 55, 194 n.9
Cuninghame, P. G.   208 n.5
Cyberfeminism and Artificial Life (Kember)   115
cyborg   191 nn.1, 2–3
    theory   26
    Vandana Shiva on   122–3

Dante Alighieri   29
Darwin, C.   51, 94, 118, 120, 124, 125, 216 n.1, 217 nn.4–5, 227 n.11
Darwin, E.   215 n.6, 217 n.5
Davies, T.   199 n.2
death of God, notion of   50–1
Death of Man (Foucault)   xii
de Beauvoir, S.   46, 68–9, 70, 204 n.2, 205 nn.7, 11
de Broglie, L.   167
de Chardin, Pierre Teilhard   29, 86, 195 n.4, 230 n.4
deconstruction   3–4, 52, 58, 61, 177, 193 n.1
"Deconstruction and Excision in Philosophical Posthumanism" (Roden)   138
dehumanization   79–80, 82, 84, 85, 98
DeLanda, M.   158, 164–5, 225 n.16
de las Casas, B.   78–9, 206 n.2
Deleuze, G.   160, 179, 180, 181, 192 n.8, 225 n.17
de Maupertuis, P-L .M.   215 n.6
Democratic Transhumanism   31, 32, 136, 138
Derrida, J.   4, 52, 193 n.1
designer babies   128–9, 133–4
    genetic discrimination and   134
"Development of a Eugenic Philosophy" (Osborn)   129
DeWitt, B. S.   228 n.8

"Diachrony and Representation" (Lévinas)   85
difference, dialectics of   xiii
dignitas   209 n.16
Discipline and Punish: the Birth of the Prison (Foucault)   74
Discourse, notion of   193 n.5
double, notion of   173
Doudna, J.   128, 129
dualism   4, 6, 44, 52, 54, 79, 110, 124, 144, 148, 159, 165, 185, 187, 194 n.2, 201 n.28
    Cartesian   37, 163–4
    hierarchical   46, 60, 109, 161
    strict   168, 171, 177, 178

Earth   105–7
earth democracy   152–3
eco-technology   118
"Eight Stages of Genocide, The" (Stanton)   79
Eliot, T. S.   29
embodiment
    alternative types of   155–6
    dream   156–7
    of life   115–17
    and perspectivism compared   154–5
    physical and biological   155
    Posthumanism on   131
    Turing on   146
End Of Education (Spanos)   193 n.4
End of Modernity, The: Nihilism and Hermeneutics in Postmodern Culture (Vattimo)   56
Enframing, modern technology as   41–3
Enlightenment and Transhumanism   36, 47, 48
entanglement   127, 159, 167, 229 n.22
epigenetics
    meaning of   126
    mechanism of   126–7
    as relevant to Philosophical Posthumanism   127
epiphanies, types of   86, 208 n.6
episteme   52, 58, 61, 199 n.10
    anthropocentric   69
    Foucault on   47
    Heidegger and   40

epistemology
  and cognitive science, difference
    between 142
  feminist 151
"Essays of Theodicy on the Goodness
    of God, the Freedom of Man
    and the Origin of Evil" (von
    Leibniz) 175
essentialism 214 n.3
"Ethical Issues in Human Enhancement"
    (Bostrom and Roache) 132
Ethics (Spinoza) 160
Ettinger, R. 107
eugenics 129–30
Eurocentric partiality 93–5
Everett, H. 172, 173, 228 nn.7–8
evolution 37, 38, 186, 215 n.6. *See also*
    multiverse
  cognitive autopoiesis and 140–7
  human enhancement and 133–9
  as intra-action 105
  life according to 120–3
  posthuman bioethics and 128–32
  posthumanities and 124–7
exclusion, from a posthumanist
    perspective 92
Extropianism 3, 32
"Extropian Principles: A Transhumanist
    Declaration" (More) 33
Extropy Institute 32

fact, notion of 150–1
Fanon, F. xiii
feminism xiii, xv, 23, 26, 50, 54–6, 59,
    75, 83, 115, 116, 122–3, 151–3,
    159, 187, 211 n.2, 214 n.12
  corporeal 158
  cyborg and 122
  magic and 80
  objectivity 151
  as pivotal in posthuman approach to
    technology 44
  politics of location and xiii
  "private is political" as 46
  radical constructivism and 224 n.4
  US 153
  womanliness as masquerade and 207
    n.3
feminist epistemology 151–2

feminist theory 68, 224 n.4
  Butler on 71
  de Beauvoir on 68–70
  Irigaray on 70–1
feminization, of magic 80
Ferrando, F. 191 n.1, 194 n.1, 197 n.6,
    200 n.16, 204 nn.3, 4, 207 n.14,
    208 n.8, 213 n.10, 218 n.9,
    230 n.31
Ferraro, G. 193 n.7
Fiedler, L. 80
Figueroa-Sarriera, H. J. 213 n.1
Finlayson, C. 210 n.1
flat ontologies 164–5, 225 nn.15, 17
Flesh and Machine (Brooks) 127
Fluehr-Lobban, C. 210 n.11
Folch, J. 217 n.3
Foucault, M. xii, 34, 44, 46–7, 48, 74, 83,
    111, 181, 192 n.9, 198 n.13,
    199 n.10, 200 n.13, 205 n.3,
    207 n.2, 230 n.32
Freaks: Myths and Images of the Secret Self
    (Fiedler) 80
French Philosophies of the Sixties
    (Cattani) 199 n.1
Freud, S. 173, 201 n.29, 205 n.10
Frey, R. G. 143
Friedlander, H. 206 n.5
frog experiment 142, 221 nn.13–14, 16
  explicit and implicit assumptions
    of 144
"From the Pre-Human to the Ultra-
    Human: The Phases of a Living
    Planet" (de Chardin) 86
Frost, S. 158, 161, 224 n.1
Fukuyama, F. 132, 133, 194 n.4, 197 n.5,
    219 n.10
Future of Human Nature, The
    (Habermas) 130
Future of Mankind, The (de Chardin) 29,
    86

Gaia hypothesis 105–6
  criticism against 106
Gairdner, W. D. 222 n.2
Galton, F. 129
Garver, B. 129, 218 n.4
Garver, K. 129, 218 n.4
Gaskill, M. 207 n.7

Gattaca (film)   134, 189
"Gattaca argument"   134
gender   68
    significance of   204 n.1, 205 n.7
    unneutral nomenclature   215 n.4
Gender Trouble (Butler)   71
genetic determinism   217 n.8
genetic discrimination   134, 218 n.3
genetic manipulation   218 n.5
genocide   79–80
germline genetic modification   218 n.4
Ghiselin, M.   121
Goldberg, D. T.   207 n.12
Gordijn, B.   218 n.1
Gould, S.   118
Graham, E. L.   197 nn.3, 10
Gray, C. H.   213 n.1
Great Chain of Being   94
Greene, B.   226 n.2
Guattari, F.   179, 180, 181, 192 n.8,
    225 n.17
"Guidelines for Non-Sexist Use of
    Language" (Warren)   75

Habermas, J.   130, 218 n.5
Hamer, D.   134, 218 n.2
Handbook of Nonsexist Writing (Miller
    and Swift)   75
Han-Pile, B.   47
Haraway, D.   2, 26, 44, 61, 103, 104, 105,
    107, 122, 141, 151, 152, 153,
    191 nn.3, 4, 214 n.4, 215 n.7
Harding, S.   151
Harman, G.   163, 164, 225 n.11
Harris, J.   197 n.4
Hassan, I.   25, 54, 193 n.6, 203 n.18
Hay, D.   199 n.6
Hayles, K.   2, 26, 39, 54, 116, 144,
    192 n.5, 193 n.8, 197 n.1,
    221 nn.13, 18
Hazen, R. M.   215 n.5
"Hedonistic Imperative, The"
    (Pearce)   35, 196 n.1
Heidegger, M.   2, 4, 39–43, 44, 57, 89,
    164, 181, 193 n.1, 197 nn.2–3,
    198 nn.5–7, 199 n.9, 202–3 n.8,
    203 n.11
Heilbron, J. L.   226 n.1
He Jiankui   218 n.3

Her (*film*)   114
Hidden Reality (Greene)   227 n.10
hierarchical dualism   46, 60, 109, 161
Hill, J.   219 n.9
History of the Indies (de las Casas)   78
Hitler, A.   218 n.4
Hlavajova, M.   202 n.40
Hochachka, P. W.   212 n.6
*Homo Sacer: Sovereign Power and Bare
    Life* (Agamben)   109
Homo Sapiens, etymology of   94–5, 96–7
hooks, b.   214 n.12
horizontal gene transfer   216 n.10
*How America's First Settlers Invented
    Chattel Slavery* (O'Rourke)   78
How We Became Posthuman (Hayles)   2,
    26, 54, 116, 141, 192 n.5,
    221 n.13
Hubbard, R.   130
Hubble's law   228 n.5
Hughes, J.   31, 33, 197 n.2
human/humanizing   68–72, 185–6. See
    also anthropological machine
    comprehensive analysis of   77–9
    etymology of   89–92
    genocide and dehumanization
        and   79–80
    Homo Sapiens and   96–7
    life and   111
    in Object-Oriented Ontology
        (OOO)   164
    "outsiders" and   80–1
    outcomes of   85–6
    overview effect and   86–8
    posthuman multiverse and   180–1
    vocabulary definitions of   87–8
Human Condition, The (Arendt)   192 n.11
human enhancement   31, 81, 133–9,
    197 n.4
    Posthumanist approach to   136–8
    precautionary principle and   135–6
    regulation of   133–5
    Speculative Posthumanism and   138–9
human exceptionalism   30, 136, 161
    Posthumanism and   160
human fixity   26
Human Germline Modification
    (HGM)   135
human intelligence   38

humanitas   57, 89, 91–2, 209 n.14
"Humans Have Always Been Posthuman"
        (Ferrando)   204 n.4
Hunger Games, The (film)   205 n.5
Huxley, A.   196 n.1, 227 n.11
Huxley, J.   29, 30, 86, 227 n.11
Huxley, T. H.   170, 227 n.11

*Il Tramonto dell'Uomo. La
        Prospettiva Post-Umanista*
        (Marchesini)   58
India   216 n.14
Indiani Metropolitani   208 n.5
interpermeating dimensions   230 n.31
intra-action   105, 163
intra-change   217 n.7
Irigaray, L.   46, 70, 205 nn.9–11
Islam   156
"Is Life Worth Living?" (James)   175
Istvan, Z.   31, 195–6 n.1

Jablonka, E.   217 n.6
Jainism   148
James, W.   175
Jenks, C.   224 n.3

Kaku, M.   227 n.10
Kant, I.   221 n.19
Kasser, T.   154
Kaufmann, W.   200 n.16
Keck, D.   199–200 n.11
Keevak, M.   210 n.9
Kember, S.   115
Kete, K.   79
King, P.   229 n.20
Kline, N.   191 n.2
Knowledge of Life (Canguilhem)   220 n.7,
        225 n.8
Knuuttila, S.   229 n.20
Koller, J. M.   149
Kristeva, J.   207 n.10
Kuhn, T.   58, 211 n.3
Kukkonen, T.   229 nn.17–18
Kurzweil, R.   37, 38

La Divina Commedia (Dante)   29
Lamarck, C.   125, 127, 215 n.6, 217 n.4
Lamarckism   125
LaMotte, S.   218 n.3
landscape, notion of   169

Langton, C.   115, 116, 214 n.5, 229 n.20
Lao-Tzu   60
Larson, E. J.   215 n.6
last universal ancestor (LUA)   120, 121,
        215 n.8
Latour, B.   104, 106, 107, 164, 191 n.4,
        203 n.19, 222 n.2
Lawrence, J. G.   216 n.10
Lemaître, G.   228 n.5
Lemke, T.   218 n.3
less-than human, notion of   78, 80–1, 98
"Letter on Humanism" (Heidegger)   2,
        57, 89
Lettvin, J.   220 n.11
Lévinas, E.   85, 208 n.1
Lewis, D.   175–6, 229 n.21
Libertarian Transhumanism   31
life
        scientific definition of   109–10
*Life on the Screen: Identity in the Age of the
        Internet* (Turkle)   191 n.3
Lind af Hageby, L.   143, 144
linguistic imperialism   210 n.12
Linnaeus, C.   93–4, 95–6, 210 nn.3, 6–12,
        211 nn.15–16, 19
logos   90, 110, 115, 193 n.5
Lovelock, J.   106
Luhmann, N.   141, 220 n.5
Lukàcs, G.   45
Lykke, N.   224 n.1

McCulloch, W.   142
McElheny, V. K.   121
McLuhan   76
Macy Conferences   220 n.10
Maggi, J.   216 n.13
Malovany-Chevallier, S.   205 n.6
mammals, etymology of   95–6
man, essence of   57
Man, humanist ideal of   xii
"Manifesto for Cyborgs, A"
        (Haraway)   26, 153
Mankind in Amnesia (Velikovsky)   202 n.7
many-worlds hypothesis   172, 228 n.8
"Many Worlds in Context"
        (Tegmark)   171
Marchesini, R.   58, 86, 203 n.14, 205 n.1
Margulis, L.   141
Marino, S.   193 n.7
Marx, K.   158, 201 n.29, 203 n.21

Masahiro Mori   112, 228 n.10
mathematical structures and
      universe   173–5, 228 n.9
Maturana, H.   140, 141, 142, 144–5,
      147, 212 n.7, 219 n.3, 220 n.6,
      220 n.9, 221 nn.18, 19, 223 n.16
measurement problem. *See* observer effect
mechanical worldview   117
Medea hypothesis   211 n.5
Meeting the Universe Halfway
      (Barad)   159
Megonigal, J. P.   216 n.13
Meillassoux, Quentin   165
Mentor, S.   213 n.1
Metahumanism   53, 202 n.37
Metahumanity   53
Metamorphoses: Towards a Materialist
      Theory of Becoming
      (Braidotti)   24
metamorphoses of spirit   48–9
Miah, A.   23
micro-physics, of power   205 n.3
milieu, notion of   220 n.7
Miller, C.   75
Milsom, C.   215 n.2
mind uploading   194 n.2
Minsky, M.   214 n.6, 220 n.8
modal essentialism   229 n.22
modal realism   176
Modernism   58
modern technology   41–2
Monocultures of the Mind (Shiva)
      192 n.7
Moravec, H.   214 n.6
More, M.   27, 32, 33, 36, 48, 135, 196 n.2,
      219 nn.5, 7
morphological freedom   36
Moser, I.   168
Mozdzer, T. J.   216 n.13
multispecies justice   152, 154
multiverse   6, 171, 227 n.10, 228 n.13,
      229 n.19
   in philosophy   175–7
   posthuman   177–82
   as related to string theory   169–70
   in science   171–2, 227 n.4
     levels   172–5, 228 nn.6–7, 9

Naho Kitano   111
Nasuto, S. J.   116

Native Americans   78
natural selection   124
natureculture   5, 127, 168, 191 n.4
nature-culture   xiv, 154, 191 n.4
negative eugenics   129
Negro Act   206 n.1
network theory   229 n.26
New Bottles for New Wine (Huxley)   29
New Materialism   5, 53, 55, 224 n.1.
      See also Object-Oriented
      Ontology (OOO)
   agential realism and   159–60, 162–3
   meaning of   158
   origin of   158–9
   risks in   160–1
   vital materiality and   161–2
Nichols, S.   208 n.9
Nicomachean Ethics (Aristotle)
      203 n.21
Nietzsche, F.   4, 5, 47–9, 52, 86, 149, 154–5,
      200 nn.13, 19, 201 nn.23, 29, 31,
      222 nn.8, 11, 223 nn.17–18,
      224 n.22, 229 n.28
   on body   223 n.15
   Bošković's influence on   224 n.21
   on death of God   50–1
   as relevant in daily life   51
   on thing   224 n.20
"Nietzsche, the Overhuman, and
      Transhumanism" (Sorgner)   48
Nietzsche and Transhumanism: Precursor
      or Enemy? (Tuncel)   48
Ninkovic, V.   223 n.13
Noble, D.   35–6
nomophobia   112
nondualism   61, 156
non-human perspectives   152–3
noosphere   230 n.230 n.4
"Nutrix Noverca" (Linnaeus)   95

objectivity   25, 83, 95, 96, 107, 110, 144,
      150–2, 222 n.5
Object-Oriented Ontology (OOO)   53,
      225 nn.11–12
   differences with Philosophical
     Posthumanism   164–5
   flat ontologies and   164–5
   meaning of   163
   similarities with Philosophical
     Posthumanism   163–4

Object-Oriented Ontology (Harman)
 225 n.11
observer effect 168, 226 n.7
Of Grammatology (Derrida) 193 n.1
"Of Posthuman Born: Gender, Utopia
 and the Posthuman"
 (Ferrando) 204 n.4
Okin, S. M. 222 n.12
Onishi, B. 196 n.3, 197 n.9
On the Genealogy of Morals
 (Nietzsche) 149, 150–1
On the Origin of Species (Darwin) 51,
 120, 227 n.11
On the Plurality of Worlds (Lewis) 176
onto-epistemological perspective 28,
 45–6, 60, 107, 113, 144
ontological privilege 57–8
Oparin, A. 215 nn.1, 3
Open, The: Man and Animal
 (Agamben) 73
oral history, feminist embrace of 83
Order of Things, The (Foucault) 46, 111,
 192 n.9, 199 n.10
organic worldview 117
Orientalism (Said) 46
Origin of Life, The (Oparin) 215 n.1
O'Rourke, D. 78
Osborn, F. 129
Other/otherness xiii, 75, 205 n.11
 absolute 85–6
 "human" project and 78, 81
 woman and 68–71
Our Posthuman Future (Fukuyama)
 194 n.4
overabundance, problem of 173–4,
 176–7
"Overhuman in the Transhuman, The"
 (More) 48
overview effect 86
 as significant to posthuman
 approach 86–8
*Overview Effect, The: Space Exploration
 and Human Evolution*
 (White) 86

paradise engineering 35
parallel universe 228 n.7, 230 n.31
Parikka, J. 105
Parry, R. 198 n.4

Pearce, D. 35, 196 n.1
Pearson, K. A. 200 n.18
penis-envy 205 n.10
Pepperell, R. 55
perspectivism 5, 28, 87, 147, 222 n.8,
 223 n.17, 224 n.22
 affinity and identity and 153
 and embodiments 154–7
 and fact, notion of 150–1
 of Nietzsche 149–50
 non-human perspectives and 152–3
 origin of 148–9
 and relativism compared 148
 standpoint theory and 151–2
 strategic essentialism and 153–4
perversion, discourse of 81
Peters, T. 218 n.7
phenomenology 223 n.16
Phenomenon of Man, The (de
 Chardin) 29
Philosophical Posthumanism 54–9,
 105, 185. *See also* Post-
 anthropocentrism; Post-
 dualism; post-humanism
 and Advaita compared 156–7
 artificial life and 117–18
 autopoesis and 141
 definition of 22
 Earth and 107
 epigenetics and 127
 fields of investigation of 187
 and Jainism compared 148–9
 meaning and significance of 54
 non-human agency as relevant to
 161–2
 notion of human and 87
 and Object-Oriented Ontology (OOO)
 compared 164
 similarities 163–4
 onto-epistemological approach
 of 113
 ontology 166–70
 pluralism and 151
 as post-humanism 98, 103, 105, 152,
 164, 185
 as praxis 188
 purpose of 188–9
 as radical response to human
 primacy 98–9

rhizome and 179–80
  technology as relevant to 186–7
  as transhistorical attitude 22
Philosophie Zoologique (Lamarck) 125
Piaget, J. 112
Pitts, W. 142
Plautus, T. M. 91
Plessner, H. 130
plurality/pluralism 5, 6, 23, 26, 45, 54,
    55, 57, 71, 82, 86, 103, 111, 118,
    147–9, 155, 164, 167–8, 176,
    180, 182, 183, 185, 188, 199 n.3,
    223 n.15
  as incorporation 194 n.10
  and Posthumanism 150–1
  rejection of 156–7
poiesis 40–1
  historical 46
Politics (Aristotle) 90
positive eugenics 129
possible worlds, notion of 175, 176,
    229 nn.17–20
post-anthropocentrism 54, 55, 56, 98,
    136, 143, 183, 211 n.4
  in Anthropocene 103–8
    paradigm shift 105
  Object-Oriented Ontology (OOO)
    and 164
  perspectivism in 152
  perverse form of 123
  technological developments and
    119
post-centrism 56, 186
post-dualism 54, 55, 60, 99, 154,
    183, 186
  human enhancement and
    136–7
  importance of 60–1
  perspectivism in 152
  significance of 189
post-exclusivism 56
Post-human (Marchesini) 203 n.14
Posthuman, The (Braidotti) 55
posthuman bioethics 128–32
  designer babies and 128–30
  eugenics and 129–30
*Posthuman Condition, The: Consciousness
    Beyond the Brain*
    (Pepperell) 56

Posthumanism 154, 193–4 n.8
  agency and 181–2, 187
  coining of 25
  compost and 107–8
  Critical 2, 25–6, 54–5
  Cultural 2, 26, 55, 194 n.9
  on death of God 51–2
  embodiment and 131, 155
  Eurocentric partiality and 93–5
  fact and 150–1
  Homo Sapiens and 97
  human enhancement and 136–8
  and humanism 23
  life and death separation and 107
  meaning of 24–5, 54
  metanarrative perspective of 58, 59
  multiverse and 173–4, 176–82
  non-hierarchical perspective of 2
  on notion of technology 119
  origin of life and 120–1
  performative approach 159, 160
  as post-anthropocentrism 3, 55,
    56, 58
  as post-centralizing 39
    as post-dualism 3, 25, 33, 54, 60
  as post-humanism 2–3, 55, 58
  post of 23, 24
  as praxis 76, 144, 181
  significance of 2–3
  Speculative 53, 138–9
  on subject and object 149
  technologies of the self and 82–3
  technology and 39–44
  and Transhumanism compared
    27–8, 42
  vitalism and 160
post-humanism xi, 3, 22, 25, 28, 54–6,
    58, 60, 98, 103, 113, 118, 175,
    184, 196 n.3, 197 n.9
  human enhancement and 136
  perspectivism in 152
  Philosophical Posthumanism and 98,
    103, 105, 152, 164, 185
  Posthumanism and 2–3, 55, 58
  in relation to other species 186
  significance of 65–7
  technological developments and
    119
Posthumanism (Badmington) 52

"Posthumanism, Transhumanism,
        Antihumanism, Metahumanism,
        and New Materialisms"
        (Ferrando)   191 n.1
Posthumanities   53, 124–7
        meaning of   125–6
posthuman life   109–10
        animate/inanimate and   110–14
        bios and *zoē* dualism and   109–10
Posthuman Life (Roden)   139, 225 n.12
"Posthuman Movement, The"
        (Nichols)   208 n.9
post-modern   58, 202 n.6
Postmodernism   2, 3, 22, 24, 25, 159
postmodernity   3, 21, 24, 32, 45, 159
Postmodern Turn, The (Hassan)   25
post-structuralism   xii–xiii, 52, 59, 159,
        224 n.4
praxis   28
        ironic   208 n.5
        Philosophical Posthumanism as   188
        post-hierarchical   119
        Posthumanism as   76, 144, 181
precautionary principle   135, 137–8
        of proactionary   135–6, 219 n.5
pre-dualistic worldview   156
"Primo Posthuman" project   36–7
progress, notion of   34
"Prometheus as Performer: Toward
        a Posthumanist Culture?"
        (Hassan)   25
Prospect of Immortality, The
        (Ettinger)   107

quantum entanglement   167
quantum physics   168, 172–3
"Question Concerning Technology, The"
        (Heidegger)   4, 40

radical constructivism   219 n.1, 221 n.19,
        224 nn.2, 4
Rae, A.   168
Raffoul, F.   208 n.1
Rambachan, A.   156
Randall, L.   166–7
Ranisch, R.   194 n.1
reason, notion of   34
reductionism   37, 168–9
relationality   xii, xiii, xv, xvi, 6, 23, 34, 44,
        52, 54, 66, 82, 86, 119, 154, 159,
        163, 165, 166, 167, 168, 174,
        177, 179, 181, 182, 186, 187
relational ontology   5, 44, 155, 157, 159,
        168, 225 n.20
relativism/relativity   35, 45, 56, 70,
        111, 133, 136, 145, 148,
        221 nn.17–18, 222 n.2
religion   31, 35, 36, 50–1, 84, 93, 149,
        155, 156, 162, 197 n.2, 201
        nn.27–8, 207 n.7, 213 n.12, 230
        n.31
Religion of Technology, The (Noble)   36
Representations of the Post/Human
        (Graham)   197 n.10
Resnik, D.   217 n.8
rhizome   176, 179–80
        and metaphor of multiverse   180
Ricoeur, P.   201 n.29
Rigby, S.   215 n.2
Riviere, J.   207 n.3
Roache, R.   132
robots   114, 127, 140, 145–6, 187, 198 n.8,
        204 n.3, 221 n.20, 228 n.10.
        See also artificial intelligence;
        artificial life; cyborg
        relationship with humans   113
        as spiritual beings   111–12
Roden, D.   138–9, 212 n.1, 225 nn.12, 16
Roman Humanism   57
Romaniello, G.   209 n.1
Rosch, E.   223 n.16

Said, E.   46, 199 n.6
Sandberg, A.   36
Sangster, J.   83
Saxton, M.   130
Schartau, L. K.   143, 144
Schatzki, T. R.   230 n.3
Schiebinger, L.   95, 96, 210 nn.12–13,
        211 nn.16, 19
Schmitt, F. F.   142
Schrödinger, E.   167, 172–3
"Schwarzenegger mice"
        experiment   133–4
Scipionic Circle   89–90
Scott, B.   219 n.1
Scotus, J. D.   175, 229 n.20
Seckbach, J.   215 n.5
*Second Self, The: Computers and the
        Human Spirit* (Turkle)   191 n.3

Second Sex, The (de Beauvoir)   68
Segrè, E.   226 n.1
Seitz, J.   135
self   23, 44, 54, 66, 85, 86, 112, 120, 131,
   149, 150, 155, 162, 173, 178,
   183, 223 n.15, 229 n.28. *See also*
   deconstruction; technologies of
   the self
   alterity within   189–90
self-assurance, rational   xii
self-harm and morphological freedom,
   distinction between   36
self-recognition   96–7, 203 n.12
Sepúlveda, J. G.   78
Setia, A.   229 n.19
sexism   153
sexuality   xiv, xv–xvi, 31, 39, 69–70,
   198 n.13, 205 n.9, 218 n.2, 224 n.4
Shambles of Science, The (Lind af Hageby
   and Schartau)   143
Shea, R.   227 n.12
Shiva, V.   122, 152–3, 154, 168, 192 n.7,
   216 nn.14, 16
Signs of Wonder and Traces of Doubt
   (Braidotti)   80
Silantsyeva, T.   204 n.2
Simondon, G.   213 n.15
singularity   21, 25, 37, 45, 56, 115, 188
   feminism and   xiii
*Singularity Is Near: When Humans
   Transcend Biology*
   (Kurzweil)   37
Sloterdijke, P.   218 n.6
Smith, D.   151
Smith, J.   224 n.3
Smith, M.   78
Smolin, L.   167
Society of Mind, The (Minsky)   220 n.8
software-based humans   37
solipsism   145
   anthropocentric   176
Somero, G. N.   212 n.6
Sorgner, S. L.   48, 134, 138, 155, 194 n.1,
   201 n.20, 222 n.8, 224 n.20
Spanos, W.   193 n.4
species
   cyborg and   122–3
   from genetic perspective   121–2
   post-anthropocentric perspective
   of   122

Speculative Posthumanism   53, 138–9
Speculum of the Other Woman
   (Irigaray)   70
Spinoza, B.   160
Spinoza: Practical Philosophy
   (Deleuze)   160
spirituality, significance of   36, 42, 47, 84,
   112, 148, 155, 156, 208 nn.7–8,
   230 n.31
Spivak, G.   153
standpoint theory   xiii, 151–2
Stanton, G.   79, 206 n.3
Stapp, H. P.   227 n.7
Stengers, I.   106
Stevens, E.   210 n.14
Stiegler, B.   42
Stoermer, E.   104
Strange Days (film)   69–70
strategic essentialism   153–4
"Striking a Balance: Policy Considerations
   for Human Germline
   Modification" (Seitz)   135
string theory   166–7, 169, 180, 226 n.3
   as related to multiverse   169–70
strong objectivity   152
Structure of Scientific Revolutions, The
   (Kuhn)   58
Stubley, P.   214 n.15
Studley, J.   227 n.3
"Studying Artificial Life with Cellular
   Automata" (Langton)   115
subject, as multiplicity   229 n.28
subjectivity   xiii, 24, 46, 68, 74, 77, 82,
   85, 107, 149, 150, 151, 154,
   156, 193 n.5, 205 n.2, 221 n.16,
   222 n.5
Susskind, L.   168, 169
Swift, K.   75
sympoiesis   141
Systema Naturae (Linnaeus)   93, 95,
   210 n.2

Tao of Physics, The (Capra)   61
Tao Te Ching (Lao-Tzu)   60
"Taxonomy for Human Beings"
   (Schiebinger)   95
techne   40, 41
*Technica and Time, 1: The Fault of
   Epimetheus* (Stiegler)   42
technogenesis   39

technologies of the self   21, 44, 82–4, 181,
        192 n.4, 198 n.13
    accessing non-hegemonic perspectives
        on human notion and   83–4
    meaning of   83
    spirituality and   84
Technologies of the Self (Foucault)
        198 n.13
Technology   198 nn.5. *See also specific*
        entries
Tegmark, M.   171, 172, 173, 174–5, 177,
        227 nn.1–2, 4, 228 nn.6–7, 9
"Telling our Stories: Feminist Debates
        and the Use of Oral History"
        (Sangster)   83
Tempier, E.   229 n.16
Terentius Afer, P.   91
Theory of the Universal Wave Function
        (Everett)   172
therapy and enhancement, difference
        between   131–2
Theses on Feuerbach (Marx)   203 n.21
thing, Nietzsche on   224 n.20
thingification   225 n.20
Thompson, E. T.   223 n.16
thought experiment and multiverse
        177–8
    humans within posthumanist
        multiverse and   180–1
    in relation to "you"   178–9
    posthuman agency and   181–2
    purpose of   177
    rhizome and   179–80
    significance of   178–9
Thousand Plateaus, A: Capitalism and
        Schizophrenia (Deleuze and
        Guattari)   179
Thus Spoke Zarathustra (Nietzsche)   47,
        48, 201 nn.23–4, 31, 223 n.15
Totality and Infinity: An Essay on
        Exteriority (Lévinas)   85
Transhumanism   3, 81, 127, 131, 194 n.3,
        195 n.1, 196 nn.2–3, 200–1 n19
    birth of   29–30
    contemporary   30, 31–2
    Democratic   31, 32, 136, 138
    devaluation of human body and
        197 n.9
    Extropianism and   32
    and humanism compared   33

human redesigning to   36–8
    Libertarian   31
    life and death separation and   107
    and Posthumanism compared
        27–8, 42
    proactionary principle and   135–6
    roots of   33–4
    self-identified   197 n.2
    and techno-enchantment   35–8
    Übermensch (overhuman) and   48
    as ultra-humanism   33
Transhumanist Declaration   33
Transpositions: On Nomadic Ethics
        (Braidotti)   110
Tree of Knowledge, The: The Biological
        Roots of Human Understanding
        (Maturana and Varela)   141,
        212 n.7
Tuana, N.   207 n.1
Turing, A.   145
Turing test   145–6
Turkle, S.   191
Turner, Q.   214 n.14
2,600 Years of the History of Western
        Philosophy Without Women
        (Warren)   207 n.1
Tylor, E. B.   213 nn.11–12

Übermensch (overhuman)   4, 47–53,
        200 n.16
    Philosophical Posthumanism and   50
    posthuman discussion and   48
ultra-humanism   33, 196 n.3, 197 n.9
"Uncanny, The" (Freud)   173
uncanny, notion of   173, 228 n.10
uncanny valley theory   213 n.13
Undoing Gender (Butler)   74, 207 n.13
"Universal Ancestor, The" (Woese)   121
universe, expansion of   172

Valladolid debate   78
Varela, F.   140, 141, 142, 144–5, 147,
        212 n.7, 219 n.3, 220 n.9, 223 n.16
Vasterling, V.   224 n.4
Vattimo, G.   56, 202 n.6
"Veiled Testimony: Negro Spirituals
        and the Slave Experience"
        (White)   84
Velikovsky, I.   202 n.7
vertical genetic exchange   216 n.10

Vibrant Matter: A Political Ecology of Things (Bennett)   161
Vico, G.   221 n.19
Villarreal, L. P.   212 n.8, 213 n.9
Vincent, A.   78
virtuality   39, 43, 66, 115, 140, 155,
        191 n.3, 192 n.5, 214 n.5
vitalism   160, 161–2, 225 nn.8, 10
    and agential realism compared   162–3
Vital Machine, The (Channell)   116
vital machine worldview   117
Vita-More, N.   36, 194 n.3, 19 n.7
Viveiro de Castro, E.   155–6
Voltaire   228 n.15
Von Glaserfeld, E.   221 n.19, 224 n.2
von Leibniz, G. W.   175
Vorhaus, D.   217 n.8

Wall-E (film)   198 n.9
Ward, P.   211 n.5
Warren, K. J.   207 n.1
Warren, V. L.   75
Warwick, K.   116
"wastefulness worry"   174
Watts, A.   60
wave-particle duality   167
Weinstone, A.   204 n.5
Western biology   93–5
wet-nursing   95, 210 n.14, 211 n.15
What is Posthumanism? (Wolfe)   26, 141

Wheaton, B. R.   226 n.5
White, F.   86, 87, 208 n.6
White, J.   84
Whitlock, G.   224 n.21
"Who is afraid of designer babies?"
        (Hamer)   134
whole brain emulation. *See* mind
        uploading
Wilkinson, T.   229 n.16
Will to Power, The (Nietzsche)   149,
        224 n.22, 229 n.28
will to power doctrine   155
Wilson, R. A.   227 n.12
Woese, C.   121
Wolfe, C.   26, 141, 194 n.10
Wolfendale, P.   163, 225 n.19
woman. *See also* feminism
    notion of   68–92
    as other   68–71
womanliness, as masquerade
        207 n.3
Wootson, Jr., C. R.   214 n.13
"Wrestling with Transhumanism"
        (Hayles)   39

Zimmer, C.   218–19 n.4
Zinnbauer, B. J.   208 n.7
zoë   xiv, 5, 109, 110, 212 n.4
Zoroastrianism   201 nn.23–5, 28
Zylinska, J.   219 n.8